10 DAYS That Shaped Modern Canada

10 DAYS That Shaped Modern Canada

AARON W. HUGHES

UNIVERSITY *of* **ALBERTA** PRESS

Published by
University of Alberta Press
1-16 Rutherford Library South
11204 89 Avenue NW
Edmonton, Alberta, Canada T6G 2J4
amiskwaciwâskahikan | Treaty 6 |
Métis Territory
uap.ualberta.ca | uapress@ualberta.ca

Library and Archives Canada Cataloguing in Publication

Title: 10 days that shaped modern Canada / Aaron W. Hughes.
Other titles: Ten days that shaped modern Canada
Names: Hughes, Aaron W., 1968– author.
Description: Includes bibliographical references and index.
Identifiers: Canadiana (print) 20220259526 | Canadiana (ebook) 20220259550 | ISBN 9781772126327 (softcover) | ISBN 9781772126624 (EPUB) | ISBN 9781772126631 (PDF)
Subjects: LCSH: Canada—History—Miscellanea. | LCSH: Canada—Miscellanea.
Classification: LCC FC176 .H84 2022 | DDC 971—dc23

First edition, first printing, 2022.
First printed and bound in Canada by Houghton Boston Printers, Saskatoon, Saskatchewan.
Copyediting by Audrey McClellan.
Proofreading by Kay Rollans.
Indexing by Siusan Moffat.

University of Alberta Press is committed to protecting our natural environment. As part of our efforts, this book is printed on Enviro Paper: it contains 100% post-consumer recycled fibres and is acid- and chlorine-free.

University of Alberta Press gratefully acknowledges the support received for its publishing program from the Government of Canada, the Canada Council for the Arts, and the Government of Alberta through the Alberta Media Fund.

Canada

Canada Council for the Arts Conseil des Arts du Canada

Alberta Government

For Liliana

Who believed when I doubted

Contents

Introduction

NOT ALL DAYS ARE CREATED EQUAL. While the vast majority of days ebb and flow in a repetitive fashion, some become so singularly momentous to a nation's formation and outlook that, although their importance is recognized at the time, the true significance becomes apparent only after the fact. Such days often start out normally enough—indeed, like all others—but through their course something of such import happens, whether positive or negative, that things are never quite the same thereafter. While the historical record attaches significance to the past as a whole, certain days in that past are often clearly more significant than their peers.

This book compresses the history of Canada's last half century into just ten days. Each chapter focuses on one date, describing what happened on it and what happened as a result of it. When understood both contextually and in terms of their causes and effects, these days help to provide a portrait of how Canada has become the country that it is today. Taken together, these days have played a crucial and formative role in shaping the way Canadians view both themselves and their place in the world.

Which days have I chosen for their significance?

- **October 13, 1970.** The day Prime Minister Pierre Elliott Trudeau uttered the phrase "Just watch me" when a CBC reporter asked how far he intended to go to end the FLQ crisis. Three days later he invoked the War Measures Act, which curtailed the civil liberties of Canadians across the country.
- **September 28, 1972.** The day Paul Henderson scored his famous goal in the dying seconds of the final game with the Russians in Moscow to win the Summit Series for Canada in the middle of the Cold War. The come-from-behind victory—which united the nation in a way never seen before—revealed as much about Cold War politics as it did about contrasting hockey styles.
- **April 17, 1982.** The day the Constitution was patriated and the Charter of Rights and Freedoms enshrined within it. The Charter would go on to shape many features of Canadian life, including preventing discrimination on the basis of sexual orientation and allowing women safe and legal access to terminate pregnancies.
- **July 21, 1988.** The day the Multiculturalism Act was signed into law, thereby continuing the trend of transforming what had been a largely white and Christian Canada into one of the most diverse countries on earth.
- **December 6, 1989.** The day of the École Polytechnic Massacre in Montreal, which began a national conversation on violence against women and subsequently led to a debate on gun ownership.
- **May 25, 1995.** The day the Supreme Court of Canada ruled on *Egan v. Canada*, a case brought to the Supreme Court by two gay men who sued Ottawa for the right to claim a spousal pension under the Old Age Security Act. Though the Court ruled against them, all nine judges agreed that sexual orientation was a protected ground and that protection extends to partnerships of lesbians and gay men, paving the way for same-sex unions and the redefinition of marriage.

- **October 30, 1995.** The day the Quebec Referendum brought Canada to the brink of a constitutional crisis, one it had been moving toward for years.
- **June 2, 2015.** The day the Truth and Reconciliation Commission (TRC) released its Executive Summary documenting decades of injustices against Indigenous populations in, for example, the residential school system, and setting a path forward for reconciliation.
- **August 20, 2016.** The day of The Tragically Hip's last concert, in the band's hometown of Kingston, Ontario. The Hip, with its Canadian-infused lyrics, had often functioned as a symbolic antidote to the hegemony of American imports.
- **March 8, 2018.** The day federal finance minister Bill Morneau and Bank of Canada governor Stephen Poloz unveiled the new ten-dollar bill with its portrait of Viola Desmond.

These days, I argue, have been crucial not only because of what happened on them but, just as importantly, by virtue of what happened because of them. Even the quickest of glances at the list should show the far-reaching consequences of these days. I would like to think that if you were to pick up any Canadian newspaper today, you would be able to connect contemporary stories or news items therein—whether through a chain of cause and effect or association—to one of these ten days. For example, the national outpouring of grief on May 27, 2021, when the remains of 215 nameless and faceless Indigenous children were discovered on the grounds of the Kamloops Indian Residential School in British Columbia, only makes sense when situated against the history of these schools in the country, something the TRC commission sought to call attention to and to redress. Though the full repercussions of the later dates, especially those in chapters 8 and 10, remain to be seen, they represent the culmination of historical wrongs, and it will be up to Canadians to ask ourselves how to move forward in their light. In other words, these days inform what we have become and, equally important, how we became it.

Each chapter focuses on one date, describing it and the events or circumstances that led up to it in detail. Most importantly, though, the greater part of each chapter examines the reverberations that each of these days set in motion. Taken as a whole, the book presents an interlocking set of vignettes.

My argument is that certain days in a nation's history take on a much broader significance than was often apparent even on the day itself. Allow me to give but one example from the pages that follow. The patriation of the Canadian Constitution from Britain in 1982 was duly noted as significant at the time, as can be seen in the media coverage and the grand ceremony that took place on Parliament Hill, with Prime Minister Pierre Trudeau, Queen Elizabeth II, and other dignitaries in attendance. However, the new Charter of Rights and Freedoms, which was entrenched in the Constitution, ushered in sweeping changes to Canadian society over the ensuing years that could not have been foreseen in 1982. At the same time, that day of celebration thinly papered over some of the long-simmering tensions between the forces of federalism and those in favour of greater provincial powers. In so doing, the day further exacerbated tensions with Quebec, where both separatists and leading federalist politicians saw—and in many cases continue to see—the Charter as an illegitimate assault on Quebec's sovereignty.

While technically isolated from one another across the span of decades, on a fundamental level these ten days are intimately connected and interwoven. They reveal how modern Canada has been forged through massive political, social, cultural, and demographic changes. These days thus create a whole that is much greater than the sum of their actual parts.

I also want to draw attention to the fact that modern Canada has been shaped as much by the repercussions associated with major political events such as the murder of Pierre Laporte during the October Crisis of 1972 (chapter 1) or the failure of the Meech Lake or Charlottetown Accords in 1987 and 1992 (chapter 3) as by, say, a momentous hockey game (chapter 2) or even pride in a Canadian rock band that never attained a huge level of success across the border (chapter 9). The goal of understanding these ten days in their complexity is to get us to understand the past, but also to help us understand our present and future.

I thought a lot about which dates to include. In selecting the final list, I unfortunately had to leave out other formative and important dates: for example, the abolition of the death penalty in 1976, the same year that the Parti Québécois took power in Quebec for the first time; Terry Fox's Marathon of Hope in 1980; the takeover of Tim Horton's by Wendy's in 1995; the attacks of 9/11 in 2001 and the subsequent Canadian military deployment in Afghanistan; or the Canadian women's hockey team's Olympic gold medal victory over the Americans at the 2002 Olympics. But I stand by the dates ultimately chosen and would like to think the majority of Canadians would agree. I should also add that, though all equally important, they are so for different reasons. Some of these days changed everything we know about modern Canada (such as the invocation of the War Measures Act or the entrenchment of the Charter in the Constitution); others ratified or made official something that was latent or already well-known (such as the Multiculturalism Act); some signal the end of an era (The Hip's final concert); and others mark possible turning points that depend on what comes next (such as the days on which the TRC report and the new ten-dollar bill were released). All of these days, in other words, share the category of being monumental, but all for quite different reasons.

Perhaps you might have chosen days that are closely connected to mine. For example, you could easily argue that the day in 1971 when Pierre Trudeau announced in the House of Commons that the Government of Canada would henceforth pursue multiculturalism as its official policy was more important than the signing of the Multiculturalism Act in 1982. Or you might argue that the most important date for same-sex marriage was its legalization in 2005, as opposed to the day in 1995 when the Supreme Court ruled against a gay couple's claim for a spousal pension under the Old Age Security Act, even though all the judges agreed that sexual orientation was protected under the law. Or you might argue that the day of Gord Downie's death could just as easily replace the day of The Hip's final concert. The effect of such replacements, however, would be the same in either case.

All of the days on my list—unlike some of the others mentioned above—have the distinct advantage that people who were teenagers or adults at the time are likely to remember them. While I certainly hope that some will agree with the list I have chosen, others might disagree. I would hope that such disagreement would encourage you to create your own list of dates, thereby facilitating a much larger conversation about the modern history of Canada that will be productive and generate debate.

The ten days I focus on in the chapters that follow are the types of days that created headlines and sustained media coverage. One of the main issues I had to deal with when writing was how to handle sources in such a manner that they did not become unwieldly. My study is informed by a lifetime of reading what are often technical analyses of Canadian history and politics, but in order to keep the prose and the narrative as accessible as possible, I have opted to refer to such studies only when necessary to make or inform a particular point. Rather than bombard you with technical studies and a myriad of footnotes, I have found it more productive to use references and citations from contemporary television interviews, newspaper articles and op-eds, and memoirs of politicians and other significant players, in addition to various polls that have surveyed Canadians about a range of related topics.

At the end of each chapter I include two brief sections that provide additional resources for those interested in reading more on the particular topic or digging a little deeper into some of that chapter's related contents. The first section is a brief bibliography of some of the works, both technical and popular, that have informed the chapter in question, and the second provides a set of digital resources, such as movies and documentaries.

While in many quarters today it is fashionable to ignore history or downplay historical forces, the days highlighted in this book reveal clearly that in order to understand what we, as a country, have become, it is essential to be aware of where we have been. It is important, in other words, to be aware of the connection between then and now.

Before I move on to an examination of the dates in question, I should note that a certain vision of Canada, one that I trust is shared by a majority of Canadians, connects all of the following chapters. This vision is largely liberal, progressive, anglophone, and centralist. As universal as it may seem, however, it is nonetheless important to realize that it is, by definition, also particular—indeed, just as particular as the vision of those opposed to it. For this reason, I have tried to give some attention to the latter voices that oppose and dissent from this vision. Quebec nationalists, Prairie populists, and Indigenous activists all fought—and, indeed, continue to fight—for a very different Canada than the one characterized in these pages. Any narrative of modern Canada, then, must also include their voices since they have all played a role in shaping the modern nation.

A final word is in order here. One particular date figured highly in the writing of this book: March 11, 2020. On that day the World Health Organization declared COVID-19 to be an international pandemic. This project was conceived just prior to this date and was largely written under its shadow. Though the date receives no chapter of its own, its consequences only now beginning to reverberate as they will undoubtedly do for years to come, it does make brief appearances, especially in the last chapters. Yet, in many ways, March 11, 2020, makes its presence felt even in the stories of days that came before it. The National Hockey League, for example, was temporarily restructured so that for the 2020–2021 season, Canadian teams played only one another (originally in empty arenas; then with a few fans by the time the playoffs started in the spring of 2021) so they didn't have to cross the forty-ninth parallel; Charter rights were upended to prevent free movement into some provinces; immigration was curtailed by border closures; and concerts like The Tragically Hip's were an impossibility until well into 2022. Just as the book was going to press a large truck convey rolled into Ottawa and blocked some border crossings with the United States, protesting COVID-19 vaccine mandates and restrictions. The convoy and its protests ended after Prime Minister Justin Trudeau temporarily invoked the Emergencies Act, thereby suspending the rights of citizens to free movement or assembly. Clearly, modern Canada is still in the process of being shaped.

1

OCTOBER 13 1970

"Just Watch Me"

THE OCTOBER CRISIS represented one of the greatest challenges to Canadian Confederation, particularly the concept of the equality and unity of federal and provincial governments. If the Canadian project was, as several historians have argued, rooted in the Enlightenment idea of liberalism and the protection of individual human rights and freedoms,[1] the federal government's response to the crisis called into question the very idea of Canada. Just three short years after the celebration of its centennial year, perhaps best symbolized for the world by Montreal's Expo 67, the country found itself in considerable disarray and on the verge of becoming a police state. No one foresaw in 1967 that the city which hosted one of the most successful world's fairs would soon be surrounded by tanks and helicopters, its streets patrolled by the Canadian army. Though perhaps, in hindsight, Charles De Gaulle's famous "Vive le Québec libre!"—yelled to an appreciative crowd from a balcony when he came to the city to visit Expo—offered a fleeting glimpse of some of the problems to follow.[2]

October 1970 began normally enough. September, not untypically, had ushered in a warm Montreal autumn. The hapless Expos had finished at the bottom of the National League in what was only their second season in major league baseball. In contrast, the Canadiens of the National Hockey League were preparing for what turned out to be a Stanley Cup–winning season.

Little did anyone expect that a few days into October, Quebec—and, by extension, the entire country—would be plunged into a chain of events with major repercussions. Given the historical tensions between francophones and anglophones, which predated Confederation in 1867, it surprised no one that there were certain individuals and groups in Quebec that desired political autonomy and independence. What shocked many Canadians that October, however, was the level of resentment that existed among some of these groups, and the violence they carried out with the aim of terrorizing Canadian and anglophone institutions in the province to achieve that autonomy. As 1970 was nearing its end, Canadians in all regions watched the evening news on their television sets as the violence unfolded in the streets of Montreal. Significantly, these events demonstrated the relative popular support among francophones for Quebec independence. Just as significantly, the federal government's response demonstrated the degree of its opposition to that independence, going so far as to invoke the War Measures Act and severely, if temporarily, curtailing the rights of all Canadians.

I

The year 1970 started out strongly enough for the development of a new Canadian sense of identity in the same vein as Expo 67. On March 2, for example, Keith Spicer was appointed as the first Official Languages commissioner. The commissioner, who reported directly to Parliament as a nonpartisan officer, functioned as a national language ombudsman whose mandate was to uphold French and English language rights in all federal institutions under the 1969 Official Languages Act. Prior to that act, Canada's federal government operated predominantly in English, something that made many French Canadians feel like second-class citizens, far removed from the corridors of federal power. The commissioner was tasked with the promotion of English and French as languages of both service and work, and facilitating the teaching of French immersion in English-language schools across Canada as a long-term support for the creation of an officially bilingual Canada.

On May 22, 1970, the Canadian Radio and Television Commission issued the first set of guidelines for Canadian content regulations for television and radio. This meant that all radio and television broadcasters needed to air a certain percentage of content that was at least partly written, produced, presented, or otherwise contributed to by Canadians. Such attempts to encourage bilingualism and the creation of a national identity were undermined by the events of October 1970. While the October Crisis did not put an end to these endeavours, it exposed the fragility that lay at the heart of the Canadian experiment. The success of Expo 67 was based on the cooperation between Canada's French- and English-speaking communities, but October 1970 reinforced what Hugh MacLennan once poignantly called Canada's "two solitudes."[3]

On April 29, 1970, Robert Bourassa became premier of Quebec after his Liberal Party defeated the Union Nationale party. The latter, a conservative and nationalist party, had held power in Quebec from 1936 to 1939, 1944 to 1960, and then again from 1966 to 1970. Bourassa's Liberals won the election on the slogan "100,000 jobs," with the aim of exploiting the province's rich hydroelectric resources as the most effective means of sustaining job creation and furthering Quebec's "Quiet Revolution," which, since the early 1960s, had increasingly modernized and secularized the province. Bourassa, the youngest premier in the province's history, appointed the older Pierre Laporte—a central figure in the events of this chapter—as his deputy premier, parliamentary leader, minister of immigration, and minister of labour and manpower.

An early sign of tension between the forces of federalism and those of Quebec nationalism appeared in the episode known as "le coup de la Brink's." On April 26, only three days before the provincial election, and with the separatist Parti Québécois doing very well in the polls, nine armoured Brink's trucks lined up outside the Royal Trust Company in Montreal to transfer gold, bonds, and other valuables from Montreal to Toronto. This dramatic scene of capital assets fleeing the province, seemingly staged by the federal government led by Pierre Trudeau, was meant to symbolize to Quebecers the troubles that would occur should a separatist party assume power in Quebec. It certainly seems to have been effective as the Parti Québécois ended up electing only seven members out of a possible 108, even though it received 23 per cent of the popular vote. To Quebec nationalists, of course, le coup de la Brink's also revealed clearly the lengths to which the federal government was willing to go to curtail their ambitions.

II

The relationship between anglophone and francophone Canada has long been a fractured one that has played a defining role in the shaping of modern Canada. Since this complicated relationship weaves through so many of the following chapters, it is worth supplying a very basic overview of it here, with the aim of getting at the source of these tensions.

On April 20, 1534, the King of France commissioned Jacques Cartier to set sail in search of a western passage to Asia. Cartier, unwittingly, was among the first Europeans to set foot on what is now Canada and, in the process, claimed the land for France. Despite this initial French presence—solidified by the first permanent settlements, established in the early 1600s under Samuel de Champlain—New France, as it was then called, was soon under attack by British forces in an extension of Europe's Seven Years War. The antagonism between the two nations culminated in the Battle of the Plains of Abraham, which took place on a plateau just outside the walls of Quebec City on September 13, 1759. British victory meant that the French evacuated the city, and their remaining military force in Canada and the rest of North America came under increasing pressure. The battle itself, it should be mentioned, did not simply pit anglophone against francophone; religious differences (Protestant versus Catholic) and different relationships to the Crown were further exacerbated by the opponents' different languages and modes of living.

The Treaty of 1763 ceded Canada and most of New France to Britain within the larger context of the Seven Years' War.[4] To avert conflict in Britain's newly acquired French-speaking territory, the British Parliament passed the Quebec Act of 1774, which expanded Quebec's territory to the Great Lakes and Ohio Valley. To appease the French, it re-established the French language, the Catholic faith, and French civil law in the region. To accommodate English-speaking Loyalists in Quebec, the Constitutional Act of 1791 divided the province into French-speaking Lower Canada (later

Quebec) and English-speaking Upper Canada (later Ontario), granting each its own elected legislative assembly.[5]

The tensions surrounding all these distant events have never completely disappeared. "Je me souviens," the official motto of Quebec, intimates that French Canadians will forever remember their lineage, their dreams, and, most importantly for some, the injustice suffered at the hands of the English. When transferred to a more modern register, there is the implication that today's francophones will never forget their own mistreatment by anglophone Canada. Indeed, it is probably no coincidence that in 1978, two years after René Lévesque and his Parti Québécois came to power on a large wave of popular support for separation, the phrase "Je me souviens" was added to all provincial licence plates.

The Parti Québécois was but one iteration of this separatist sentiment. Because of perceived mistreatment, both historic and contemporary, the province has witnessed, especially since the 1960s, a strong desire for autonomy. This movement is not just political and is predicated on the perceived uniqueness of the language, culture, values, and ideas shared by Quebecers, which is in turn coupled with the resentment of having been wronged and exploited by anglophone structures of power in Ottawa and beyond. While there have been numerous explicitly nationalist and indépendantiste parties—such as the provincial Union Nationale, the aforementioned Parti Québécois, and subsequently the federal Bloc Québécois—even the provincial Liberal and Conservative parties, while rejecting the idea of the province's political sovereignty, have tended to be at odds with numerous federalist policies over the years, which they maintain impinge on Quebec's sovereignty. Most of these parties, with few exceptions, have sought to provide a political solution to Quebec independence, often through, for example, provincial referendums. As is frequently the case, however, those who seek more forceful means often speak with the loudest voices.

III

In retrospect, perhaps the October Crisis was inevitable. It could be argued that the differences between Canada's two founding cultures—their respective languages, religions, and customs—were irreconcilable. That the British took control of their new colony from the French through war meant that the nature of their relationship in the "New World" was predicated on resentment and mistrust. As early as 1839, Lord Durham, the Governor General and High Commissioner of British North America, expressed this in his *Report on the Affairs of British North America* (also known as the *Durham Report*):

> Those who have reflected on the powerful influence of language on thought, will perceive in how different a manner people who speak in different languages are apt to think; and those who are familiar with the literature of France, know that the same opinion will be expressed by an English and French writer of the present day, not merely in different words, but in a style so different as to mark utterly different habits of thought.[6]

This was exacerbated, he noted in the report, by the different educational systems in the two Canadas, which, he argued, heightened the tensions between their peoples.[7] He even went so far as to say that the French inhabitants "have no culture nor literature."[8] This phrase would resonate loudly through the years as Québécois writers and artists sought to create—with a great deal of success—a distinct culture of their own. This culture, as we shall see shortly, was at the heart of Quebec nationalism.

The immediate result of Durham's report was the Act of Union, which in 1840 created the united Province of Canada, initially with its capital in Kingston.[9] Notwithstanding the amalgamation, however, the former Upper Canada (now referred to as Canada West) maintained English common law, whereas the former Lower Canada (Canada East) maintained the French civil code.[10] This, of course, allowed the tensions between anglophone and francophone populations to remain.[11] In retrospect, it may have been the catalyst for all future conflict.

Over the course of the ensuing century, various prime ministers made overtures, with varying degrees of success, to integrate French- and English-speaking Canada. One of the most concentrated efforts was announced on July 19, 1963, when recently elected Liberal prime minister Lester B. Pearson struck a Royal Commission on Bilingualism and Biculturalism in order "to recommend what steps should be taken to develop the Canadian Confederation on the basis of an equal partnership between the two founding races."[12] Though other groups objected, with some degree of success to the idea that there were only "two founding races" (see chapter 4), the approaching date of Canada's centenary on one hand and rising separatist sentiment in Quebec on the other meant that the commission was, at least initially, focused on redressing Canada's perceived failure to establish the equality of English and French within governmental institutions and the country more generally.

The commission was also to examine the existing state of bilingualism and biculturalism, with the goal of reporting "on the role of public and private organizations, including the mass communications media, in promoting bilingualism, better cultural relations and a more widespread appreciation of the basically bicultural character of our country and of the subsequent contribution made by the other cultures; and to recommend what should be done to improve that role."[13]

After noting the underrepresentation of francophones in the nation's political and business communities, and the fact that incomes of French Canadians lagged behind those of other ethnic groups, with the exception of Indigenous communities, the commission went on to make several recommendations that would usher in large-scale changes in Canadian life. These included that bilingual districts be created in regions of Canada where members of the minority community, be they French or English, made up 10 per cent or more of the local population; that children be able to attend schools in the language of their parents' choice in regions where there was sufficient demand; that Ottawa become a fully bilingual city; and, perhaps most symbolically, that English and French be declared the two official languages of Canada.

Prime Minister Pierre Trudeau, who succeeded Pearson in 1968, used the commission's recommendations as one of the foundations for his new government's policies. In 1969, for example, the Official Languages Act / Loi sur les langues officielles made Canada officially bilingual within the larger context of multiculturalism (see chapter 4). Trudeau's vision was that the next generation of Canadians—from Victoria to Whitehorse to Quebec City to St. John's—would speak both languages fluently. This would be no easy feat, of course. It required that Canada's education system be overhauled as schoolchildren across the country learned both official languages. While the vision was certainly bold and unprecedented, in hindsight it was clearly virtually impossible to achieve. The country was just too big, and francophone communities outside Quebec too sparse.

Perhaps tellingly, and a symbolic sign of things to come, soon after passage of the Official Languages Act, Quebec decided to make French its only official language and began to actively limit instruction in English to certain qualified families.[14] In like manner, French-language instruction in western provinces remained limited because of both scarcity of resources and resistance. Not for the first time, an attempt to achieve national unity was undone by the pressures of provincialism and regionalism.

However, if the Official Languages Act / Loi sur les langues officielles failed to make Canada a truly bilingual nation, it did succeed in giving French-speaking Canadians greater access to positions of power and to government services in their own language. Of course, not all Quebecers agreed. Many felt strongly that such accommodations prevented francophones from realizing a new society with its own language and culture, and from determining their own economic and legal policies.

IV

By the time Robert Bourassa and his Liberals won the provincial election in April 1970, troubles were festering behind the scenes in Quebec that would soon erupt into the open, becoming evident to Canadians of all stripes. While the anger and the violence might have come as a shock to those living outside Quebec, in retrospect, they perhaps should not have been unexpected. They were, in many ways, the inevitable result of events that had occurred over the previous two centuries and had been simmering in the ensuing years.

Since the early 1960s, a number of individuals, growing increasingly frustrated with the slow pace of political solutions to Quebec's alienation from the rest of Canada, began to take matters into their own hands, seeking alternative ways to force the issue. Some of these individuals established what they called the Front de Libération du Québec (or "Liberation Front of Quebec," frequently known by its abbreviation: the FLQ), a Marxist-Leninist terrorist group—though, of course, they would have considered themselves "freedom fighters" as opposed to "terrorists"—that would draw attention to what they perceived to be the inherent righteousness of their cause. Deriving inspiration from other such groups in the 1960s—for example, the Palestine Liberation Organization (PLO), the Basque Homeland movement (ETA) in Spain, and the National Liberation Front (FLN) in Algeria—the FLQ called for radical deeds to put an end to what they described as "Anglo-Saxon" imperialism and colonialism.[15] Indeed, one leading member of the FLQ, Pierre Vallières, went so far as to write a book with the provocative title *White N-----s of America*, comparing the status of Quebecers in Canada to that of African Americans in the United States.[16] To address historical wrongs, members of the FLQ made it their goal to, in this order, overthrow the provincial government by violent means, gain independence from Canada, and establish a French-speaking workers' society.

Like other groups seeking to overthrow the yoke of colonial oppression, the FLQ argued that the people of Quebec were the direct descendants of a conquered people who—not unlike Palestinians, Basques, Algerians, and others—were now entitled to political independence and national sovereignty. The FLQ gained the support of left-leaning students, teachers, and academics, many of whom publicly expressed their solidarity. Some FLQ members travelled abroad, where they received guerrilla training from the PLO in Jordan. And, like other liberation organizations, the group tended to operate in secretive cells.[17]

In 1963, the same year Pearson struck his Royal Commission on Bilingualism and Biculturalism, the FLQ commenced its activities. And from 1963 to 1970, its cells committed over 160 violent actions, including bombings, bank robberies (to fund their activities), kidnappings, and at least five killings (three from bombings and two from gunfire). In 1966 they prepared their *Revolutionary Strategy and the Role of the Avant-Garde*, a document outlining the group's long-term strategy, which included successive waves of robberies, bombings, kidnappings, and further violence. All of this, they imagined, would lead to their goal of instilling fear in anglophone Canada, while creating the necessary conditions for revolution and independence.

Groups like the FLQ clearly represented a different vision from that put forward by the Liberal governments of Pearson and Trudeau, but one no less valid to their followers and supporters. If the federal Liberals hoped to paper over difference by encouraging more people to speak French, the FLQ sought to call attention to the structural injustices that federal policy had created and continued to aggravate. While some members of the FLQ were extreme in their actions, it cannot be denied that the movement tapped into a real sense of dissatisfaction and resentment that many

Quebecers felt toward "Anglo-Saxon imperialism." In its place, they sought to create an independent nation, which would reverse years of injustice and linguistic discrimination. Many of these supporters engaged in public strikes in solidarity, right up to the October Crisis. Indeed, many francophone artists and other important supporters of the FLQ, several of whom were jailed during the October Crisis, remained important figures of Quebec culture after 1970.

On February 13, 1969, an FLQ cell detonated a powerful bomb in the Montreal Stock Exchange that severely damaged the building and seriously injured twenty-seven people. Showing their solidarity with other guerrilla organizations, most notably the PLO, another cell tried, but failed, to kidnap an Israeli envoy in Montreal in February 1970. And on May 5, almost exactly one year before the election of Bourassa's Liberals, another cell hijacked an American airplane with seventy-five passengers aboard—National Airlines Flight 91, which had been scheduled to fly from New York City to Miami—and forced it to land in Havana, Cuba.

These apparently random and scattered acts of violence culminated in what became known as the October Crisis. It began in the late afternoon of October 5 when two members of the FLQ's Liberation Cell, disguised as delivery men, kidnapped James Cross, the British Trade Commissioner, from his home at 1297 Redpath Crescent in Montreal's Square Mile neighbourhood. The kidnappers subsequently issued a set of demands that outlined their conditions. They would release Cross, they said, in exchange for the release of a number of jailed FLQ members (referred to as "political prisoners"), in addition to having the Canadian Broadcasting Corporation (CBC) broadcast on radio, in both French and English, the FLQ Manifesto.[18] The latter set out a rambling list of resentments about anglophone domination, argued for the need to secure rights and autonomy for francophones, and denounced capitalism, the Catholic Church, Bourassa, and Trudeau. It ended with the following:

> We are Quebec workers and we are prepared to go all the way. With the help of the entire population, we want to replace this society of slaves by a free society, operating by itself and for itself, a society open on the world. Our struggle can only be victorious. A people that has awakened cannot long be kept in misery and contempt.

Long live Free Quebec!
Long live our comrades the political prisoners!
Long live the Quebec Revolution!
Long live the Front de Libération du Québec![19]

On October 10, a warm Saturday afternoon, members of the FLQ's Chénier Cell kidnapped Pierre Laporte, Quebec's deputy premier, at gunpoint from his home in Montreal while he was playing on the front lawn with his young nephew. Once again, a set of demands were released that would involve the swap of another twenty-three "political prisoners" for Laporte, whom they pejoratively referred to as the "Minister of Unemployment and Assimilation."

Needless to say, Canadians from all regions of the country were watching these events unfold on their television screens. At the same time, members of Parliament in Ottawa were figuring out how to respond to the crisis. It was soon apparent that the federal government would have to intervene in the matter lest events escalate even further. On October 12, using provisions of the National Defence Act, Canadian Forces troops were called out to support the police in Ottawa, and on October 15, at the request of the Quebec National Assembly, they began to patrol the streets of Montreal as well.

Perhaps the most telling response came from the mouth of the prime minister. When Tim Ralfe, a CBC reporter, asked Trudeau on October 13 whether the government would deploy the Canadian military to protect cabinet ministers and other senior officials in Quebec, Trudeau remarked, "Society must take every means at its disposal to defend itself against the emergence of a parallel power which defies the elected power" and that sought to establish its authority by kidnapping and blackmail. Ralfe objected that if the government went further, it would have repercussions in terms of "the kind of society [we] live in." Trudeau responded: "Well, there's a lot of bleeding hearts around who just don't like to see people with helmets and guns. All I can say is, go on and bleed, but it's more important to keep law and order in this society than to be worried about weak-kneed people." Ralfe then asked how far the prime minister would go to deal with the FLQ, to which Trudeau responded with the famous phrase, "Well, just watch me."[20]

When pushed further, and now visibly losing his patience with Ralfe's line of questioning that asked if he would use wiretapping and begin the process of reducing civil liberties, Trudeau remarked that he was willing to "go to any distance" to stop the FLQ from terrorizing the streets of Montreal.

While English Canadians were aghast at the violence they were seeing on their television screens, French Canadian support for the FLQ seemed to be rising with each passing day. Such differing takes on the events further exposed the fault lines between the two founding communities, setting in motion repercussions that would, in many ways, culminate in the provincial referendum of October 30, 1995 (chapter 7). Two days after Trudeau's famous comments to the CBC reporter, for example, the trade union leader Michel Chartrand remarked at a rally that popular support for the FLQ was very high, adding, "We are going to win because there are more boys ready to shoot Members of Parliament than there are policemen."[21] The rally frightened many anglophone Quebecers in particular, and Canadians in general, who heard in such comments the threat of a full-blown insurrection in Quebec.

In response, Trudeau implemented the War Measures Act, a statute of the Canadian Parliament that represented the federal means to respond to a declaration of war, invasion, or insurrection, and set out the types of emergency measures that the federal government could take as a result. Such measures included, but were not limited to, censorship, the suspension of habeas corpus (the right of a detained individual to have a judge confirm that the detention is legal), and the granting of wider-than-normal powers to the police—precisely the types of curtailments of civil liberties that Ralfe had questioned Trudeau about in his interview. It is worth noting that the invocation of this act was not confined to Quebec, but included all of Canada, from Victoria, British Columbia, to St. John's, Newfoundland.

In an address to the nation on October 16, Trudeau said that although he was reluctant to invoke the act and realized it "suspends the operation of the Canadian Bill of Rights," the precursor to the Charter of Rights and Freedoms (see chapter 3), it also "gives sweeping powers to the Government." He continued:

> I recognize, as I hope do others, that this extreme position into which governments have been forced is in some respects a trap. It is a well-known technique of revolutionary groups who attempt to destroy society by unjustified violence to

goad the authorities into inflexible attitudes. The revolutionaries then employ this evidence of alleged authoritarianism as justification for the need to use violence in their renewed attacks on the social structure. I appeal to all Canadians not to become so obsessed by what the government has done today in response to terrorism that they forget the opening play in this vicious game. That play was taken by the revolutionaries; they chose to use bombing, murder and kidnapping.[22]

This was only the third time in Canadian history that the War Measures Act had been implemented. It was used to strip Ukrainian Canadians of their rights and allowed their internment during the First World War, and it was used to intern Japanese Canadians during the Second World War. The October Crisis was the first time it had been activated in peacetime.

Trudeau's invocation of the act was, in many ways, unprecedented. For one thing, it curtailed the rights of all Canadians, not just those residing in Quebec. Despite this, however, he was overwhelmingly supported by Canadians, from all regions of Canada. According to a December Gallup poll, the majority of both Quebecers (86 per cent) and Canadians (89 per cent) approved of Trudeau's implementation of the War Measures Act.[23]

There were certainly vocal critics of the federal government's response. Some argued that it was an overreaction on the part of Trudeau and the federal government. Others claimed that Trudeau invoked it to crush Quebec separatism. Perhaps most notably, Tommy Douglas, the leader of the New Democratic Party, remarked that "the government, I submit, is using a sledgehammer to crack a peanut."[24]

Prescient also were the comments of René Lévesque, a former journalist who had founded the Parti Québécois in 1968 (and who, ten years later as premier, would become the first to attempt to negotiate the political independence of Quebec through a referendum). Lévesque argued that Quebecers were no longer in charge of their own destiny and that the Bourassa government now essentially functioned as "a puppet in the hands of the federal leaders." Of the presumed size of the revolutionary army, he wrote, "Until we receive proof to the contrary, we will believe that such a minute, numerically unimportant fraction is involved, that rushing into the enforcement of the War Measures Act was a panicky and altogether excessive reaction, especially when you think of the inordinate length of time they want to maintain this regime."[25]

On October 17, one day after the invocation of the War Measures Act, the FLQ released a statement saying they had executed Pierre Laporte, whom they again referred to as the "Minister of Unemployment and Assimilation." The statement shocked the nation. Police soon found Laporte's strangled body stuffed into the trunk of a car that had been abandoned on the outskirts of Montreal. James Cross's kidnappers also released a statement that said they had decided to suspend the death sentence against Cross, but would only release him once a number of their demands had been met. These included publication of the FLQ Manifesto; release of twenty-three political prisoners; provision of an airplane to take them to either Cuba or Algeria; a payment, which they called a "voluntary tax," of $500,000, to be loaded aboard the plane prior to departure; and the name of a police informer who had reported on the FLQ earlier in the year.

With tanks on the streets of Montreal and in other parts of Quebec, and with movement drastically curtailed, police begin making raids on FLQ houses and arrested nearly five hundred people. On December 4, after almost two months of conflict, negotiations with the FLQ Liberation Cell finally led to the safe release of James Cross.[26] The five known kidnappers were granted safe passage to Cuba—flown there in a Canadian Forces aircraft—after Cuban prime minister Fidel Castro granted approval.[27]

From that moment forward, it seemed to be agreed that independence could only come about by means of the political process—such as provincial referendums—as opposed to acts of violence or terrorism. Nevertheless, for many of the FLQ's supporters, including those who did not endorse kidnapping or murder, the sight of the Canadian army in Quebec, and the detention of hundreds of their fellow citizens, reflected exactly the type of imperialism that led to their resistance in the first place.

V

The facts of the October Crisis, including its prehistory in nationalist resentment, are relatively easy to recount, but its effect on the shaping of modern Canada is a little trickier to articulate. In part this stems from the date that one chooses to determine its importance. For example, if I chose October 5, the day that Cross was kidnapped, as the date that signals the beginning of the crisis, we could argue that it symbolizes the day subterranean tensions between francophone and anglophone Canada—tensions that, as we saw, predated Confederation—were exposed to the light of day. If Canada was to proceed as a nation, such tensions would have to be acknowledged and addressed using political processes as opposed to acts of violence. While the conflict ended fairly quickly—by January 1971 all was restored to normal in the sense that most detainees had been released and the War Measures Act was lifted—the tensions never disappeared (see chapters 3 and 7). They were now out in the open for all Canadians to see.

In this context, virtually all the other chapters of this book circle back to the crisis and all that led up to it. In the provincial election of 1976, for example, René Lévesque's Parti Québécois (henceforth PQ) formed the provincial government for the first time. The PQ ran on a platform of national sovereignty that involved Quebec's independence from Canada. While many francophone Quebecers greeted the PQ victory with celebration, many of the province's anglophone residents began to relocate to other places, particularly Toronto. Foreshadowing the 1995 provincial referendum on Quebec sovereignty (chapter 7), the PQ held the first independence referendum on May 20, 1980, asking Quebecers if the province should pursue a path toward sovereignty. Sixty per cent, a fairly sizable majority, of Quebecers said no.

When the Canadian Constitution was patriated in 1982 (chapter 3), all the provincial governments eventually endorsed the new Constitution, except for that of Quebec. The province refused to sign because it would not be granted a veto over future constitutional issues. Unlike the other provinces, Quebec regarded the new Constitution as an illegitimate assault on its sovereignty. The province asked the Quebec Court of Appeal and the Supreme Court of Canada if, given Canada's history, Quebec had a veto to block amendments to the Constitution. The Supreme Court ultimately ruled that granting Quebec a veto would undermine the principle of equality of all ten provinces. "From a political view," said René Lévesque, "it is as clear as spring water that this marks the end of a 115-year-old illusion."[28] The Government of Quebec also objected to the inclusion of a Charter of Rights, which it claimed would subsume provincial matters under federal jurisdiction.

These tensions between anglophone and francophone Canada have also structured the issue of the rights of Indigenous populations (chapter 8). While there is now a general recognition that Canada came into existence from three founding groups—French, English, and Indigenous—the history of Canada's treatment of the last group certainly does not reflect this reality. While the PQ was the first provincial government to recognize the rights of Indigenous peoples to self-determination, it did so only to the extent that such self-determination did not infringe on the territorial integrity of Quebec. Indigenous leaders in Quebec have tended not to support separation because of what it would mean for their land claims with the province, especially since they have never been consulted on the legal matters of separation. In this context, some of the most dramatic confrontations between Indigenous and non-Indigenous Canadians have taken place in Quebec, such as the Mohawk blockades at Oka and the Mercier Bridge near the Kahnawake Reserve near Montreal, both of which occurred in the summer of 1990.

VI

As important as October 5 was for the history of anglophone-francophone relations, I have chosen instead to highlight October 13. This date structures the importance of the event very differently. October 13 was the day that Trudeau uttered the famous words "Just watch me." That remark signalled that he—and the federal government—was willing to do anything, including curtailing the rights of all Canadians, to attain his objectives. It is on October 13, then, that we see just how easy it was—and potentially still is—for the federal government to limit the basic rights of its citizens.

Under the powers of the War Measures Act, for instance, police conducted over three thousand searches and detained close to five hundred individuals.[29] All those arrested under the act were denied due process, and habeas corpus was suspended. That meant the Crown could hold suspects for seven days before charging them with a crime and, if necessary, for another twenty-one days if the extension was ordered before the first seven days had passed. Prisoners had no recourse to legal counsel, and many were not allowed to communicate with family. Simple membership in the FLQ became a criminal offence. Innocence and guilt were determined by executive decree rather than in a court of law.

This use of emergency powers resulted in the subversion of many features of the democratic process, in addition to human rights abuses. Newspapers, especially student ones, were subject to censorship. Police cautioned editors at the *McGill Daily* not to attack the War Measures Act or express sympathy with the FLQ. Printers of student newspapers in Toronto and Halifax refused to publish the FLQ Manifesto, and police visited student papers as far away as Victoria, British Columbia, to remind student editors that it was forbidden to publish the document.[30] Prominent media personalities were arrested and interrogated, including Louis Fournier, a radio host at the major Montreal radio station CKAC, and journalist Pol Chantraine. E.S. Hallman, vice president at Radio-Canada, the French-language unit of the CBC, forbade his reporters from commenting on the crisis. When Michel Bourdon did, he was suspended and then fired for insubordination. Gérard Pelletier, a former journalist who was secretary of state in the Trudeau government, visited Claude Ryan, editor of *Le Devoir*, a major French-language newspaper in Montreal, to ensure that he and other editors engaged in self-censorship.[31] This intimidation of the media was unprecedented in modern Canada.

The effects of the War Measures Act reverberated across Canada in ways that did not relate directly to the crisis precipitated by the FLQ's actions. In Hull, for instance, the Sûreté du Québec raided the home of a woman who had been photographed at a demonstration to protest the imposition of the War Measures Act. In British Columbia, police arrested seven members of the Vancouver Liberation Front, a fringe group sympathetic to the aims of the FLQ, for distributing copies of the FLQ Manifesto in Vancouver. British Columbia premier W.A.C. Bennett issued an order-in-council that forbade teachers in the province—including college and university professors—from expressing sympathy with the FLQ. The order, dated October 22, 1970, proclaimed that "no person teaching or instructing our youth in educational institutions receiving government support shall continue in the employment of the educational institution if they advocate the policies of Le Front de Liberation du Quebec, or the overthrow of democratically elected governments by violent means."[32] Such a threat of dismissal represented a direct limit on free speech, and at least one individual, a high school teacher in Dawson Creek, was dismissed for discussing the FLQ in his classroom.[33] Vancouver's mayor, Tom Campbell, announced that he would use the emergency powers granted by the War Measures Act to run hippies and draft dodgers out of town.[34] Though Campbell never followed through, the fact that civil liberties could be abrogated—or that abrogation could be threatened—in places so far removed from the actual crisis was a serious issue. That the overwhelming majority of Canadians had no problem with this violation is equally problematic.

When national security concerns trump human rights, many problems can follow. In early 1971, for example, Quebec's minister of justice, Jérôme Choquette, supported the creation of an identity card—including photograph and fingerprints—for all citizens.[35] Choquette also encouraged Ottawa to revoke the citizenship of FLQ prisoners who were deported during the crisis. And Jean-Pierre Goyer, the federal solicitor general, mused in public about the possibility of enacting peacetime emergency legislation to allow the government to act quickly and decisively in any future crisis.[36]

Although none of these ideas came to fruition at the time, that they were raised meant they were now in the public domain. And many of them were revisited in Parliament after the terrorist attacks in the United States on September 11, 2001—a fact that is perhaps most clearly visible in the passage of Bill C-51, the Anti-terrorism Act.[37] This controversial bill, put forward by Stephen Harper's government in 2015, allowed governmental agencies to share information on Canadians and strengthened the powers of the Canadian Security Intelligence Services. In light of Trudeau's invocation of the War Measures Act and the passage of bills such as C-51, any time a particular group—political, ethnic, or religious—is seen as a problem, civil liberties, and by extension the democratic principles on which they rest, are now potentially threatened. The most recent version of this occurred on February 15, 2022, when Justin Trudeau invoked the Emergency Act (drafted in 1988 to replace the War Measures Act), which curtailed citizens' rights to free movement and assembly, in an attempt to end the blockades and protests over COVID-19 measures. In this context it is worth noting that abusive states have frequently used such measures to harass peaceful, if politically or ethnically problematic, citizens. This restricts freedom of movement and speech, just as it invades the privacy of citizens.

VII

Reflecting on the October Crisis years later, Lorne Nystrom—at the time of the crisis a twenty-four-year-old rookie NDP MP from Saskatchewan, who, along with his fifteen NDP colleagues, voted against the implementation of the War Measures Act—argued that Trudeau's response ultimately hurt the prime minister and Canada more generally. "If you were against the act," he reminisced in 1990, "you were made to feel un-Canadian." But, he said, Trudeau "lost the support of all those civil libertarians who had previously regarded him as one of their own, and I do not think he ever got it back."[38] In the same interview, he compared the situation in 1970 to that of the Oka crisis in the summer of 1990. The latter was a land dispute between the Mohawk Nation and the town of Oka, Quebec, over a proposed golf course. "When the War Measures Act was declared, there was an open debate about it. When the army was called in this summer [to Oka], there was not even a recall of the House to discuss the situation. So how far have we progressed in our respect for civil liberties?"

For many Canadians, the October Crisis was about a quickly escalating situation between francophone and anglophone Canadians in Quebec. Despite the chaos and uncertainty surrounding those events, the situation was quickly dealt with. However, Trudeau's "Just watch me" on October 13 has had a lasting significance on Canadian democracy and the rights and freedoms of individuals in Canada, stretching to the present and into the future.

SUGGESTIONS FOR FURTHER READING

Dominique Clément. "October Crisis." *Canada's Human Rights History*. https://historyofrights.ca/history/october-crisis/.

John English. *Just Watch Me: The Life of Pierre Trudeau. Volume 2: 1968–2000*. Toronto: Knopf Canada, 2009.

Marian Botsford Fraser. *Acting for Freedom: Fifty Years of Civil Liberties in Canada*. Toronto: Second Story Press, 2013.

Louis Hamelin. *October 1970: A Novel*. Translated by Wayne Grady. Toronto: House of Anansi Press, 2013.

D'arcy Jenish. *October Crisis: Canada's Long Nightmare of Terrorism at the Hands of the FLQ*. Toronto: Doubleday Canada, 2018.

William Tetley. *The October Crisis, 1970: An Insider's View*. Montreal and Kingston: McGill-Queen's University Press, 2006.

Pierre Vallières. *White N-----s of America: The Precocious Autobiography of a Quebec "Terrorist."* Translated by Joan Pinkham. New York: Monthly Review Press, 1971. (The French original appeared in 1968 as *N----s blancs d'Amérique*).

SUGGESTIONS FOR FURTHER VIEWING

Catherine Annau. *Just Watch Me: Trudeau and the '70s Generation*. National Film Board of Canada, 1999.

Robin Spry. *Action: The October Crisis of 1970*. National Film Board of Canada, 1973. www.nfb.ca/film/action_the_october_crisis_of_1970/.

2

SEPTEMBER 28 1972

Team Canada's Most Famous Goal

"CANADA IS FIRST IN THE WORLD IN TWO THINGS," Team Canada coach Harry Sinden remarked in the summer of 1972, "hockey and wheat. In that order."[1] Canadians then and now have prided themselves on the fact that no one plays better hockey than we do. And we certainly have the evidence to legitimate such claims—and our bragging rights. The first indoor game, for example, occurred on Canadian ice, in Montreal, on March 3, 1875. Even the Stanley Cup, the championship trophy of the National Hockey League (NHL), and today the symbol of professional supremacy throughout the world, was first awarded in 1893 to recognize the Canadian amateur champion. Indeed, 381 Canadian players (both active and non-active) participated in the 1972–73 NHL season, compared to eighteen Americans and four from all other nationalities.[2] During a few short weeks in September 1972, however, this myth of supremacy was severely put to the test.

I

Sports, especially when played at the international level, are never just about friendly competition. In the background, often but not always hidden, lurks a host of political issues. In 1972, for instance, the Cold War had been in place for nearly a quarter century, with the result that any sporting event between the Soviet Union and a Western country was destined to be about more than just sports. Hockey rinks and other sports venues became one of the major arenas where rival powers could meet to assert their dominance without actually going to war with one another. One did not just want to win; one had to win at all costs to demonstrate that one's socio-economic system was superior to that of one's rivals. As Phil Esposito, Team Canada's assistant captain for the 1972 Summit Series, put it immediately after his team had been booed for losing Game 4 by a score of 5–3 in Vancouver: "As I was doing [the interview], people were yelling and screaming at us, calling me names, 'Communism is better, don't you admit it now,' and all this other stuff. This is Vancouver! Guys in the stand were yelling 'Communism is best. It is supreme.' That's when I really realized, man we are in a war here. This is no game. This is war."[3]

Further proof, if needed, that international sporting competitions were highly charged political events came from Munich at the same time as the events recounted in this chapter. On September 4, just as Game 2 between the Soviets and Canada's best NHL players was wrapping up in Maple Leaf Gardens, members of Black September, a Palestinian terrorist organization, sneaked into the Olympic Village and took Israeli athletes hostage. The murder of the athletes two days later made clear, if it was ever in doubt, that the world of sports has always been used to make political statements.

While these events in Munich, based as they are on nationalism and political resentment, evoke the spirit of the previous chapter, the story this chapter seeks to tell is one of catharsis, as Canadians of all stripes came together to cheer for a Canadian men's hockey team against an unknown group of supposed amateurs from the Soviet Union. For the first time in their history, the Canadians were known simply as "Team Canada," and it was assumed that they would demolish their opposition. The reality turned out to be rather different than anticipated. In four short weeks, tensions boiled over amid accusations of spying, attempts at manipulation off the ice, and bad-tempered behaviour on it. For what? The Summit Series, as it came to be known, was neither a championship nor a world hockey tournament. It was little more than a pre-season exhibition series. There was no trophy. No gold medals. Only bragging rights.

II

Relations between Canada and the USSR leading up to September 1972 were, as was to be expected, tense. Though lacking the paranoia and blacklists seen in the United States, Canada's relations with the Soviets are best summed up by the so-called Gouzenko Affair, which had occurred nearly thirty years earlier and had exposed a purported spy ring of Canadian communists who were passing secret information, including government files, to the USSR. Igor Gouzenko, a clerk at the Soviet Embassy in Ottawa, defected three days after the end of the Second World War, bringing with him a set of documents that showed how the Soviets were spying on the West using, among other things, sleeper cells. Some have gone so far as to call this defection the Cold War's point of origin.[4] Canada's prime minister, William Lyon Mackenzie King, established a Royal Commission with the intention of investigating and exposing Soviet espionage in Canada.

The Kellock-Taschereau Commission was responsible for the arrest of the Canadians named in Gouzenko's documents. Those detained were not provided with legal counsel and were allowed no contact with the outside world until they were summoned before the commission. The most well-known to be charged was Fred Rose, a communist and the MP for the Labor-Progressive Party in Montreal. He became the only sitting MP convicted of spying for a foreign country, after which he was expelled from the House of Commons. After four-and-a-half years in jail, he moved to Warsaw, at which point he had his Canadian citizenship revoked.[5]

Most Canadian prime ministers maintained the same mistrust of the Soviet Union. In 1949, for example, Canada joined the North Atlantic Treaty Organization (NATO), the most important Western alliance against the Soviet Bloc. In 1950, Canadian forces joined those of the United Nations in the Korean War, an important theatre of the Cold War. After the Soviet Union acquired nuclear weapons, Canadians were worried that any Soviet attack on the United States would have to go through Canadian airspace.

This led to Canada's entry into the North American Aerospace Defense agreement (NORAD) with the US.

Liberal governments tended to be more interested in developing good relations with the Soviets. After the death of Stalin, for example, Lester B. Pearson—secretary of state for external affairs and a future prime minister—visited Moscow in 1955 for talks with the new leader, Nikita Khrushchev. In so doing, he became the first foreign minister of a NATO country to visit the Soviet Union.

When Pierre Trudeau came to power in 1968, Canadian policy changed dramatically. He was much more favourably disposed and sympathetic to communist nations than were the leaders of other Western nations, especially those of the United States. It was perhaps no coincidence that Trudeau had decided, years earlier, to engage in doctoral-level work at the London School of Economics, where he went to study with Harold Laski, former chairman of the British Labour Party and a noted Marxist economist.[6] Though Trudeau kept Canada in NATO when he was prime minister, he often pursued an independent path from other leaders when it came to international relations. In 1970, for example, he was among the first Western leaders to establish diplomatic relations with the People's Republic of China, and he went on an official visit to Beijing in 1973 where, among other things, he met with Mao Zedong. He was also a friend and admirer of Cuba's Fidel Castro.

These actions were driven by Trudeau's desire to lessen Canada's reliance on the United States by forging closer ties with other countries, while also trying to liberate Canada from the same Cold War mentality that had hamstrung the United States. During a trip to the Soviet Union in 1971, he remarked that the United States, just across the border, posed a much bigger existential threat to Canada than the Soviet Union, which was farther away. "The Americans," he declared at a press conference in Moscow on May 20, to the consternation of many, are a greater "danger to our national identity from a cultural, economic and perhaps even military point of view."[7]

Despite Trudeau's sympathies, any hockey game or series between the two countries could only be scheduled after the organizers had waded through decades of ignorance and mistrust. And while sports, like other cultural events, were meant to thaw tensions, they could just as easily further contribute to them.

III

It is within this larger context of Cold War mistrust, and thawed or thawing relations between Canada and the Soviet Union, that we must situate what would become the most famous goal and the most famous game in the history of Canadian hockey, if not hockey more generally. Since the Summit Series took place in the midst of the Cold War, preparations for its organization could be neither simple nor straightforward. While Canadians and Soviets had played against one another before the series, this was to be the first competition between a Soviet national team and a Canadian team made up of professional players from the NHL.

The intention of the Summit Series was to showcase a best-on-best hockey competition: the best Canadians were to play the best Soviets. Though the Canadians had long been dominant in international hockey, it is worth noting that their success on the international stage had waned in the years leading up to the series. Before the Soviet Union's entrance into international competition in 1954, Canada had won six out of seven gold medals at the Olympic Games and ten world championships. However, for the next thirty years, from 1962 to 1993, Canada won neither an Olympic gold medal nor a world championship.

The Soviet rise and Canadian diminution were a direct result of the fact that international competitions favoured the Soviets because professional players were deemed ineligible to participate. This ruled out Canadians playing in the NHL, and since the USSR had no "professional" leagues, Soviets were allowed to send their best players to such competitions. To protest, Canada withdrew from all official events run by the International Ice Hockey Federation (IIHF), the world governing body for hockey, in 1970 and suspended their national team program after being refused permission to use semi-professional players (though they would later return to the IIHF in 1977).

In the winter of 1971–1972, Gary Smith, a diplomat at the Canadian embassy in Moscow responsible for sport and cultural exchanges with the Soviet Union, learned of the Soviets' interest in developing a hockey series with Canada. He approached Soviet hockey boss Andrei Starovoitov, who told Smith that he would like to see a series between the USSR national team and Canadian professionals. Smith passed the idea on to Ottawa with the aim of figuring out the logistics. That spring, matters were finalized.

The two sides agreed on the terms:

- Four games to be played in Canada—in the Montreal Forum, Toronto's Maple Leaf Gardens, the Winnipeg Arena, and the Pacific Coliseum in Vancouver—and four games to be played in the Soviet Union, all of them in the Luzhniki Ice Palace in Moscow.
- The Canadians agreed to hold the series in September and play the games under international rules.
- IIHF amateur referees would officiate the games played in Canada, and European referees would work those to be played in Moscow.
- The international two-referee system would be used, as opposed to the NHL system of one referee and two linesmen.

Alan Eagleson—indefatigable organizer, Hockey Canada director, first executive director of the NHL Players Association, and later disgraced fraudster—played a particularly important role in promoting the series as he was able to garner support from a large network of players, NHL team owners, and Hockey Canada executives. At Eagleson's insistence, Harry Sinden was chosen as the coach of the team, which for the first time was known simply as Team Canada. Eagleson, who had originally wanted to call the team the "NHL All-Stars," was also responsible for the decision to exclude those stars who had signed with the World Hockey Association (WHA)—a rival league to the NHL that had been founded in 1971 and played its first game in October 1972. The most famous players to be excluded from Team Canada were Bobby Hull of the Winnipeg Jets and goalie Gerry Cheevers, who was on the verge of signing with the Cleveland Crusaders. Even a personal appeal from Prime Minster Trudeau was unable to change this.[8]

Team Canada was a veritable who's who of hockey players familiar to any Canadian of a certain age: Ken Dryden, Phil Esposito, Bobby Clarke, Frank Mahovlich, Yvan Cournoyer, Serge Savard, Stan Mikita, and Paul Henderson, to name only a few. (Bobby Orr was out with an injury.) Though the Canadian government had wanted to call the series the Friendship Series, at the time it was simply called the Canada–USSR Series. It was only given the name Summit Series after the fact.

IV

Both teams knew very little about one another. There were, after all, no Russian players in the NHL (the first ones would only begin to arrive in the late 1980s). While the Canadians were confident in their belief that they would win—if not actually sweep—the series, the Soviets were equally convinced that their team was as good as, if not better than, any team found in the NHL. For their whole lives, Canadians—including all those who were to play on Team Canada—had been taught that no one played better hockey than they. Many Canadian fans, and most Canadian media, expected a one-sided romp with eight straight victories. Father David Bauer, who created and coached Canada's first amateur national team in 1962, wrote in the *Toronto Sun*, "I expect total victory from the National Hockey League All-Stars in their series against the Soviet Union." He continued by remarking that "what they'll have to do, however, is dedicate themselves to this eight-game series from start to finish. By that I mean from training camp right on until after the last game. If they do that, I cannot see how they could fail."[9] Failure, in sum, was not an option.

Canadian journalists echoed this sentiment. Milt Dunnell (*Toronto Star*), Jim Coleman (Southam News), and Claude Larochelle (*Le Soleil*) all predicted that Canada would win the series seven games to one. American journalists Gerald Eskenazi (*New York Times*) and Frank Rosa (*Boston Globe*) both predicted eight wins to none, while Mark Mulvoy (*Sports Illustrated*) predicted seven wins to one for the Canadians.[10] A dissenting opinion was offered by the *Montreal Star*'s John Robertson, who wrote at the time that Team Canada was too ill-prepared and too out of shape to win. He blamed not the players, but the NHL: "This, the most important hockey event of our time, has been tacked onto the front of the NHL season as something only tolerated by the owners, and endorsed by the players as a means of enriching their pension plan."[11]

On August 23, members of Team Canada arrived in Toronto and began training for what they thought would be a whitewash. Coach Sinden named four co-captains: Phil Esposito, Frank Mahovlich, Stan Mikita, and Jean Ratelle. As the players admitted in the documentary *Cold War on Ice*, they did not take training very seriously. Esposito joked that the only ice he had seen that summer was in his vodka.

The team trained for three weeks in Toronto, arrived in Montreal on August 31, and held a practice on September 1 at the Forum. With Orr injured and Hull ineligible, some of the younger or lesser-known players would soon get their chance to shine, including the forward line of Bobby Clarke, Ron Ellis, and Paul Henderson.

The first game took place in an overly hot Forum at 8 p.m. on the evening of September 2 in front of close to nineteen thousand fans, with millions more watching at home on their television screens. The Soviets refused to release their starting lineup until Team Canada released theirs. Sinden had wanted to start the Ellis-Clarke-Henderson line against the line of Soviet star Valeri Kharlamov, but since Kharlamov's line did not start, he put Phil Esposito's line on for the opening faceoff.[12] The decision proved to be prescient, as Esposito scored after just thirty seconds of play. Six minutes later, Henderson made it 2–0 for Team Canada. All seemed to be on course to show the world that Canadians were truly the best hockey players on the planet.

However, that was not to be. After their initial shock, the Russians regrouped and began to attack. Most worrisome for the Canadian bench, they seemed to have no problem getting through Canada's defence.[13] Reminiscing on the forty-year anniversary of the Summit Series' first game, Gerald Eskenazi, the hockey reporter for the *New York Times*, described the situation as the young Russian team came to life and scored its first goal:

> I watched the Soviets move the puck toward Dryden. They passed the blue line, and my view was extraordinary: the Soviets stopped suddenly and got into position—pieces in a chess match. Canadian skaters blocked the middle. But Alexander Yakushev sent the puck darting into the players in front of him. Somehow, as if guided by some out-of-this-world technology, it slithered through untouched to Evgeny Zimin, who was standing whispering distance from Dryden. Zimin swatted at the puck. It flew past Dryden, the prettiest goal I had ever seen.[14]

By the end of the first period, the Soviets had recovered enough to tie the score at 2–2. The game ultimately ended 7–3 in their favour.

Canadians were shocked. Coach Sinden remarked after the game that the Soviets "outplayed us in goaltending, shooting, passing," to which a journalist for the *Gazette* wrote: "And he could have added, 'in bodychecking, forechecking, backchecking—and sportsmanship.'"[15] Commenting on the game, former Canadiens coach Claude Ruel remarked that the Soviet forwards were one of the most finely honed units he had ever seen. "They are always moving, never standing around, they head-man the puck as well as anyone has ever done—and they always seem to be in the right place."[16] The Canadians, by contrast, were all over the place: "We didn't play our game at all," said goalie Dryden. "After they tied it up, we started playing a panic type of game. Sometimes there were five men all going for the puck at once."[17]

To make matters worse, after the game was over, Team Canada—whether by accident or out of frustration—returned directly to the dressing room without shaking hands with the Soviets.[18] The stage had been set for a battle, not just a series of hockey games. And it was a battle that began to draw on stereotypes. The Canadians were perceived as overconfident, even arrogant; the Russians as robots without personality. Coming out of the summer off-season, the Canadian players were perhaps not as fit as they should have been, and they did not practise well, so assured were they of victory. The Soviets, on the other hand, were tough, lean, and out to prove a point not just to the world of hockey, but to the world more generally. Whereas the Canadians thought it would be an easy series against the equivalent of a junior team, the Soviets sought to show their domination to a stunned West.

The second game was played in Toronto's Maple Leaf Gardens two days later, on September 4. Having been roundly outclassed, the Canadians decided to change their tactics from Game 1. They now sought to intimidate the contact-averse Soviets with aggressive play and hard bodychecking. The change proved successful as they went on to win the game, 4–1, and tie the series. In a motif that would weave throughout the series, the Soviet coaches blamed the loss on poor refereeing, arguing that the American referees had favoured the Canadians. When the game ended, Andrei Starovoitov, head of the USSR Hockey Federation, barged into the officials' dressing room and kicked chairs over as he berated the two referees.[19] The pair had been scheduled to referee the fourth game in Vancouver, but Team Canada agreed to the Soviet demand to replace them.

After tying the third game 4–4 in Winnipeg on September 6, the series moved to Vancouver's Pacific Coliseum on the 8th for the fourth and final game to be played on Canadian soil. During the warm-up, Team Canada players were surprised to hear boos ring out from some in the crowd. Canada went on to lose the game 5–3, and the players were booed off the ice. This caused Phil Esposito, who had emerged as the team's unofficial leader over the course of the series, to lash out at the Canadian fans. In an interview aired on national television at the end of the game, he remarked,

> I cannot believe it. Some of our guys are really, really down in the dumps. We know, we're trying like hell. I mean, we're doing the best we can, and they got a good team, and let's face facts. But it doesn't mean that we're not giving it our 150 per cent, because we certainly are. I mean, the more—every one of us guys, thirty-five guys that came out and played for Team Canada. We did it because we love our country, and not for any other reason, no other reason. They can throw the money, uh, for the pension fund out the window. They can throw anything they want out the window. We came because we love Canada. And even though we play in the United States, and we earn money in the United States, Canada is still our home, and that's the only reason we come. And I don't think it's fair that we should be booed.[20]

As Roy MacGregor from the *Globe and Mail* put it: "The Americans have their great speeches from Gettysburg, and Kennedy's 'Ask not what your country can do for you' speech, but our great speech was by a sweaty hockey player in a rink in Vancouver."[21]

In the span of one week, having lost two games and tied another, Team Canada and Canadians across the nation had to confront the uncomfortable fact that they were not genetically predisposed to be superior hockey players. The series was quickly demonstrating the superior preparation and conditioning of the Soviet players. The latter's skill, discipline, and long passes that were able to split the Canadian defence were starkly juxtaposed with the individualistic and aggressive play of the Canadians. On display were two different styles of hockey—styles that had never confronted one another in the highest echelons of hockey and that would, in the years to follow, increasingly come together to change the game forever.

After the Canadian half of the series was done, Team Canada took a few days off, then travelled to Sweden for a pair of exhibition games before arriving in Moscow to play the remaining four games of the series. Canada lost the first game of the series on Soviet ice, and the fifth game overall, by a score of 5–4.

Team Canada now had to win all the remaining games if they were to take the series. Though they won the sixth game 3–2, the Canadians criticized the poor officiating of the two German referees. Coach Sinden called them "entirely incompetent—the worst officials I've ever seen in my life." And team leader Esposito complained that the referees would, among other things, drop the pucks at faceoffs before the Canadian players were ready. He complained to the Canadian reporters, "So while I'm saying 'Bergey [Gary Bergman], take that guy,' the dummy drops the puck. Bang-bang and it's in the net. Hell, that's awful. It's not bad, it's worse than bad. I thought I saw some bad refereeing when I was a kid, but they're even worse than my old man."[22]

Game 6 proved to be the turning point in the series, for better and worse. Team Canada decided to target Valeri Kharlamov, the Soviet forward, who had greatly impressed the Canadians. In the second period, Bobby Clarke, in retaliation for a hit by Kharlamov, rubbed the latter's face with his glove and a fight ensued. Peter Mahovlich later elbowed Kharlamov, who retaliated by shoving Mahovlich to the ice. Later, Clarke raced down the ice to catch a streaking Kharlamov and deliberately slashed his already sore ankle, fracturing it. It was subsequently reported that Clarke had been told by John Ferguson, the assistant coach, to deliberately target the ankle because he knew Kharlamov was favouring it. At any rate, it was a cheap shot. As Kharlamov made his way to the dressing room, he skated by the Canadian bench and yelled at the Canadians. Clarke was given a minor penalty for slashing and an additional ten-minute misconduct.

On the thirtieth anniversary of the series, Henderson called the slashing incident "the low point of the series," though he apologized when Clarke publicly complained.[23] The Russians condemned the slash, and Russian fans became increasingly disgruntled at what they perceived to be the dirtiness of the Canadian style of play.

After Team Canada won Game 7 by a score of 4–3, to even the series 3–3–1, all eyes turned to the final game, to be played in Moscow's Luzhniki Ice Palace on September 28. There was now sufficient ill-will on both sides. "To me, it was war," Esposito said in 1989. "There's no doubt in my mind that I think I would have killed to win." On the forty-year anniversary of the series, Ron Ellis, Clarke's linemate, remarked, "The pressure put on both teams to win was unbelievable. I found myself doing things that were uncharacteristic for me as well, and it was because of the emotion. We felt like we were representing our way of life."[24]

Game 8—a hockey game-cum-ideological battle—thus took place in a highly charged atmosphere, as veritable a theatre of the Cold War as one could imagine. With Clarke's mean-spirited slash in everyone's minds, and amidst rumours that the KGB had been spying on the Canadian players to learn their tactics, there were also charges, again on the part of the Canadians, that the referees and timekeepers were actively working to scupper a Canadian victory. The tension was so electric that Canadian team executives nearly came to blows with their Soviet counterparts, both on the bench and in the stands. Prior to the eighth game, the Soviets wanted to back out of the refereeing agreement. They sought to return the two German referees—the ones Esposito had remarked were "even worse than my old man"—in place of the referees who had originally been scheduled to officiate. Eagleson threatened to prevent Team Canada from playing. Eventually a compromise was reached: one of the Germans would officiate, and the second German would be replaced by another official.

Team Canada took a number of questionable penalties early in the game. With two Canadian players in the penalty box, the Soviets scored the first goal of the game. Violence was not far from erupting. The officials charged J.P. Parise for interference. Moments later they called him for misconduct after he banged his stick on the ice. When he skated across the ice with stick raised and threated to swing it at the German official, he was given a match penalty. As he remarked years later, "I had never gotten a misconduct penalty—I don't know if I was ever kicked out of a game before, ever."[25] To signal his displeasure, Sinden threw a chair on the ice.

With the Soviets leading by a score of 5–4 in the third period, Cournoyer scored to tie up the game. However, the goal judge did not put on the goal light, despite the fact it was clearly a goal and had been signalled as such by the referee. Eagleson, sitting across from the Team Canada bench, leaped out of his seat and sought to confront the goal judge. Soldiers of the Red Army moved to arrest him before the Canadian players and a few of the Canadian fans—there were roughly three thousand in Moscow for the Soviet half of the series—headed over to protect him, while Peter Mahovlich jumped over the boards to confront the soldiers with his stick. Eagleson was freed, and the Canadian coaches and players escorted him across the ice to the Canadian bench. Eagleson shook his fist at the Soviet crowd and saluted them with the middle finger.

The tensions and anger that had built up over the month were, in short, boiling over. With the score 5–5, the teams entered the last minutes of play. If the game had ended in a tie, the Soviets would have won the series on goal difference.

In the final minute of play, Henderson came on the ice and skated to the Soviet goal. Esposito took a shot on goal. Henderson fell behind the net but got up and went to the front of the net, where he was uncovered. He recovered the rebound of Esposito's shot and made an initial shot that Tretiak, the Soviet goalie, saved. Henderson got a second rebound and, with Tretiak down, scored with only thirty-four seconds to play. In the inimitable words of Foster Hewitt, the Canadian announcer, "Here's a shot. Henderson made a wild stab for it and fell. Here's another shot. Right in front, they score! Henderson has scored for Canada!"

And with that goal, Team Canada won the series four games to three (with the one tie)—a far different margin than had been predicted on the eve of the series.

While Canada formally won the series, there was neither a cup nor a gold medal awaiting the players. In many ways, both teams could claim victory. The Soviets, who felt they should have won the series, continued to complain bitterly about the dirty tactics of the Canadians. And they certainly earned the respect of Canadians, players and fans alike. The Soviet team that gave the Canadians such a difficult time throughout the series was not the one that the Canadians originally teased as backward and afraid to get hurt because they wore helmets. If anything, the Soviets proved that their skill, talent, and conditioning was at the very least equal to that of the Canadians.

Team Canada arrived back in Canada on October 1. They were met by Prime Minster Trudeau and Jean Drapeau, the mayor of Montreal, and a crowd estimated to be in the vicinity of ten thousand people. A city that had been wracked by sectarian and nationalist violence only two years earlier now produced a crowd of both anglophones and francophones to celebrate Canadian victory. Those players not from Montreal then travelled on to Toronto. There, an estimated crowd of eighty thousand attended a ceremony at Nathan Phillips Square to celebrate the victory and congratulate the players.

The Summit Series was, in many ways, unprecedented. Though Henderson's goal on September 28 ended what was the most important hockey game a Canadian national team had played, the game itself was the culmination of a month of courage, mutual mistrust, and villainy, both on and off the ice. Young men who had been hockey players suddenly, over the course of that September, were transformed into political and national symbols.

V

More people watched television on the afternoon of September 28 than ever before in the history of Canadian television broadcasting. Television sets were brought into school classrooms and gymnasiums as children, teachers, and principals cheered on Team Canada together. People took the day off work. The whole country gathered as a collective to cheer on the Canadians. Estimates put the viewing audience in Canada at 16 million. With a combined national population of some 22 million, according to the 1972 census, that translated into something close to three-quarters of all Canadians watching Henderson score Canada's game- and series-winning goal.

Viewers did not just watch a hockey series, however. They watched a reflection of themselves and what they perceived as Canada's place in a much larger world. But it was a new place. Lester Pearson had won a Nobel Peace Prize in 1957 for "saving the world" during the Suez Crisis, solidifying Canada's reputation as a peacekeeper. Winning the Summit Series was, however, quite a different prize for Canadians. It was not based on peacekeeping, but on aggression, bad temper, the need to validate the type of hockey that Canada played and, ultimately, a larger ideology that made such play possible in the first place.

The eight games of the Summit Series not only changed the way hockey would be played, but also, and more importantly, became a defining national event. If October 13, 1970, was one of Canada's darkest hours, September 28, 1972, proved to be one of its brightest. If the October Crisis saw a fringe group using terrorism to tear the country, and its values, asunder, the Summit Series win represented a collective catharsis. And if the country looked like it was going to unravel in the fall of 1970, the fall of 1972 saw Canadians come together in a celebration of their national sport and, by extension, their nation.

Hockey, in other words, was able to do what no Royal Commission on Bilingualism and Biculturalism, Canadian content rules, or Official Languages Act could. Transcending law and language, Henderson's goal securing Canada's victory from the jaws of defeat brought not just celebration, but also legitimation for the Western way of life and its ideology. For that one moment, it was Canada, and not its stronger and more vocal neighbour to the south, that carried the torch of freedom and represented the West's values. Canadians could be proud of their team, their sport, and, most importantly, themselves.

Indeed, Henderson's last-minute goal became one of the few events since Confederation that has bound the country together. By 1972, Confederation was merely legal and theoretical, the act of distant politicians in another era; the Canadian victory over the Soviets, however, touched all Canadians: French and English speakers, those living in big cities like Montreal and Toronto, and those in small towns in the Prairies and in Quebec's Eastern Townships. Team Canada reflected the country, and the citizens of the country saw themselves in the national hockey team.

Dryden, Canada's goalie for half of the series, wrote retrospectively that that final game, and especially Henderson's goal, was "the one wholly Canadian event that has left a similar trail of memory" to what the assassination of John F. Kennedy left for Americans.[26] But if the Kennedy assassination brought Americans together in mourning and tragedy, Team Canada's victory was of a wholly different order. It was based on collective celebration and joy. In the words of the *Globe and Mail*'s Roy MacGregor, "Americans tend to remember where they were, what they were wearing, and who they were with the day Kennedy was shot. Canadians tend to remember where they were, what they were wearing, who they were talking to, and who they were with the moment that Paul Henderson scored that goal. That is how important it is in our history."[27]

Like any good story, of course, it was grounded in the heroic and the mythic. It was a tale of good versus evil, and of right versus wrong. It was a tale of hubris, near loss of reputation, and the hard work needed to salvage it. The series was not so much a set of hockey games as it was a national drama that changed the way Canadians thought about themselves. If one myth—that of simple and naïve Canadian hockey supremacy—was dismantled that September, it was replaced by another one that was much grittier. On display was a new form of national pride grounded in hard play and aggression, perhaps best symbolized by Clarke's slash in Game 6. But the series was, and is, remembered for Henderson's goal. That goal, as symbolic as it was real, revealed how Canadians perceived themselves: what they valued, what they held dear, and how anything was possible. Canadians, after all, had never really celebrated together. Expo 67 in Montreal had tried to remedy that. But it was ultimately Henderson's goal in the dying seconds of Game 8, in a Soviet ice rink a continent away, on the afternoon of September 28, 1972, that brought Canadians from all walks of life together.

VI

Over the course of one month, these eight hockey games captured the imagination of both nations. Far beyond any sporting event, the series began to take on a much broader significance in the two countries. East was pitted against West, the countries behind the Iron Curtain against the so-called Free World, as the competing ideologies of communism and capitalism faced off against one another at centre ice. The players, no longer mere hockey players, were transformed in their own minds, and in the minds of those watching, into soldiers in a classic Cold War battle.

The series did not just pit two opposing sides of the Cold War against one another, two rival political and ideological systems, but also two very different styles of hockey. Each team thus had to justify and validate for themselves the kind of hockey they played. The story still circulates that when Canadian scouts travelled to the Soviet Union with the aim of watching the Soviets play, trying to ascertain the nature of the opposition Team Canada would face, they watched Vladislav Tretiak, the Soviet goalie who would go on to be one of the stars of the Soviet team, let in eight goals, not realizing that he had celebrated his wedding the night before. Others said that the Soviets had known all along the Canadian scouts would be in attendance, so they made him play poorly on purpose. Regardless, prior to the first game, and seriously underestimating Tretiak's ability, Jacques Plante, the former multi-Stanley Cup–winning goaltender, was so worried about the possible embarrassment the Soviet goalie might face, he went into the Soviets dressing room and asked to speak to him through an interpreter to give him advice on NHL forwards.[28]

The story is further proof that the Canadian team woefully misjudged the quality of the Soviets. Since the Canadians thought there was only one way to play hockey—their way—they assumed the Soviets would simply play a poorer version. They made fun of the fact that they all wore helmets and were in possession of flimsier hockey sticks. These were taken as omens of Soviet inferiority. While the Canadians played an aggressive and punishing game, after the first half of the first period of Game 1, as the Soviets composed themselves, it became clear to all watching that their playing style was swift, precise, and very skillful.

We should never forget that, on the most fundamental level, the series was about hockey, and at that level the two teams played two very different games. The Soviets played as a well-organized and highly coordinated unit that knew, at any given moment, where all its individuals should be. The collective was thus more important than the individual. The Canadians, by contrast, emphasized the individual at the expense of the collective. The two styles of play manifested the competing political ideologies. The Summit Series had the unintended effect of opening these two styles up to one another, exposing what would later become a point of mutual repose. Some North American coaches, for example, were so impressed with the Soviet style that they began to imitate aspects of it, including their clearly superior training techniques. When Philadelphia Flyers head coach Fred Shero, clearly a fan of the Soviet style, adopted it in the NHL, his Flyers won back-to-back Stanley Cups in 1974 and 1975, losing in the finals in 1976.

The series also demonstrated the superior preparation and conditioning of the Soviet players. Though, admittedly, the Canadian players were just coming from their off-season, it was clear that two different styles of hockey were going head-to head. Instead of having a Canadian sweep, which so many anticipated, the series proved that the gap between the best Canadian NHL players and those who played in the top national teams of Europe—such as the USSR, Sweden, and Czechoslovakia—was much narrower than most observers had anticipated. The success of the Summit Series paved the way for other series, including the Canada Cup, a world championship tournament open to both pros and amateurs that ran between 1976 and 1991, in addition to regular series of games between Soviet and NHL clubs, which became known as the Super Series. Such series became redundant with the fall of the USSR in 1991, and the appearance of Russians on NHL teams.

In time, more and more European players entered the NHL, initially from Sweden and what was then Czechoslovakia, but later from the Soviet Union and then Russia. European training and conditioning methods became increasingly accepted in North America. And, going the other way, more Canadian players travelled overseas to play hockey, where Canadian styles and attitudes were slowly incorporated into the international game. This blending of the North American and European styles produced the swift, skillful, and rugged game that we have today. The Summit Series, on the level of sport, changed hockey for the better.

VII

If the 1972 series was a reflection of Canada, a quick look at eyewitness footage and other contemporaneous scenes reveal it to be a very white country. This stems from the fact that, until the late 1960s and early '70s, Canadian immigration policies had largely favoured those coming from Britain and other Western European countries. It was not until 1967, five years before the Summit Series, that a federal order-in-council established new standards for assessing potential immigrants and determining their admissibility.[29] The result was the creation of a points system, one still in use today, whereby potential immigrants were given a score in nine categories: education and training; personal character; occupational demand; occupational skill; age; prearranged employment; knowledge of French and English; the presence of a relative in Canada; and employment opportunities in their area of destination. Individuals receiving a score above a certain threshold were then admitted as independent immigrants, regardless of ethnicity or place of birth. This greatly facilitated immigration from Asia, the Caribbean, Latin America, and Africa.[30] The Immigration Act of 1976 further contributed to this more inclusive pattern of immigration to Canada. It sought to "ensure that any person who seeks admission to Canada on either a permanent or temporary basis is subject to standards of admission that do not discriminate on grounds of race, national or ethnic origin, colour, religion or sex."[31] As a result of these changes, in the 1970s and '80s Canada underwent a momentous demographic change. Up until then the country had been largely white, European, and Christian. Afterward it became increasingly multicultural, multiethnic, and multireligious (see chapter 4).

Sport tends to reflect society, and hockey in the 1970s was still very white. Though Larry Kwong, the first non-white player in the NHL, played in one game for the New York Rangers in 1948, the league had to wait until 1958 for its first Black player. Willie O'Ree, born and raised in Fredericton, New Brunswick, played two games for the Boston Bruins in 1958, and then another forty-three games in the 1961–1962 season. After him, there were no Black NHLers until the Washington Capitals drafted Mike Marson, from Scarborough, Ontario, in 1974. So by the time the best Canadian players were about to take on the best from the Soviet Union, there had been only a small handful of non-white faces in professional hockey. By way of comparison, both the Canadian and National (US) Football Leagues had their first Black players in 1946, Major League Baseball in 1947, and the National Basketball Association in 1950.

While recent years have seen more players of colour and of different ethnic backgrounds—Grant Fuhr of the Oilers; Robin Bawa of the Canucks; P.K. Subban of the Devils; Justin Abdelkader of the Red Wings; and Kailer Yamomoto and Jujhar Khaira of the Oilers—hockey remains a fairly white sport, especially when compared to other sports leagues. Today only 5 per cent of players in the NHL are Black, compared to 67 per cent in the NFL and 77 per cent in the NBA.[32] According to a 2013 Nielsen report, 92 per cent of NHL viewers are white.[33]

A sport that was able to unify Canadians that September afternoon in 1972 has, since that date, not often been able to repeat that task. Perhaps this was never on starker display than when, in November 2019, famed commentator Don Cherry made negative remarks about immigrants to Canada—so-called new Canadians—who he believed were not honouring Canada's fallen soldiers appropriately because he did not see them wearing poppies on Remembrance Day. "You people that come here...," he said on air, "you love our way of life, you love our milk and honey, at least you can pay a couple of bucks for a poppy or something like that."[34] The comments—especially the "you people" phrasing—bothered the majority of Canadians to such an extent that Sportsnet fired Cherry. Nevertheless, his comments reveal the extent to which hockey's demographic is out of sync with a multiethnic Canada, and just how far hockey has to go to overcome that disparity,[35] though the fact that Canada's iconic *Hockey Night in Canada* television program now has a Punjabi edition offers hope that the sport can unify Canadians as it has in the past. In the words of Harnarayan Singh, co-host of that program, "If we were talking about the pure game of hockey, in terms of how great a sport it is, how we can be fans of the sport together no matter who we are, what language we speak or how we look... that definitely does bring people together."[36]

When I was first thinking about including a sports date among the days that have shaped modern Canada, for a moment I thought of September 24, 1988, and former world record–holding sprinter Ben Johnson. His rivalry with the arrogant and loud-mouthed American Carl Lewis evoked some of the same types of nationalist sentiment as the Canada-Soviet series. As a Black man, Johnson also showed just how much the face of sports had changed in the country. As with the Summit Series, all Canadians and, indeed, most of the world had heard of him. And when Johnson and Lewis took their rivalry to the 1988 Summer Olympic Games in Seoul, Canadians from all over watched the men's 100-metre final on September 24. Johnson won the gold medal in a world record time of 9.79 seconds, breaking his own record of 9.83, and Canadians rejoiced—in a manner that was reminiscent of September 28, 1972—in the fact that, for the first time since 1928, a Canadian had won the gold medal (while breaking the world record, no less) in the 100 metres at an Olympic Games. Immediately after his victory, Prime Minister Brian Mulroney called Johnson to say that "it is a marvelous evening for Canada."

Three days later, however, Johnson was stripped of his medal when a banned substance was found in his urine sample. The gold medal was then awarded to Lewis, who had finished in second place, and who, it was later revealed, had tested positive for banned substances at the Olympic trials, two months before the Games, which he said he had inadvertently consumed.[37] Johnson forever after was, in the words of a CBC documentary, a "hero disgraced."[38] Canadians began to turn on Johnson, and he was quickly transformed from a Canadian sprinter to a Jamaican or Jamaican Canadian sprinter. It is worth noting that the Canadian-ness of Phil Esposito was never called into question, even when Canada was down three games to one, nor was his Italian background mentioned pejoratively.

VIII

In 2000 the Dominion Institute compiled a list of the ten most famous events in Canadian history.[39] While Confederation in 1867 topped the list, Henderson's goal came in at a respectable number five, just after Canadian troops' capture of Vimy Ridge in the First World War and just above Canada's role in the Second World War.[40] Canadians ranked it higher than the Battle of the Plains of Abraham, the creation of the Canadian flag, the repatriation of the Constitution, and even the recognition that women were "persons" and therefore eligible to be appointed to the Senate.

It is, to be sure, a large role for one goal, or even one hockey game, to fill. But this was much more than a hockey game. Because so much Canadian identity had been based on what we were not (i.e., not Americans), and because we tended not to perform as well as other countries in international competitions, such as the World Cup or the Olympics, Henderson's goal allowed Canadians to celebrate victory.

Would a hockey game played today take on such national significance? It seems unlikely. Canadians are no longer outliers at the Olympics, and they regularly perform at the same level as Americans and others in swimming, track, skiing, and other team or individual sports. Though Canada is still a hockey country, other sports now compete for fans and viewers alike. The Toronto Blue Jays' World Series titles in 1992 and 1993 or the Toronto Raptors winning the NBA championship in 2019 are cases in point. And, come World Cup time, crowds cheering for their favourite teams in the streets of cities like Toronto, Montreal, and Vancouver reveal that soccer is growing in popularity, with many avid fans among new Canadians and increasingly among old ones as well.

But for that one defining moment on the afternoon of September 28, 1972, Canadians came together in a way they never had before and perhaps never will again.

SUGGESTIONS FOR FURTHER READING

Ken Dryden (with Mark Mulvoy). *Face-Off at the Summit*. Boston: Little, Brown and Co., 1973.

Paul Henderson (with Roger Lajoie). *The Goal of My Life: A Memoir*. Toronto: Random House, 2011.

Andrew C. Holman. *Canada's Game: Hockey and Identity*. Montreal and Kingston: McGill-Queen's University Press, 2009.

Roy MacSkimming. *Cold War: The Amazing Canada-Soviet Hockey Series of 1972*. Vancouver: Greystone Books, 1996.

Lawrence Martin. *The Red Machine: The Soviet Quest to Dominate Canada's Game*. Toronto: Doubleday Canada, 1990.

Scott Morrison. *The Days Canada Stood Still: Canada vs USSR 1972*. Toronto: McGraw-Hill Ryerson, 1989.

Harry Sinden. *Hockey Showdown: The Canada-Russia Hockey Series*. Toronto: Doubleday Canada, 1972.

SUGGESTION FOR FURTHER VIEWING

George Roy. *Cold War on Ice: Summit Series '72*. Flagstaff Films & NBC Universal, 2012.

3

APRIL 17 1982

The Patriation of the Constitution

ON APRIL 17, 1982, Prime Minister Pierre Trudeau and Queen Elizabeth II signed into law the Constitution Act, 1982. The act successfully patriated the Constitution and enacted the new Charter of Rights and Freedoms. Thousands of onlookers braved the pouring rain as the dignitaries assembled under a canopy on Parliament Hill for the official event. In an iconic photo a smiling Trudeau signs the document while a stone-faced Queen looks into the distance. The smile was certainly heartfelt, but it could not completely conceal the tensions of the previous year, which heard grumblings from the provinces and saw the unwillingness of the Government of Quebec to agree to the act. The moment was so full of emotion that when Trudeau signed the document, his pressure on the pen broke its nib. As Jean Chrétien, in his role as foreign minister, moved to sign the document, he found the pen broken. "Merde!" he whispered under his breath. The Queen let out a quiet giggle, and another pen was quickly found.[1]

On the same day, storm clouds of the metaphorical kind were brewing in Quebec, as René Lévesque ordered that the provincial flag be flown at half-mast to symbolize that although Quebec was bound by the new Constitution and Charter, it wanted no part of it.

I

Canada was, for all intents and purposes, a legal colony of the United Kingdom until April 17, 1982. Since then, although the country may still retain the English monarch as its figurative head-of-state, and a Governor General as the monarch's official representative, Canada has been an independent, self-governing nation. Most people think Canada gained its independence from the UK on July 1, 1867, when the British North America Act signalled Canada's birth, but the fact is that until 1982 the country's Constitution remained firmly embedded within the British Parliament. If a constitution reflects and is reflected in the spirit of a nation, defining a set of values its citizens hold dear, the fact that Canadian politicians had to ask the British Parliament to make amendments to our Constitution was deeply problematic. Further, a Constitution that was defined by British values and common law at the same time as the country was becoming increasingly bilingual and multiethnic, with new Canadians coming from all walks of life and from all over the globe, was increasingly out of sync with the reality of Canadian life.

To become its own country, both literally and symbolically, Canada needed to take possession of its Constitution, to have the power to amend it as it saw fit, and to make it a living and breathing document in tune with the needs of a growing and increasingly diverse population. Since Canada was not the United Kingdom, its demographics, its official languages, and, indeed, its very future needed to be addressed by Canadians and not British parliamentarians. If July 1, 1867, was the day of the creation of Canada, April 17, 1982, heralded its "canadianization"—though, as we shall see, the way this was accomplished was not without its detractors.

If the Constitution and Charter were to do what they set out to do, the federal government would need to address old wounds and seek to move forward in an honest and transparent manner. That this was not done only intensified the severity of these wounds and led to a series of grievances and disputes that reverberated throughout the nation in the coming decades.

Because the Government of Quebec refused to sign on to the idea of patriating the Constitution to Canada and refused to endorse the Charter of Rights and Freedoms, the day that was meant to showcase the country's unity just as clearly revealed some of its deep and fundamental rifts.

II

A nation's constitution consists of the basic principles and established precedents that determine not just how and by whom it is to be governed, but also its basic values. The history of Canada, perhaps like that of any country, is intertwined with the history of how such values came to be enshrined in its Constitution. If a constitution enshrines, however, it also exposes. In the case of Canada, something as fundamental as the "law of the land" necessarily poses the question "Whose land?" Answering this question put on clear display many of the tensions—between francophones and anglophones, and between white Canada and Indigenous peoples—that had been thinly papered over since Confederation. That Canada did not have its Constitution patriated from the United Kingdom until 1982—115 years after its formation as a country—is telling.

It was the British North America Act, 1867, that was directly responsible for establishing the Dominion of Canada as a federation of provinces on July 1 of the same year. The Declaration of Union in the act states the matter clearly:

> It shall be lawful for the Queen, by and with the Advice of Her Majesty's Most Honourable Privy Council, to declare by Proclamation that, on and after a Day therein appointed, not being more than Six Months after the passing of this Act, the Provinces of Canada, Nova Scotia, and New Brunswick shall form and be One Dominion under the Name of Canada; and on and after that Day those Three Provinces shall form and be One Dominion under that Name accordingly.[2]

This British North America Act thus succeeded in combining "the Province of Canada" (now Ontario and Quebec) with Nova Scotia and New Brunswick into a Dominion within the British Empire. The new Dominion adopted a Westminster style of government, and included the appointment of a Governor General to fulfill the constitutional duties of the British monarch on Canadian soil. Despite giving the new country autonomy, the United Kingdom still had the power to legislate for Canada, making the latter a self-governing British colony. There were several more British North America Acts (e.g., of 1871, 1886, 1907), all of which the Canadian government subsequently renamed Constitution Acts.

It was the Statute of Westminster—an act of the UK Parliament that was passed into law on December 11, 1931—that established the legislative independence of the self-governing Dominions, including Canada, Australia, New Zealand, and Newfoundland (which was not yet part of Canada). The Statute removed nearly all of the British Parliament's authority to legislate for the Dominions, making them largely sovereign nations. This was an important first step in the transformation of former Dominions into separate and autonomous states—until 1931, these Dominions had been legally self-governing, but remained colonies of the United Kingdom.

The Statute of Westminster meant that the British Parliament could no longer make laws for the Dominions, except at the request and consent of their governments. This limited the legislative authority of the British Parliament over Canada, giving the country legal autonomy and transforming it into a self-governing Dominion. The Statute also enabled Canada to open up embassies in foreign countries, with the first one established in Washington, DC, in the same year. Before this, Canada's interests were represented solely by Britain. It is also worth noting, in part to show the tremendous influence Britain had on Canadian policy, that it was not until January 1947 that Canadian citizenship, as a status distinct from British nationality, was officially created by the Canadian Citizenship Act.

Despite the Statute of Westminster, however, the British North America Acts—the core documents of the Canadian Constitution until that time—remained in the hands of the British Parliament because of disagreements between the provinces, especially Quebec, and the federal government over how the Constitution might be amended. This meant that changes to the Constitution could not be made by the Canadian government, but only by the British Parliament at the request of the Canadian government. While the British North America Act, 1949, gave the Canadian government some power to make constitutional amendments related only to matters of federal jurisdiction, full Canadian control over its own Constitution remained limited.

Canada's patriation of its Constitution from Britain was precipitated by the Canada Act, 1982, which was passed by the British Parliament at the behest of the Canadian government. The new act effectively ended the power of the British Parliament to amend Canada's Constitution. Until passage of the Canada Act, the British North America Act, 1867 (subsequently known in Canada as the Constitution Act, 1867), had functioned as the "supreme law of Canada." Now the Constitution Act, 1982, which included the Charter of Rights and Freedoms, became the supreme law. The Constitution and Charter were attached as a schedule to the Canada Act and came into force on April 17, 1982.

It had always been Prime Minister Pierre Trudeau's goal to have the Constitution in Canada and not have to ask Britain's approval to change it. He also sought to create a sweeping Charter of Rights and Freedoms that would guarantee all citizens (and non-citizens) basic protections from arbitrary actions of either provincial or federal governments. Not everyone shared this vision, however. Provinces were afraid that such a proposal would limit their influence at the expense of federal centralization, and would transfer power from elected officials to a non-elected judiciary.

As a result, when Trudeau attempted to gain provincial consensus for the patriation of the Constitution, there was grumbling from many of the provincial leaders, who saw it as an attempt by the federal government to impose its will on the provinces, and downright opposition from Quebec premier René Lévesque, Trudeau's nemesis and leader of the separatist Parti Québécois. In response to numerous legal challenges by the provinces, Canada's Supreme Court ruled that while provincial consent was not legally necessary, a unilateral act on the part of the federal government on so weighty a matter without substantial consent would contravene a long-standing constitutional convention.

Trudeau brought the premiers to Ottawa for a last ditch set of meetings in November 1981. After a late-night bargaining session orchestrated by Jean Chrétien (the federal minister of justice), Roy Romanow (attorney general of Saskatchewan), and Roy McMurtry (attorney general of Ontario) in the fifth-floor kitchen of the Government Conference Centre, an agreement was struck—now known as the "Kitchen Accord"—by which nine provinces would support patriation. Lévesque had not been part of the late-night negotiations because he was staying at a hotel in Hull (now Gatineau) and had left the conference centre earlier in the day to return there. He arrived at breakfast the next morning to learn that a deal had been reached without him, at an event that he called "the night of the long knives." "I have been stabbed in the back during the night," he later remarked, "by a bunch of carpetbaggers,"[3] to which he added that his fellow premiers were a bunch of "rug merchants who wouldn't hesitate to walk over their mother for an ice cream cone."[4]

This is as good a place as any to mention that there are at least two accounts of this famous—even mythic—event, and two historiographies that sprang from it. These accounts, moreover, are often irreconcilable. Lévesque and his supporters complain that he was left out of the final agreement achieved in the late evening/early morning of November 4, 1981. "La nuit des longs couteaux," in the separatist mythos, represents one more time that anglophone Canada conspired to sidetrack Quebec's ambitions. To this day, many Quebecers still remember it as English Canada and francophone federalists (such as Trudeau and Chrétien) making a fool out of Lévesque and, by extension, the separatist movement and indeed all Quebecers. As well, to this day Quebec has not signed the Charter, and many Quebecers, including leading federalist politicians in the province, see it as an illegitimate assault on the sovereignty of Quebec.[5]

From the other side, those who support the Trudeau narrative argue that Quebec never would have agreed to patriation, owing to the fact that, despite his defeat in the 1980 provincial referendum, Lévesque was committed to separation. For him to agree with the rest of Canada on constitutional patriation, he would have to renounce his own political principles, the ones that had brought his government to power in Quebec in the first place. This, at least according to the likes of Chrétien, Romanow, and McMurtry, was why they were not so worried about Quebec coming on board. They felt that Lévesque never would have given his assent.

These competing narratives bear witness, even in what was one of Canada's finest hours, to the fundamental tension that dates back to Confederation, if not earlier. The Quebec government's unwillingness to sign on with the other provinces once again manifests a fracture at the heart of the Canadian project. The next few years would see the provinces and federal government try to iron out these tensions—at Meech Lake

(1987) and at Charlottetown (1992), both to be discussed below—but with little or no success.

In many ways, Trudeau and Lévesque were the main protagonists in the eighteen-month battle that led up to the events of April 17. Trudeau, ever the federalist, and the separatist Lévesque were classic adversaries: both were articulate, charismatic, and in possession of strong convictions. At a first ministers' conference held in September 1980, which ended in fury and disarray, Trudeau responded angrily to Lévesque and the majority of the other premiers who objected to his idea of patriation: "I'm telling you now, we're going to do it alone." After the Supreme Court ruled that Trudeau did not need unanimity, and when all the provinces except Quebec were ready to agree to patriation, Lévesque remarked to Trudeau, "You won't get away with this. The people will stop it." To which Trudeau responded, "The people have already spoken, René, and you lost."[6]

Lévesque and Trudeau represented two different visions of Canada. Trudeau was a hardline federalist, believing that the future of Canada lay in a strong federal government. Lévesque was a proud Quebecer who sought to free the province from the economic, political, and cultural yoke of a federal regime that promised much, but delivered little. As the symbol of a federal Canada that Lévesque rejected outright, Trudeau increasingly represented all that he desired to end. That they were both Quebecers only added to the tension between the two men. If Trudeau saw Quebec's rightful place in a strong Canada, Lévesque's vision for Quebec was political sovereignty, albeit with an economic partnership with Canada, that gave it freedom to levy its own taxes, pass its own laws, and deal with other nations in its own name and its own language. The conflict of two personalities was never far below the surface in the months leading up to, and away from, that day in April 1982.

In the end, Trudeau was able to convince nine provinces to endorse patriation of the Constitution, in part by agreeing—reluctantly, and much to his chagrin—to a proposal from provincial legislatures that he include a "notwithstanding clause," which would allow provincial legislatures to temporarily override certain portions of the Charter of Rights and Freedoms (discussed below). This notwithstanding clause became enshrined in the Charter as section 33: "Parliament or the legislature of a province may expressly declare in an Act of Parliament or of the legislature, as the case may be, that the Act or a provision thereof shall operate notwithstanding a provision included in section 2 or sections 7 to 15 [of the Charter]."[7]

The patriation of the Constitution immediately resulted in Canada's full legislative independence from the United Kingdom, meaning that no further British Acts of Parliament would apply to Canada as part of its law.

III

As early as 1967, when he was justice minister, Pierre Trudeau—undoubtedly inspired by Canada's centenary that same year—appointed a team of legal experts, under the leadership of the University of Saskatchewan's Barry Strayer, to look into the creation of a new bill of rights. In 1974, when Trudeau was prime minister, Strayer became assistant deputy to the justice minister, where he played a leading role in drafting what would eventually become known as the Canadian Charter of Rights and Freedoms (often referred to simply as the Charter). Also instrumental in drafting the Charter were the aforementioned Jean Chrétien, Trudeau's justice minister, and the attorneys general of Saskatchewan and Ontario, Roy Romanow and Roy McMurtry.

This new Charter was meant to supersede the Canadian Bill of Rights of 1960, which, unlike the Charter, was not a constitutional document but a federal statute that, by definition, had little bearing on provincial jurisdiction. While the new Charter includes many of the same basic rights found in its predecessor (e.g., right to life, liberty, security of person, and habeas corpus), it also goes far beyond it by, for example, enshrining bilingualism, multiculturalism, and equality rights for people with disabilities.

Writing in 1993, Pierre Trudeau said that his goal for the Charter was to create a "society where all people are equal and where they share some fundamental values based upon freedom."[8] The Charter was thus meant to define a set of principles and rights—Canadian values like bilingualism, multiculturalism, justice, liberty, and equality for all—and to function as a source of national unity by enshrining these values for future generations. It was a tall order, to be sure, and not surprisingly it met with many detractors at the provincial level.

Most Canadians would support the values included in and protected by the Charter. Polls in 1987 and again in 1999 showed that over 80 per cent of English-speaking Canadians approved of the Charter, with 64 per cent of Quebecers agreeing with this sentiment in 1987 and 70 per cent in 1999.[9]

Since the Charter's implementation in 1982, it has been responsible for notable changes in Canadian society. In 1986, for example, David Oakes argued that his arrest for possession of hashish with intent to traffic outside a bar in London, Ontario, violated his Charter right of presumption of innocence. Lawyers argued that parts of the Narcotic Control Act (i.e., the presumption of intent to traffic) contravened section 11(d), the presumption of innocence before being proven guilty, of the Charter.[10] The Supreme Court ruled in Oakes's favour, arguing that the presumption of the intent to traffic equates to a limitation of rights and freedoms which is "radically and fundamentally inconsistent with the societal values of human dignity and liberty which we espouse."[11] This led to the so-called Oakes Test, which looks to section 1 of the Charter that states that rights are guaranteed "subject only to such reasonable limits...as can be demonstrably justified in a free and democratic society." This means that the government must establish that the benefits of a law outweigh its negative impact—that is, its violation of a Charter right.

Another monumental ruling came in 1988 when Henry Morgentaler challenged the constitutionality of the federal abortion law. Though he had lost an earlier challenge in 1975—significantly, prior to the Charter's enactment—the Supreme Court now ruled in his favour, arguing that a woman's inability to terminate a pregnancy violated her right to "security of the person" under section 7 of the Charter. Significantly, since *R. v. Morgentaler*, there have been no criminal laws regulating access to abortion.

In 1991, when Delwin Vriend, an openly gay man, was fired from his job at King's College, a Christian university in Edmonton, he appealed to Alberta's Human Rights Commission but was rejected on the grounds that the Alberta human rights code did not protect people facing discrimination because of their sexual orientation. The decision was ultimately appealed to the Supreme Court, where it was known as *Vriend v. Alberta*. The Court ruled in 1998 that provincial governments could not exclude sexual orientation from the areas protected under human rights legislation. While some—particularly conservative Christian groups—thought that Alberta should invoke the notwithstanding clause, the government did not do so. *Vriend v. Alberta* would go on to become an important precedent in the argument that provincial bans on same-sex marriage throughout Canada were unconstitutional (see chapter 6).

Such cases reveal the extent to which the Charter has shaped modern Canada, liberalizing its laws and upholding the rights of Canadians when it comes to criminal law, sexual orientation, and women's access to reproductive health. In the span of twenty years, the Charter has completely transformed the lives of Canadians, though paradoxically it has done so in such a manner—namely, behind the scenes—that most Canadians might not even realize how much they have been affected.

IV

Some politicians in the United Kingdom had initially objected to the patriation of Canada's Constitution because they had been on the receiving end of endless complaints—from the Government of Quebec, other provincial governments, and Indigenous leaders—about the actions of the federal government. On a visit there to smooth the way for the Canada Act, Justice Minister Jean Chrétien was so angry at this paternalistic attitude toward Canada on the part of British lawmakers that he adjourned the meeting. He said that since Canada had no problems between Catholics and Protestants, he was going to go to Northern Ireland the following day and then come back to tell the English how they should go about solving their own problems. "You don't tell us what to do," he said, "and we won't tell you what to do."[12] Had the British not agreed to the patriation, he said in an interview, the Canadian government was prepared to take a more drastic option and simply declare Canada to be an independent country, thereby severing all ties with the United Kingdom.[13]

Before examining the repercussions of April 17, 1982, however, it is worth examining some of the internal Canadian critiques when it came to patriation. While it might seem strange that there were Canadian objections to the idea of Canada taking possession of its own Constitution, there were certainly valid reasons.

The biggest opponent to patriation at the time was René Lévesque's Parti Québécois government in Quebec. I discussed Quebec separatism in the context of chapter 1, and it's enough here to say that the raison d'être of the Parti Québécois was to separate from Canada. Such a party could not, by definition, sign on to a constitution that promoted federalism and still be able to look at itself in the mirror the following morning. Subsequent negotiations to bring Quebec into the constitutional framework, even if symbolically, tended to break down over the party's demands that Quebec:

- be recognized as a distinct society
- be given veto power over constitutional amendments
- receive funding from the federal government if it opted out of federally funded programs that were under provincial jurisdiction (for example, university funding or language training for immigrants)
- be guaranteed representation on the Supreme Court
- take control of its own immigration policy

From Trudeau's perspective, giving such privileges to one province and not the others would undermine the very nature of the Charter and its promotion of equality. At the same time, giving such privileges to all provinces would destroy Trudeau's ideal of a strong federal government.

Quebec might also point to the fact that, since 1975, it was in possession of its own Charter of Rights and Freedoms (the Charte des droits et libertés de la personne).[14] This elaborate document—which includes basic human rights (including a clause against discrimination on the basis of sexual orientation that was formulated as early as 1977), in addition to a number of important social and economic rights—forms one of the foundations of Quebec's legal system. Quebec clearly did not find itself in need of another Charter, especially not a federal one. But despite the fact that the Government of Quebec has never signed the Constitution, the Canadian Charter enjoys legal priority over the Quebec charter.

Many Indigenous leaders were also skeptical of patriation. It was unfortunate that the Trudeau government's initial proposal for patriation in 1980 made little reference to Indigenous rights and, for the most part, his government failed to consult with Indigenous leaders. As a result, many Indigenous people feared the transfer of constitutional powers from Britain to Canada would coincide with a reneging on territorial rights that had been worked out under the legal status quo. Two years of lobbying in Canada and abroad, at both the United Nations and the British Parliament, put pressure on the Canadian government to include the rights of the Indigenous population in the Constitution.

This led to the inclusion of section 35 of the Constitution:

> 35. (1) The existing aboriginal and treaty rights of the aboriginal peoples of Canada are hereby recognized and affirmed.
> (2) In this Act, "aboriginal peoples of Canada" includes the Indian, Inuit and Métis peoples of Canada.
> (3) For greater certainty, in subsection (1) "treaty rights" includes rights that now exist by way of land claims agreements or may be so acquired.
> (4) Notwithstanding any other provision of this Act, the aboriginal and treaty rights referred to in subsection (1) are guaranteed equally to male and female persons.[15]

Section 35 falls under Part II of the Constitution, meaning that it exists outside of the Charter. This has the distinct advantage of making the section exempt from the notwithstanding clause, which applies only to the Charter.[16] The federal government cannot, in other words, override Indigenous rights. As it came to be interpreted, section 35 of the Constitution paved the way for the inherent right of Indigenous groups to self-government:

> The Government of Canada recognizes the inherent right of self-government as an existing Aboriginal right under section 35 of the *Constitution Act*, 1982. It recognizes, as well, that the inherent right may find expression in treaties, and in the context of the Crown's relationship with treaty First Nations. Recognition of the inherent right is based on the view that the Aboriginal peoples of Canada have the right to govern themselves in relation to matters that are internal to their communities, integral to their unique cultures, identities, traditions, languages and institutions, and with respect to their special relationship to their land and their resources.[17]

Even after the Constitution Act of 1982, and the inclusion of section 35, there were still Indigenous objections. The most common was that the new Constitution remained rooted in colonialism since, at its foundation, the document was grounded in European notions such as individual rights and the ownership of private property. Indigenous communities—including Inuit and Métis—thus had to adapt to a system that was not their own. However, other Indigenous leaders have argued that the Charter actually helped to settle the troubled relationship between the federal government and Indigenous peoples by providing the latter with the legal wherewithal to appeal violations of their rights and freedoms.[18]

Recent years have seen attempts, on all sides, to overcome this Quebec and Indigenous skepticism. In 2017, commemorating the 150-year anniversary of Confederation and the 35-year anniversary of patriation, Quebec premier Philippe Couillard said he would be open to revisiting the idea of Quebec's signing on to the Constitution. Prime Minister Justin Trudeau, however, said he had no intention of reopening the constitutional debate, especially given the fates of the Meech Lake and Charlottetown Accords, (which I discuss next).[19] Indigenous leaders have tended to be more positively predisposed to the Constitution than their Quebec counterparts. However, the Assembly of First Nations has called for amendments to ensure that Indigenous leaders will have a place at the table in meetings of, for example, the first ministers.[20] Though Justin Trudeau did include such leaders in a first ministers' meeting on March 13, 2020, which was cancelled because of the COVID-19 pandemic, it is worth noting that the meeting with Indigenous leaders was to take place the day before the official meeting.[21]

V

In the years after patriation there were several attempts to persuade Quebec to endorse, even if symbolically, the Constitution of Canada. The first such attempt was the 1987 Meech Lake Accord, negotiated by Prime Minister Brian Mulroney and all ten provincial premiers, which was designed to make certain constitutional amendments that would give more powers to the provinces, including Quebec. In a first ministers' meeting held at Meech Lake, just north of Gatineau, Quebec, a consensus was reached that would address the five points mentioned above that had always prevented Quebec's ratification of the Constitution: Quebec was to be recognized as a distinct society; future constitutional amendments would require the agreement of *all* provincial governments and the federal government; provincial governments could receive financial compensation if they opted out of federal programs that were under provincial jurisdiction; the names of new senators would be drawn from a list assembled by the provinces; and provinces could have more say in immigration policy.

When the accord was announced, public opinion was favourable. Both Ed Broadbent, leader of the federal NDP, and John Turner, leader of the federal Liberals, supported it. The most vocal critique came, perhaps not surprisingly, from former prime minister Trudeau. In an open letter published in the *Toronto Star* and *La Presse* in Montreal, Trudeau wrote, "What a dark day for Canada was this April 30, 1987!" He explained,

> Those Canadians who fought for a single Canada, bilingual and multicultural, can say good-bye to their dream: We are henceforth to have two Canadas, each defined in terms of its language. And because the Meech Lake accord states in the same breath that "Quebec constitutes, within Canada, a distinct society" and that "the role of the legislature and government to preserve and promote (this) distinct society... is affirmed," it is easy to predict what future awaits anglophones living in Quebec and what treatment will continue to be accorded to francophones living in provinces where they are fewer in number than Canadians of Ukrainian or German origin.[22]

Trudeau, the devoted federalist, was clearly dead set against the idea of giving more power to the provinces at the expense of a strong centralized government. It was only the latter type of union, Trudeau maintained, that could assure a creative equilibrium between the provinces and the central government. With a Charter binding on both the provinces and the federal government, he had hoped that Canada's "constitutional evolution" would take place in such a manner that the federal government could function as a state without either provincial preconditions or blackmail. But with the changes contained in the Meech Lake Accord, Trudeau warned, all of the provinces—not just Quebec—could promote their own interests at the expense of the collective.

The idea that any provincial government could jeopardize future constitutional amendments was anathema to Trudeau. "For those Canadians who dreamed of the Charter as a new beginning for Canada," he wrote, "where everyone would be on an equal footing and where citizenship would finally be founded on a set of commonly shared values, there is to be nothing left but tears."[23]

The provision stipulating that the provinces, rather than the federal government, would be responsible for choosing Supreme Court justices and senators also risked politicizing these institutions.

Trudeau was furious that everything he had worked for—the patriation of the Constitution and its subsequent "canadianization"—was now on the verge of being undermined from within. The Meech Lake Accord, he feared, threatened to balkanize the country, with various provinces and/or regions competing with one another for special favour. He was particularly upset with the clause that would prove to be the accord's undoing: namely, the recognition of Quebec's distinctiveness within Canada. Indigenous groups and other minorities (including anglophones) in the province feared that the acknowledgement of Quebec's status as a "distinct society" might lead the province to disregard those constitutional protections afforded by the Charter under the guise of preserving Quebec's so-called distinct culture.

Ultimately, the critics prevailed. Although the amendments were originally backed by all provincial legislatures, elections in New Brunswick, Manitoba, and Newfoundland brought in governments opposed to the accord. Perhaps the final nail was pounded into the Meech Lake Accord coffin the following year, when the Supreme Court ruled on *Ford v. Quebec*, a series of cases that involved Bill 101, which defined French as the official language of Quebec. The Court ruled that Bill 101's ban on English-language signs was in clear violation of the federal Charter. In response, Robert Bourassa's governing provincial Liberal Party amended Bill 101 with Bill 178, which made French the only language on "public signs, posters and commercial advertising." Though in clear violation of the Charter, Bourassa invoked the notwithstanding clause.[24] This caused a backlash in the rest of Canada, with many of the other provinces asking themselves what the consequences of accepting Quebec's distinctiveness might be.

One more attempt to bring Quebec into the constitutional fold occurred in 1992 with the Charlottetown Accord, another set of proposed amendments to the Constitution. In addition to the notion of Quebec as a distinct society within Canada, other issues such as Indigenous self-government and Senate reform (the so-called Triple-E Senate—elected, effective, and equitable—which was popular with the newly created Reform Party) were included in the new agreement. Unlike the Meech Lake Accord, however, a national referendum was required to ratify the Charlottetown Accord because three provinces—Quebec, Alberta, and British Columbia—had, since Meech Lake, passed provincial legislation that necessitated public referendums to decide all future constitutional amendments. Rather than have three provinces use a referendum and the others not, Prime Minister Mulroney decided to have a national referendum. Quebec opted to have a provincial referendum, while all the other provinces had a federal referendum overseen by Elections Canada.[25]

On October 26, 1992, the question was put to all Canadians: "Do you agree that the Constitution of Canada should be renewed on the basis of the agreement reached on August 28, 1992?" (and in Quebec: "Acceptez-vous que la Constitution du Canada soit renouvelée sur la base de l'entente conclue le 28 août 1992?"). In the end, 54.3 per cent of Canadians voted "no," with 45.7 voting "yes." In Quebec, the "no" vote was 56.7 per cent.

Despite the fact that every first minister in the country, all the federal parties, and the overwhelming majority of media outlets had endorsed the "yes" position, it was perhaps telling—and a sign of the future—that the overwhelming majority of Canadians voted against the accord. Pundits and pollsters argued that the defeat was the result of sheer frustration on the part of Canadians and showed both their desire to leave the constitutional debate behind and their growing disaffection with politicians of all stripes.[26]

Almost a year to the day later, on October 25, 1993, a federal election was held. The Progressive Conservatives under Mulroney's successor, Kim Campbell—technically Canada's first female prime minister—were reduced to just two seats in Parliament, the worst defeat ever of a sitting federal government. Their defeat came at the hands of the Liberals, who won a massive victory under new leader Jean Chrétien. He had played an instrumental role in the patriation of the Constitution and the drafting of the Charter, but, undoubtedly sensing the frustration of the majority of Canadians, Chrétien vowed not to revisit constitutional issues.[27]

Although theoretically nothing had changed—the Constitution still existed, just as it had before both the Meech Lake and Charlottetown Accords—the country was, paradoxically, more divided than ever. Most disconcerting for proponents of federalism was the fact that the majority of seats lost by the outgoing Progressive Conservative government had been picked up by two relatively new parties—the Reform Party in the West and the Bloc Québécois in Quebec. These parties, both of whom had opposed the Charlottetown Accord, were predicated on the disaffection with federalism in their respective provinces/regions, and thus a strong resentment of and alienation from Ottawa. As a consequence, both parties were more interested in promoting regional causes at the expense of national unity, much less some inchoate sense of national identity. All of this would lead directly to the Quebec referendum in 1995 (chapter 6), an event that pushed the country "to the cliff of a constitutional crisis."[28]

The alienation of Quebec nationalists and Prairie populists was real and should not be dismissed out of hand. Many in the Bloc Québécois (to be discussed in greater detail in chapter 6) built on the strategies of the Parti Québécois, seeking an independent Quebec that was free to support and develop fully its own economic, political, and cultural potential. Unlike the PQ, however, they did this at the federal rather than the provincial level. Like the PQ, they saw the Charter as the symbol par excellence of Canada's illegitimate assault on Quebec's political sovereignty. The Reform Party, fully aware of the wrestling between Quebec and Ottawa, argued—from the perspective of the other side of the country—that both the federal Liberal and Progressive Conservative parties, because of their obsession with Quebec, were consistently indifferent to the interests of Western Canada. And they had good reason for this view. Not infrequently, Reformers noted that the National Energy Program, which was introduced by Trudeau's Liberals in 1980 and which intervened in Canada's energy markets to regulate prices, resulted in economic losses to Alberta and benefits to Eastern Canada.

VI

April 17, 1982, was, in many ways, just as important as July 1, 1867, if not more so. The Dominion of Canada was formally created in 1867, but April 17, 1982 saw the conclusion of what the earlier date had set in motion: full constitutional independence and political autonomy. The two dates thus mutually reinforce one another. "After 114 years," said Pierre Trudeau on the eve of patriation, "Canada will become in a technical and a legal sense an independent country once and for all."[29]

As important as patriation was, of even greater significance for the shaping of Canada was the inclusion of the Charter. It is not without its detractors. For example, the Charter was criticized in certain quarters for granting too much power to the courts at the expense of elected officials, giving judges the power to strike down legislation enacted by democratically elected legislatures.[30] In defending the Charter, former Supreme Court justice Louise Arbour has argued that since Canadian courts, unlike American ones, lack partisan politics and allegiances, "Charter litigation has provided a high-quality intellectual forum in which to debate issues that are not best left to majority diktat."[31] Others have argued that the Charter allows the federal government, with its own agenda, to limit the powers of the provinces.[32]

And if the Charter was ready to create a new Canada, one that reflected the country's bilingual and multicultural heritage, Canadians were not always ready for the boldness of the Charter's vision. A case in point occurred in 1989 when a new recruit to the RCMP, a young Sikh by the name of Baltej Singh Dhillon, wanted to continue wearing his beard and turban while in uniform. The RCMP's dress code forbade long hair, facial hair, or a head covering other than the usual flat-brimmed Stetson hat. Since beards and turbans are important components of Sikh religious faith, it was obvious, when the case went before the Supreme Court, that the RCMP requirements were in clear violation of the Charter, which upholds the freedom of religion and also makes provisions for the protection of multicultural rights. The RCMP—whose commissioner was, incidentally, not opposed to Dhillon retaining beard and turban—was forced to change its dress code as a result of the case. Yet despite the clear violation of Dhillon's Charter rights, and the fact that the RCMP could not dismiss him, Canadians were not quite so forgiving. Dhillon received anonymous death threats in the mail; over ninety thousand Canadians signed petitions against the wearing of the turban in the RCMP; retired Mounties launched a legal challenge to the changes in the dress code; and the Reform Party—the federal party arising from the alienation of western provinces—campaigned against the changes in the name of "tradition."[33] Reflecting on these events on the eve of his retirement, Dhillon remarked,

> I didn't join to change anything. I didn't change to be a charter hero. I didn't join to be an icon. I didn't join to be any of those...terms that have been associated to me and the journey. I'm humbled by it all. I'm thankful for the journey, I'm thankful to the creator that I had the tenacity and the courage and the capacity to move through that time.[34]

The issue of multiculturalism will be the subject of the next chapter, but in the context of the Charter, I should point out here that in 2016 the RCMP once again made a change to its dress code, this time to allow hijabs—the head scarves worn by some Muslim women.[35] Perhaps as a sign of the times, or a sign that the principle of equality embedded in the Charter had taken root, the new exemption did not cause nearly so much controversy. To coincide with the change in attire, Scott Bardsley, spokesperson for public safety minister Ralph Goodale, announced that "the Royal Canadian Mounted Police is a progressive and inclusive police service that values and respects persons of all cultural and religious backgrounds."[36]

The Charter has been instrumental in shaping the worldview of Canadians, whether they have liked it or not. If, on the verge of patriation, the Constitution was something that Canadian politicians had to ask the British Parliament for permission to amend, a mere ten years later the Charter of Rights and Freedoms became a living document that was actively shaping and being shaped by the lives of Canadians. In an interview with CBC Radio, Alan Cairns, professor of political science and expert on the Constitution, remarked:

> It has become, to a huge majority of Canadians—including those within Quebec—the fundamental constitutional instrument with which they identify. So it has transformed the

psyche of Canadians. This document is not just an external arrangement of rules by which we live, this is an attempt to transform who we are and who we actually feel and think we are. On the whole I think it has had that effect.[37]

Addressing Canadians in the ceremony that immediately followed the signing of the Constitution Act, 1982, Trudeau remarked, "We now have a charter which defines the kind of country in which we wish to live, and guarantees the basic rights and freedoms which each of us shall enjoy as a citizen of Canada."[38]

VII

Writing on the front page of the *New York Times*, American journalist Adam Liptak lamented the fact that the Constitution of the United States no longer functioned as a model for other democracies, since there now existed "the availability of newer, sexier and more powerful operating systems in the constitutional marketplace." The US Constitution, he wrote, "is terse and old, and it guarantees relatively few rights...failing to protect, at least in so many words, a right to travel, the presumption of innocence and entitlement to food, education and health care." According to Liptak, the US Constitution has been overshadowed on the global stage by the Canadian Charter of Rights and Freedoms. The latter document, he continued, "is both more expansive and less absolute. It guarantees equal rights for women and disabled people, allows affirmative action and requires that those arrested be informed of their rights. On the other hand, it balances those rights against 'such reasonable limits' as 'can be demonstrably justified in a free and democratic society.'"[39]

Liptak wrote his story to summarize the findings of a study by David S. Law of Washington University in St. Louis and Mila Versteeg of the University of Virginia that had appeared in the *New York University Law Review*.[40] "Initial analysis of the data," they argued, "reveals that the Canadian Constitution, unlike the U.S. Constitution, is increasingly in sync with global constitutionalism."[41] They then refer to the Canadian Charter as a global trendsetter:

> The fact that other common law countries have ultimately followed the same path does not necessarily prove, of course, that they did so because they were influenced by Canada. However, given Canada's relatively high prestige and goodwill as a member of the international community, as well as anecdotal evidence that Canadian constitutionalism has been influential in other countries, the most plausible inference to draw from our empirical findings is that Canada is, at least to some degree, a constitutional trendsetter among common law countries.[42]

Within this context, the Canadian Charter has been described as both the model and the leading influence on the drafting of other nations' constitutions, including the South African Bill of Rights, the Israeli Basic Laws, the New Zealand Bill of Rights, and the Hong Kong Bill of Rights, among others.[43]

VIII

In many ways, April 17, 1982, is also about the place of Pierre Elliott Trudeau within Canadian society. Despised in his own province, loathed in Western Canada, his legacy is as complicated as the man himself. He certainly succeeded in putting his stamp on Canada, and there can be little doubt that much of what the country is today is the result of both his vision and his influence. As early as 1967, for example, as minister of justice, he was responsible for introducing the landmark Criminal Law Amendment Act, an omnibus bill that, among other things, decriminalized homosexuality, allowed women access to abortion under certain conditions, decriminalized the sale of contraceptives, created more restrictive rules for gun possession, and introduced breathalyzer tests for suspected impaired drivers. Speaking to reporters outside Parliament about the act, Trudeau said, "In terms of the subject matter it deals with, I feel that it has knocked down a lot of totems and overridden a lot of taboos. And I feel that in that sense it is new, but it's bringing the laws of the land up to contemporary society." This segued into perhaps one of his most famous statements: "The view we take here is that there is no place for the state in the bedrooms of the nation.

I think that what is done in private between adults does not concern the Criminal Code."[44]

As prime minister, he was able to maintain national unity in the face of the rising tide of Quebec sovereignty including, as seen in chapter 1, bringing a successful end to the October Crisis. It was his federalist vision, moreover, that helped to create a national identity implemented by sweeping institutional reform, such as official bilingualism, official multiculturalism, and, as this chapter has shown, the patriation of the Constitution and its articulation of a set of Canadian values and rights through the Charter of Rights and Freedoms.

But this tells only part of the story. Critics accused him of economic mismanagement that led to an increase in the federal deficit. Others might argue that his desire to unify the country along federalist lines actually had the opposite effect, fanning the flames of regionalism. In so doing, he alienated both the inhabitants of Quebec and those in the West, in addition to harming the Alberta economy through the highly unpopular (especially from an Alberta perspective) National Energy Program. This led directly to the formation of federalist parties, the Bloc in Quebec and the Reform Party in the West, that sought to reassert provincial (in the case of the Bloc) and regional (in the case of the Reform Party) interests. Finally, Trudeau's detractors point to his desire to centralize the decision-making process by increasing the powers of the courts at the expense of provincial legislatures.

Despite this, neither critics nor admirers can deny just what an effect Pierre Trudeau has had on Canada. And April 17, 1982, the date that his entire political career led to and which characterizes him more than any other, is perhaps the most important day in the nation's history. Few other days have had such a long-term effect on the shaping of modern Canada. Its architect was Trudeau, with the Charter forming the infrastructure that would define the country into the future. Yet the day that was meant to sustain a national identity paradoxically carried within it the seeds to undermine national identity and unity.

SUGGESTIONS FOR FURTHER READING

Michael Asch. *Home and Native Land: Aboriginal Rights and the Canadian Constitution*. Agincourt, ON: Methuen, 1984.

Jean Chrétien. *My Stories, My Times*. Translated by Sheila Fischman and Donald Winkler. Toronto: Penguin Canada, 2018.

Adam Dodek. *The Canadian Constitution*. 2nd ed. Toronto: Dundurn Press, 2016.

Ian Greene. *The Charter of Rights and Freedoms: 30+ Years of Decisions That Shape Canadian Life*. Toronto: Lorimer, 2014.

René Lévesque. *Memoirs*. Translated by Philip Stratford. Toronto: McClelland and Stewart, 1986.

Kenneth McRoberts and Patrick Monahan, eds. *The Charlottetown Accord, the Referendum, and the Future of Canada*. Toronto: University of Toronto Press, 1993.

Pierre Elliott Trudeau. *Memoirs*. Toronto: McClelland and Stewart, 1993.

SUGGESTIONS FOR FURTHER VIEWING

Maurice Bulblian. *Dancing Around the Table, Part One*. National Film Board of Canada, 1987.

4

JULY 21 1988

The Multiculturalism Act

IN 2017 JAGMEET SINGH WAS ELECTED LEADER of the federal New Democrats, becoming the first person from a visible minority to lead a national party. In the same year, Justin Trudeau's federal cabinet contained more Sikhs than the cabinet of Prime Minister Narendra Modi in India. And as of 2020, there were seven ministers from visible minorities in Trudeau's cabinet. None of this is coincidence. On the contrary, all of these facts are the result of a number of events set in motion decades earlier.

One of these events occurred on July 21, 1988, the day the Multiculturalism Act (Bill C-93) was signed into law. This legislation emphasized the right of all individuals to preserve and share their cultural heritage while retaining their right to full and equitable participation in Canadian society. But even this date had an important precedent, at least as early as Pierre Trudeau's declaration in 1971 that Canada would henceforth pursue an official policy of multiculturalism, becoming the first country to do so. These dates transformed Canada from a largely white and Christian country to one of the most ethnically, religiously, and culturally diverse countries in the world within the span of a few decades. Since 1990 over six million immigrants, from all over the globe, have chosen to make Canada their home.

Combined with the Charter of Rights and Freedoms, the Multiculturalism Act has perhaps done more than anything else to shape modern Canada. Both established the legal principles whereby the country could flourish within a distinct vision. Though multiculturalism has its detractors, it cannot be denied that it has transformed, and perhaps come to define, the nation.

I

In many ways, Canada has always had to deal with otherness. At the beginning it primarily involved the English seeking to accommodate a French minority—although in theory this should also have included accommodation of Indigenous populations. We see this as early as 1774 with the passing of the Quebec Act, which, among other things, restored the use of French civil law in the province, removed any reference to the Protestant faith in oaths of allegiance sworn by public officials, and guaranteed the free practice of the Catholic faith for those who held public office. This ability to accommodate difference, displayed so early in its historical development, set Canada on a different course than Britain, its colonial overlord at the time.

Leaving aside some of the tensions witnessed in previous chapters—which will come to the fore again in chapter 7—Canada has a lengthy tradition of having two of its founding peoples—French and English—work with one another.[1] For example, when Canada East and Canada West were united in the province of Canada in 1840 (before being separated again into the provinces of Quebec and Ontario with Confederation), provincial leadership was shared by two attorneys general, one anglophone and one francophone. Indeed, it was one such partnership—between Robert Baldwin (1804–1858) and Louis-Hippolyte Lafontaine (1807–1864)—that helped foster the notion of "responsible government" in the colony and prevented what could very easily have become a civil war.[2]

If such cooperation was the result of necessity, if not actual goodwill, Canada was less accommodating when it came to Indigenous populations, non-Europeans, and Europeans who were neither French nor

English. Indigenous peoples will be the subject of chapter 8, but in terms of non-Europeans, suffice it to say that the Canadian Parliament had, from its earliest years, enacted a number of restrictive immigration measures that prevented non-whites and non-Christians from entering the country.[3] These included the Continuous Journey Regulation of 1908, which barred immigrants who had not travelled directly from their country of birth or citizenship to Canada by a "continuous journey." The intent was to block immigrants from India and South Asia, whose ships often had to stop in Japan or Hawaii.[4] Then there was the Chinese Immigration Act, renewed as late as 1923, which banned most forms of Chinese immigration to Canada.[5] However, such legislation had to be repealed in 1947, the year Canada signed the United Nations' Universal Declaration of Human Rights, which aspired to prevent discrimination based on race or religion. This was further facilitated by the Canadian Citizenship Act of 1946, which separated Canadian citizenship from British nationality.

In addition to legislation limiting immigration, Canada also enacted legislation during both World Wars to intern Canadians of "enemy nationality." During the First World War, for example, German and Ukrainian Canadians were treated with suspicion and were interned in labour camps—something that would be repeated with Japanese Canadians in the Second World War.

Despite issues of xenophobia, there were exceptions, and remarkable signs of things to come. In 1926, for example, Kate A. Foster prepared a survey of immigration for the Dominion Council of the YWCA, and her *Our Canadian Mosaic* observed that Canadian society was comprised of a number of disparate cultural groups.[6] And in his 1938 book, titled *Canadian Mosaic: The Making of a Northern Nation*, the Oxford-educated amateur folklorist and CPR publicist John Murray Gibbon also used the term "mosaic," this time as an ideal as opposed to just a description. His book provides a chapter-by-chapter account of the various "racial groups" that comprise Canada. "The Canadian people today presents itself as a decorated surface, bright with inlays of separate coloured pieces," with the result, according to him, that "the ensemble may truly be called a mosaic."[7]

Foster and Gibbon, among the first to use the phrase "multiculturalism" to refer to Canada, sought to differentiate the Canadian experience from the "melting pot" of the United States. If the latter sought to assimilate immigrants into a dominant American culture, Canada sought to create a "mosaic" wherein each cultural group retains a distinct sense of its own identity while also contributing to the larger nation of which they are a part. This concept of a mosaic would be recycled in official multicultural policy in the 1970s, which increasingly began to define Canada as a "cultural mosaic," a term still very much in vogue.

II

So what happened? How did Canada change from a largely Eurocentric and Christocentric nation to one of the world's most multicultural and multi-ethnic societies? In many ways, what set the wheels in motion was activism on the part of ethnic minorities who were worried that they would be left out of national conversations at the time that were trying to define Canada along English and French lines. When Prime Minister Lester B. Pearson formed the Royal Commission on Bilingualism and Biculturalism in 1963, the federal government's aim was "to recommend what steps should be taken to develop the Canadian Confederation on the basis of an equal partnership between the two founding races."[8] This naturally worried all those who were neither English nor French Canadians. Ukrainian, German, Dutch, Jewish, Hungarian, Polish, and Chinese Canadians, among others, were all concerned such language relegated them to second-class citizens or inferior "races." This so-called third force, particularly vocal in Western Canada, objected to the basic idea of "bilingualism and biculturalism."[9] In a speech in the Senate, for example, Paul Yuzyk, a Progressive Conservative senator from Manitoba was critical of such cultural dualism. Noting that Indigenous peoples were on the land long before the arrival of the French and the British, he went on to argue that it was immigrants from elsewhere who had settled the western provinces and that, if anything, biculturalism should give way to multiculturalism. He reminded French Canadians that "the Ukrainians have brought under cultivation approximately 10 million acres of land on the prairies which is twice as much as the French-Canadians, who cultivated in Quebec in over three centuries some 5 million acres."[10]

Ukrainian groups, the Canadian Jewish Congress, and others particularly objected to the Royal Commission's reference to "two founding races." The large outcry forced the government—rather reluctantly—to address the role of ethnic and other minority groups. It adjusted the commission's terms of reference to encompass reporting on "the role of private and public organizations, including the mass communications media, in promoting... more widespread appreciation of the basically bicultural character of our country and of the subsequent contribution made by the other cultures; and to recommend what should be done to improve that role."[11] The commission dedicated the fourth volume of its report to addressing the contributions of other ethnic groups to Canadian society and suggesting how to go about fostering and protecting their cultural and linguistic development. It recommended that minority groups be given greater recognition and support in preserving their own distinct cultures.[12] The report would serve as the basis for the government's official policy of multiculturalism.[13]

When, on October 8, 1971, Prime Minister Pierre Trudeau unveiled his government's new policy of multiculturalism in a speech to the House of Commons, he said:

> It was the view of the royal commission, shared by the government and, I am sure, by all Canadians, that there cannot be one cultural policy for the Canadians of British and French origins, another for the original peoples and yet a third for all others. For although there are two official languages, there is no official culture, nor does any ethnic group take precedence over any other. No citizen or group of citizens is other than Canadian, and all should be treated fairly.[14]

This makes it sound like multiculturalism was the government's intention all along, but we must remember the activism of minoritized peoples that helped bring it about. As important as multiculturalism was (and is) as a legal accomplishment, we must understand the role of immigrant minorities in challenging the status quo, and in trying to make those who were neither English nor French feel at home in Canada.

Trudeau then proposed that the cultural freedom of all individuals be preserved and that the cultural contributions of diverse ethnic groups to Canadian society be recognized:

> The policy I am announcing today accepts the contention of the other cultural communities that they, too, are essential

> elements in Canada and deserve government assistance in order to contribute to regional and national life in ways that derive from their heritage yet are distinctively Canadian.[15]

The result was a policy of multiculturalism within the context of a bilingual (but not multilingual) framework. This would mean:

> First, resources permitting, the government will seek to assist all Canadian cultural groups that have demonstrated a desire and effort to continue to develop a capacity to grow and contribute to Canada, and a clear need for assistance, the small and weak groups no less than the strong and highly organized.
>
> Second, the government will assist members of all cultural groups to overcome cultural barriers to full participation in Canadian society.
>
> Third, the government will promote creative encounters and interchange among all Canadian cultural groups in the interest of national unity.
>
> Fourth, the government will continue to assist immigrants to acquire at least one of Canada's official languages in order to become full participants in Canadian society.[16]

As of 1971, multiculturalism became official government policy, and Canada became the first country in the world to adopt such a policy. A decade later, when the Trudeau government repatriated the Constitution from Britain in 1982, multiculturalism became even further entrenched in the Charter of Rights and Freedoms. Section 27 of that document, for example, reads: "This Charter shall be interpreted in a manner consistent with the preservation and enhancement of the multicultural heritage of Canadians." This officially recognizes multiculturalism as a Canadian value.[17]

The Immigration Act of 1976, mentioned briefly in the context of chapter 2, further contributed to this inclusivity of immigration.

That act, it will be recalled, ensured that admission to Canada could not discriminate "on grounds of race, national or ethnic origin, colour, religion or sex." It was the first immigration act, for example, to include refugees—as defined by the United Nations' Convention Relating to the Status of Refugees—as a distinct class. As a result of all this, in the 1970s Canada underwent a momentous demographic change, one that has continued largely unabated up to the present.

III

When Brian Mulroney's Progressive Conservatives swept to power in 1984, his new government kept the positive multicultural momentum of the Trudeau years alive. While cynics might say, as they did with Trudeau, that this was one way to secure the votes of new Canadians, it cannot be denied that making multiculturalism, like bilingualism, the law of the land would have massive repercussions on the future of the country. In 1985, Mulroney struck a House of Commons Standing Committee on Multiculturalism, which two years later issued an extensive report on the current state and future prospects of Canadian multiculturalism.

The committee found that the existing policy of multiculturalism no longer adequately reflected the needs of Canadian society. It argued that the initial policy of 1971 was based largely on preserving culture for European-born immigrants. By the 1980s, however, the majority of immigrants were arriving from Asia, Africa, and the Middle East, and these communities had very different concerns than their largely white and European predecessors. These included not just the desire for cultural retention, but also concerns over discrimination and adequate access to employment, housing, and education. The committee thus called for a new policy on multiculturalism, including the creation of the Department of Multiculturalism.

The culmination of these initiatives resulted in the passage of the Canadian Multiculturalism Act on July 21, 1988. Whereas Mulroney's failed Meech Lake Accord (see chapter 3) had attempted to recognize the language rights of minorities, the successful new act was based on promoting "the full and equitable participation of individuals and communities of all origins in the continuing evolution and shaping of all aspects of Canadian society."[18]

On one level the act would provide a legislative framework for the official policy of multiculturalism that had been adopted in 1971 by the Trudeau government. But on a much deeper level, the new act went further by seeking to remove any barriers—legal, economic, social, and cultural—that would prevent full participation in Canadian society.

The preamble to the act noted two international agreements that Canada was a party to, which underpinned the concept of multiculturalism:

> The *International Convention on the Elimination of All Forms of Racial Discrimination*, which Convention recognizes that all human beings are equal before the law and are entitled to equal protection of the law against any discrimination and against any incitement to discrimination, and...the *International Covenant on Civil and Political Rights*, which Covenant provides that persons belonging to ethnic, religious or linguistic minorities shall not be denied the right to enjoy their own culture, to profess and practise their own religion or to use their own language.

The preamble then goes on to describe the aims of the federal government's policy of multiculturalism and the goals it was trying to achieve with the new act:

> The Government of Canada recognizes the diversity of Canadians as regards race, national or ethnic origin, colour and religion as a fundamental characteristic of Canadian society and is committed to a policy of multiculturalism designed to preserve and enhance the multicultural heritage of Canadians while working to achieve the equality of all Canadians in the economic, social, cultural and political life of Canada.

The act was an attempt to reflect the changing reality of Canada's racial and ethnic diversity, fully acknowledging multiculturalism as a fundamental characteristic of Canadian society. The new policy that the act ushered in promoted inclusivity in all of Canada's social, cultural, economic, and political institutions. Government agencies and departments were now expected to provide leadership in advancing multiculturalism at an institutional level. The act also contained provisions to help federal organizations implement policies and programs that adequately reflected a sensitivity and respect for the multicultural reality of Canada.

Section 3 of the act set out Canada's new multiculturalism policy. As such, it is worth quoting at length:

> 3. (1) It is hereby declared to be the policy of the Government of Canada to
>
> a. recognize and promote the understanding that multiculturalism reflects the cultural and racial diversity of Canadian society and acknowledges the freedom of all members of Canadian society to preserve, enhance and share their cultural heritage;
> b. recognize and promote the understanding that multiculturalism is a fundamental characteristic of the Canadian heritage and identity and that it provides an invaluable resource in the shaping of Canada's future;
> c. promote the full and equitable participation of individuals and communities of all origins in the continuing evolution and shaping of all aspects of Canadian society and assist them in the elimination of any barrier to that participation;
> d. recognize the existence of communities whose members share a common origin and their historic contribution to Canadian society, and enhance their development;
> e. ensure that all individuals receive equal treatment and equal protection under the law, while respecting and valuing their diversity;
> f. encourage and assist the social, cultural, economic and political institutions of Canada to be both respectful and inclusive of Canada's multicultural character;
> g. promote the understanding and creativity that arise from the interaction between individuals and communities of different origins;

h. foster the recognition and appreciation of the diverse cultures of Canadian society and promote the reflection and the evolving expressions of those cultures;
i. preserve and enhance the use of languages other than English and French, while strengthening the status and use of the official languages of Canada; and
j. advance multiculturalism throughout Canada in harmony with the national commitment to the official languages of Canada.

Significantly, while the act makes Canada into an officially multicultural society, it does not transform it into a multilingual one. The country thus retains the Official Languages Act that had previously defined the country as bilingual.

In the next section, titled "Implementation," the act makes clear how it will attain its ends by, among other things, encouraging and assisting "individuals, organizations and institutions to project the multicultural reality of Canada in their activities in Canada and abroad." While certainly broad, on a practical level this translated into making federal funds available to ethnic groups to help them preserve their languages and cultures, and assisting "ethno-cultural minority communities to conduct activities with a view to overcoming any discriminatory barrier and, in particular, discrimination based on race or national or ethnic origin."

While there have been critics of the Multiculturalism Act over the years, some of whom I shall discuss below, I will mention here that some complained it did not go far enough. Writing in the *Globe and Mail*, columnist Jeffrey Simpson remarked that the act left out several key recommendations, such as the creation of a separate ministry devoted to multiculturalism, and provided few funds to carry out its mission.[19] Indeed, a Department of Multiculturalism and Citizenship was not created until 1991, and it was subsequently folded into the Department of Canadian Heritage.

IV

On October 8, 1971, Canada declared itself multicultural—the first country in the world to do so. On July 21, 1988, it went a step farther, becoming the first country to pass a national multiculturalism law. These dates have had a tremendous influence on shaping the country. Perhaps most significantly, the Multiculturalism Act has transformed Canada into what is arguably one of the world's most culturally, religiously, and ethnically diverse nations. In 2013, for example, the Pew Research Center showed Canada to be the only Western country to break into the top twenty most culturally diverse countries. The United States, by comparison, ranks near the middle, slightly more diverse than Russia but slightly less diverse than Spain.[20] Other studies, based on diversity of labour forces, put Canada in the top ten of the world's most diverse countries—and such studies freely admit that if they were to include ethnic diversity (their focus tended to be on gender and linguistic diversity), Canada would "would move towards the very top of the ranking."[21]

The Multicultural Act has also made Canada a country with one of the highest per capita immigration rates in the world. According to census data, Canada accepted 250,640 immigrants in 2001, with numbers ranging from 221,352 to 262,236 immigrants per year since then.[22] Indeed, the 2016 census revealed one of every five Canadians is an immigrant, with over six million immigrants arriving in Canada since 1990—not coincidentally, the second year the Multiculturalism Act was in force. And while the act did not necessarily cause immigration numbers to rise, what is certain is that the former ensured that the latter would contribute to Canada's multicultural diversity. In 2017, Justin Trudeau's Liberal government announced that the country would welcome nearly one million immigrants over the next three years.[23] And in 2018, Canada saw the highest level of new permanent residents in recent history, with just over 321,000 individuals. In that same year, Canada also became the number one resettlement country in the world, resettling over 28,000 refugees.[24]

It is important to note the extent to which these impressive immigration numbers have helped the country grow and develop economically. While many of these new Canadians arrive because of federal programs designed to reunite families and facilitate the safe settlement of refugees, the overwhelming majority come because they want to contribute to the overall economic health of the country. So successful is Canada at attracting a highly educated and productive immigrant community that one American commentator remarked in the pages of the *New York Times*, "When it comes to immigration, Canada's policies are anything but effete. Instead, they're ruthlessly rational, which is why Canada now claims the world's most prosperous and successful immigrant population."[25] This commentator noted that whereas about half of all Canadian immigrants arrive with a college degree, in the United States that figure is about a quarter. He also cited a report from the Organisation for Economic Co-operation and Development which said that while immigrant children in Canadian schools read at the same level as those who are native born, the gap in the US is much larger. Finally, he noted that Canadian immigrants are almost 20 per cent more likely to own their own homes than immigrants to the US, and are much less likely to live in poverty.

This has many repercussions. Andrew Griffith, a fellow at the Canadian Global Affairs Institute, has found that "89 percent of Canadians believe that foreign-born Canadians are just as likely to be good citizens as those born in Canada." Though, Griffith notes, Canadians also have clear ideas that multiculturalism should be about integration, with the understanding that new immigrants should adopt Canadian values and attitudes.[26] A 2012 survey by Environics, *Focus Canada* 2012, asked Canadians, "What is it about Canada that gives you the greatest sense of pride?" Multiculturalism ranked third, behind freedom and the country's humanitarian spirit.[27] The same survey also found that among new Canadians, close to 80 per cent identified more closely with Canada than with the country of their birth. Finally, the Environics survey reported that Canadians ranked multiculturalism as a greater national symbol than hockey (with the country's healthcare system ranking as the most important).[28]

In recent years, though, Canadians have become slightly less positive about immigration.[29] A 2017 poll by the federal government found that 32 per cent of Canadians said too many refugees—note refugees, and not immigrants—were coming to Canada, compared to 30 per cent in the previous year. The same poll also asked respondents about their comfort levels around people of different races and religions, with 89 per cent saying they were comfortable around people of a different race, compared to 94 per cent in 2005–2006. It is worth noting that the timing of the 2012 poll coincided with a spike in asylum seekers crossing illegally into Canada from the United States.

Another consequence of the success of Canadian multiculturalism is the fact that none of the three mainstream federal parties are anti-immigration. This suggests that Canadians value both immigration and multiculturalism. In the 2019 federal election there was one party—the People's Party of Canada, led by Maxime Bernier—that, while not in theory opposed to immigration, nevertheless sought to limit it to no more than 150,000 people per year. The party's platform also called for introduction of a "values" test for potential immigrants, and removal of the "parents and grandparents" class from the family reunification program.[30] Bernier's party promised to repeal the Multiculturalism Act and, perhaps most unpalatable to the majority of Canadians, vowed to build border fences at popular points of entry.[31] Not a single candidate from the People's Party was elected to Parliament.

While some cities are more multicultural than others—with the Greater Toronto Area, Montreal, and Vancouver leading the pack—the reach of multiculturalism can be found in virtually every medium- to large-sized city in Canada. Multiculturalism has shaped Canada and the sense that Canadians have of themselves. While in the next two sections we will examine some of the criticisms levelled against multiculturalism, it cannot be denied that multiculturalism as a political policy has forever changed the demographic makeup of Canada, and created a worldview of which the overwhelming majority of Canadians are proud.

V

Since Pierre Trudeau's announcement in 1971 that Canada would pursue a multicultural policy, every Quebec government has officially rejected the principle. Some Quebec nationalists, for example, maintain that multiculturalism was devised by Trudeau as a way to weaken and ultimately destroy the forces of separation. They levelled the same charge against him for invoking the War Measures Act to put an end to the October Crisis. Multiculturalism, they argue, stands in stark opposition to biculturalism. Others hold a view expressed succinctly by *Montreal Gazette* columnist Lise Ravary: "Quebecers know who they are: it's the rest of Canada that struggles with Quebec's identity as a nation 400 years-plus in the making, with the help of immigrants along the way."[32] At the time of Trudeau's announcement, for example, Quebec premier Robert Bourassa informed the prime minister that Quebec was already subsidizing various ethnic groups in the province through programs analogous to those envisaged by the federal policy. Indeed, the late 1970s saw the perception of Quebec nationalism metamorphose from a beleaguered minority under existential threat to the creation of more inclusive civic nationalism. With a falling birth rate, the province—originally opposed to immigration—began to encourage it, but only insofar as Quebec could be in control of newcomers to the province.

In 1981, the Lévesque government adopted a more systematic approach to immigration. In a white paper entitled "Autant de façons d'être québécois: Plan d'action du gouvernement du Québec à l'intention des communautés culturelles" ("The Diverse Ways of Being a Quebecer: The Quebec Government Action Plan for Cultural Communities"), the government developed the principle of "interculturalism," a Quebec alternative to Canadian multiculturalism. In this context, immigrants and minorities were to be welcome in Quebec and could retain their own cultures and languages, but they had to accept the idea that French was the official language of Quebec. Children of immigrants, in turn, had to attend French-language schools.[33] Significantly, Quebec's anglophones, owing to the fact that they were imagined to wield disproportionate power and influence with their established links to the anglophone majority in Canada, were not considered to be a "cultural community" as others were.

One of the most articulate framers of "interculturalism" is Gérard Bouchard, a distinguished historian and brother of Lucien Bouchard, founder of the Bloc Québécois and later PQ premier of Quebec. For Gérard Bouchard, "in the particular case of Quebec it is necessary to develop a form of pluralism that acknowledges that the francophone majority is itself a precarious minority that needs protection in order to ensure its survival and development in the North American environment and in the context of globalization."[34]

Interculturalism thus recognizes the existence of a majority culture (to wit, French-speaking), something multiculturalism does not, but also acknowledges that room must be made for other cultures to partake of and add to this majority culture. Bouchard concludes his essay on interculturalism with the following statement:

> Interculturalism is built on the basic wager of democracy, that is, a capacity to reach consensus on forms of peaceful coexistence that preserve basic values and make room for the future of all citizens, regardless of their origins or nationalities.

This path is certainly not the easiest. For the Quebec majority culture, the simplest thing would be to try to protect the old francophone identity to the point of isolating it, to freeze it—as it were—and thus to impoverish it, which would be another way of putting it at risk. The more promising but also the more difficult option is the one which offers a wider horizon to this identity and to its underlying values by sharing them with immigrants and minority groups. This last option, contrary to what is sometimes said, does not involve withdrawal or self-renunciation, but real affirmation. It means the expansion and enrichment of heritage. It also includes the important advantage of providing inspiration for all Quebec's citizens.[35]

Bouchard's discussion here is informed by the work he did with his colleague, the philosopher Charles Taylor. In 2007, Jean Charest's provincial Liberal Party formed a Consultation Commission on Accommodation Practices Related to Cultural Differences in response to public discontent around the issue of "reasonable accommodation" for minorities as defined by the Charter of Rights and Freedoms. The commission, headed by Taylor and Bouchard, was to address four key issues: (1) cultural integration, (2) collective identity, (3) church-state relations, and (4) procedures for handling cultural and religious harmonization requests. They heard testimony in various hearings and informal town hall meetings held across the province from August to December 2007, and reported their findings to the provincial government in March 2008.[36]

The so-called Bouchard-Taylor Commission on Reasonable Accommodation concluded in its 300-plus page report that the province needed to better define the principle of secularism so that minorities would feel more welcome and comfortable. This would involve prohibiting provincial judges, Crown prosecutors, police officers, and prison guards from wearing religious signs and clothing while on the job, and eliminating prayers from all municipal council meetings. Finally, they recognized that although Quebec was most certainly a pluralist society, the Canadian multiculturalism model "does not appear well suited to conditions in Quebec." Instead, they again emphasized the model of Quebec's interculturalism.

At a news conference in Montreal the day after the report was released, Taylor said, "Quebec is entering a new phase in its history marked by a shift in selfhood, which is no longer a French-Canadian identity. It has become a Quebec identity. But such identity must be an inclusive type of identity."[37] Though we might well ask: just how different is interculturalism from multiculturalism?

Despite the report, French-speaking Quebecers' sense of alienation did not go away and was in fact intensified with a perceived inundation of Muslim immigrants, with veils, burkas, and niqabs worn by many Muslim women. In 2013, the governing Parti Québécois, led by Pauline Marois, introduced Bill 60—the Charter of Quebec Values (Charte de la laïcité or Charte des valeurs québécoises)—to address the notion of "reasonable accommodation" when it came to immigrants. There was much controversy in Quebec and elsewhere about Bill 60, which proposed prohibiting public sector employees from wearing or displaying conspicuous religious symbols, and would also make it mandatory to have one's face uncovered when providing or receiving a state service. The response from civil liberty and Muslim groups, among others, was very critical. Though Bill 60 was clearly in violation of the Canadian Charter of Rights and Freedoms, Marois threatened to invoke the notwithstanding clause to pass it. However, the bill was dropped when the provincial Liberal Party formed government in 2014.

The situation did not disappear with the change in government. In 2015, the Coalition Avenir Québec (Coalition for Quebec's Future or CAQ)—a nationalist party founded in 2011, which was gradually picking up momentum in provincial politics—announced that one of its key priorities was to "exempt Quebec from the requirements of multiculturalism."[38] This would allow Quebec to establish, among other things, different immigration criteria from the rest of the country. The CAQ also proposed the creation of a "pact" with immigrants, meaning that, after three years in Quebec, immigrants would be tested on their level of French and knowledge of "Quebec values."[39] Such linguistic and cultural knowledge takes Quebec's notion of interculturalism in a new direction by attempting to define the criteria whereby immigrants are allowed to remain in the province or, presumably, are forced out.

In the 2018 provincial election the CAQ won enough seats to form government, with François Legault, CAQ leader, as the new premier. One of the planks in the CAQ election platform, was to reduce the number of incoming immigrants to the province from 50,000 to 40,000 annually, which would amount to about a 20 per cent reduction.[40] In June 2019 the Legault government passed Bill 21, the Act Respecting the Laicity of the State / Loi sur la laïcité de l'État, which limits the wearing of religious symbols while providing or receiving public services. The only reason Bill 21 can exist in Quebec is because the provincial government enacted the notwithstanding clause; otherwise, it is a clear violation of the Charter.

VI

Quebec is not the only province seeking to redefine the notion of multiculturalism. In the 1993 federal election, the recently created Reform Party—whose mantra was "The West Wants In!"—won fifty-two seats in the House of Commons. Virtually sweeping Alberta and British Columbia, the party won an impressive 19 per cent of the popular vote nationwide. Presenting itself as a populist party, and running on a platform of balanced budgets and social conservative values, the Reform Party gained Official Opposition status in the 1997 election without winning a seat outside of Western Canada.

In 1992, University of Calgary political scientists Keith Archer and Faron Ellis asked delegates to the Reform Party's national assembly to rate the amount of influence they thought certain groups had on government policy on a scale of 1 (very little) to 7 (a great amount). "Recent immigrants" averaged 2.9, just behind homosexuals at 3.5 and feminists at 4. (By comparison, the leader of the Opposition and the Senate averaged 2.3 and 2.2, respectively.)[41] When it came to multiculturalism and immigration, only 1.9 per cent of respondents agreed with the statement "The federal government should increase its efforts to further multiculturalism" (with 96.8 per cent disagreeing and 1.35 per cent undecided). Furthermore, 91.3 per cent of respondents agreed with the statement "Newly arrived immigrants should be assimilated into the Canadian mainstream" (with 3.9 per cent disagreeing and 4.8 per cent undecided).[42]

As early as 1991, the Reform Party called for an end to funding the federal multicultural program and abolishing the Department of Multiculturalism.[43] Party members saw multiculturalism as another aspect of the federal welfare state, which the Reform Party opposed, and they did not share the assessment of other federal parties that the program was essential to national unity and harmony. Reform's 1988 election platform complained that federal immigration policy was "explicitly designed to radically or suddenly alter the ethnic makeup of Canada." And the 1990 platform discussed the need to maintain a "national culture," without actually defining what such a culture was. Though party leadership was able to remove such racialized language from the federal platform, this did not stop individual constituency associations from returning to it. The Reform Party was also opposed to the federal policy of official bilingualism, imagining it as institutionalization of French elites in Ottawa.[44]

Like any populist party, the Reform Party of Canada imagined—and sought to promote—a nostalgic version of Canada and Canadian culture. Its Canada was white, Christian, rural or small-town, and monolingual, a vision that was clearly out of step with what Canada had become.[45] Although party leadership would parade the odd candidate from a minority background—especially in those ridings with large ethnic populations—the guiding ideology was anything but inclusive. Unlike nationalist parties in Quebec, the Reform Party offered no alternative to address what by then had clearly become a multiethnic and multicultural society, other than to complain that it was the result of "special interests." It is worth underscoring in this context that any attempt by a federal party to end multiculturalism would be impossible because it is supported by the overwhelming majority of Canadians and, just as importantly, because it is a principle enshrined in the Charter.

Through the late 1990s, the Reform Party worked to bring all Canadian conservatives together in one party. In 2000 it was renamed the Canadian Reform Conservative Alliance, and in 2003 it united with the federal Progressive Conservative Party to become the Conservative Party of Canada. Former Reform members took a number of the party's social conservative values with them and also became leaders of the new party.[46] Future Conservative Party leader and prime minster Stephen Harper, for example, was a founding member of the Reform Party, and its subsequent leader, Andrew Scheer, worked on former Reform leader Preston Manning's failed campaign to lead the Reform Conservative Alliance. As prime minister, Harper sought to advance an agenda with an emphasis on common Canadian values and a stress on integration rather than accommodation. Those symbols that highlighted Canadian historical connections to Britain, including the monarchy, were also emphasized. Without praising the virtues of Canadian multiculturalism, he certainly endorsed Canadian diversity.[47] In 2008, Harper moved the Ministry of Multiculturalism from the Department of Canadian Heritage to the Department of Citizenship and Immigration,[48] which seemed to signal that multiculturalism was something brought from outside the country by immigrants as opposed to something which was nourished at home by all Canadians.

Both Stephen Harper and Jason Kenney, minister of multiculturalism for many of the Harper years, focused unduly on Muslim women who wore the niqab or burqa, and accused Muslim men of spousal abuse and "honour" crimes.[49] Campaigning in the 2015 federal election, Harper's Conservatives said they would prevent Muslim women from wearing a niqab while taking the citizenship oath, and planned to create a "barbaric cultural practices" tip line. During the 2015 leaders debate, Stephen Harper said the tip line would allow "old stock" Canadians to report on their "new stock" neighbours.[50] The Conservative government, while not necessarily anti-immigrant, nevertheless severely overhauled the immigration and refugee system, making it much more difficult for those fleeing war and poverty to settle in Canada.

It was ultimately a refugee, however, who at least symbolically brought down the Harper government. About a month and a half before the 2015 federal election, Alan Kurdi, a three-year-old boy from Syria, drowned at sea as his family tried to cross from Turkey to Greece in the hope of a better life. The iconic photo of the young boy lying face down on a beach made headlines around the world. As word got out that Alan's family were trying to come to Canada, Canadians became increasingly upset at the tragic events of Alan's life and death and the larger refugee crisis, a topic that increasingly dominated the national conversation in the weeks leading up to the election. Liberal leader Justin Trudeau remarked, "All different stripes of governments in Canada have stepped up in times of crisis to accept people fleeing for their lives. Canadians get it. This is about doing the right thing, about living up to the values that we cherish as a country."[51] In contrast, Harper said that, though the event was tragic, Canada's security needs—a phrase his government had consistently used to limit refugee claims—were central, as he was afraid that Muslim extremists would take advantage of the system to enter the country. Many Canadians, with a lengthy and proud history of multiculturalism behind them, bristled at Conservative indifference to international suffering. Trudeau's

Liberals vowed to resettle 25,000 refugees as soon as possible. It worked. The Liberals won the 2015 election and, significantly, the Conservatives won only two of thirty ridings with very large visible minority populations (mainly in the Greater Toronto Area and BC's lower mainland).[52]

VII

Criticisms of multiculturalism are not confined to provinces or regions trying to promote their own concerns nor to populist parties seeking hot-button issues to put before an electorate. Some critics, for example, argue that multiculturalism promotes ghettoization and balkanization. They argue that many immigrants to Canada opt to live in their own ethnic enclaves, since it is much easier to do so than to try to fit into mainstream Canadian culture.[53] Then there are the criticisms from those who maintain that multiculturalism is a form of "political correctness" (a term that functions as a code for neo-conservative individuals or groups who use it to accuse others of oppressing or silencing them) that weakens a sense of national identity as opposed to strengthening it.[54] Rarely do such individuals offer a positive portrayal of what a national identity might look like. Also figuring in this critique is the accusation that Canada's generous immigration policy, supported by multiculturalism, poses a security threat to law-abiding Canadians.

Writing in the *National Post* after the arrest of the Toronto 18—a group of individuals who plotted a series of attacks in Toronto and southern Ontario—Robert Fulford lamented that "we had traditionally believed in old-fashioned pluralism: people of different sorts maintaining independent cultural traditions, but living side by side in an integrated society." Instead of this, he claimed that multiculturalism succeeded in creating a "land of ghettos," and that a disaffected young generation of immigrants, "who see cultural isolation as a permanent way of life tend to cripple their own possibilities, limit their ability to contribute to Canada, and create impregnable communities in which they can nourish their imported grievance and generate hatred for democracy and the West."[55] If anything, though, the Toronto 18 are the exception that proves the rule. Indeed, one could make the case that multiculturalism has prevented precisely this sort of alienation among immigrant youth, unlike what is happening in such countries as France, Germany, or even the United States.

Perhaps the most articulate critic of multiculturalism is Neil Bissoondath, a distinguished Canadian novelist who emigrated from Trinidad and Tobago in 1973. In his 1994 book *Selling Illusions: The Cult of Multiculturalism in Canada*, he argues that Canadian multiculturalism has emphasized difference and, as a result, has retarded the integration of immigrants into the Canadian mainstream while simultaneously damaging any national sense of self.[56] Instead, he says, we need to begin to focus on those ideas, events, and programs that emphasize the experiences and values of all Canadians, regardless of colour, language, religion, or ethnicity. This, and not multiculturalism, he argues, leads to acceptance of others, not just tolerance of them. But one could perhaps make the case that it is precisely the idea of multiculturalism that is the idea, event, and program that unites all Canadians rather than dividing them.

VIII

The Multiculturalism Act of 1988 was, in many respects, the culmination of a long-standing policy that began as early as the late 1960s. These two dates mark points on a continuum that witnessed the transformation of Canada from a largely white, European, and Christian country into one of the world's most diverse. Despite those critics who see multiculturalism creating barriers between Canadians or leading to balkanization or fragmentation, if the polls are to be believed this has not happened. If anything, multiculturalism has played a major role in shaping the way Canadians think about themselves. It has become a defining element of national identity.

On the eve of his first election as prime minister, Pierre Trudeau talked about the need for a "just society," a phrase that became synonymous with all the reforms he ushered in. Perhaps in response to the phrase so popular in the United States of an "all-American" girl or boy—stereotypically described as having blond hair and fair skin—Trudeau remarked that there could never be a such a thing in Canada:

> Uniformity is neither desirable nor possible in a country the size of Canada. We should not even be able to agree upon the kind of Canadian to choose as a model, let alone persuade most people to emulate it. There are few policies potentially

> more disastrous for Canada than to tell all Canadians that they must be alike. There is no such thing as a model or ideal Canadian. What could be more absurd than the concept of an "all-Canadian" boy or girl? A society which emphasizes uniformity is one which creates intolerance and hate. A society which eulogizes the average citizen is one which breeds mediocrity. What the world should be seeking, and what in Canada we must continue to cherish, are not concepts of uniformity but human values: compassion, love, and understanding.[57]

Though I think it is fair to say that Trudeau began the process of forming a multicultural society with his speech to Parliament on October 8, 1971, and enshrined it in the Charter of Rights and Freedoms, it was the signing of the Multicultural Act on July 21, 1988, under Prime Minister Brian Mulroney, where we see the concept fully integrated into Canadian legal culture. Not unlike the Charter, multiculturalism has truly changed modern Canada. To celebrate this, on November 13, 2002, Prime Minister Jean Chrétien designated June 27 of each year to be Canadian Multiculturalism Day.

SUGGESTIONS FOR FURTHER READING

Neil Bissoondath. *Selling Illusions: The Cult of Multiculturalism in Canada*. Toronto: Penguin Books, 1994.

Andrew Griffith. *Multiculturalism in Canada: Evidence and Anecdote*. Toronto: Anar Press, 2015.

Freda Hawkins. *Canada and Immigration: Public Policy and Public Concerns*. 2nd ed. Montreal and Kingston: McGill-Queen's University Press, 1988.

Michael Temelini, ed. *Multiculturalism and the Canadian Constitution*. Vancouver: UBC Press, 2007.

SUGGESTIONS FOR FURTHER VIEWING

Rohan Fernando. *Trudeau's Other Children*. National Film Board of Canada, 2005.

Lucie Lachapelle. *Mosaic Village*. National Film Board of Canada, 1996.

Anne Marie Nakagawa. *Between: Living in the Hyphen*. National Film Board of Canada, 2005.

5

DECEMBER 6 1989

The École Polytechnique Massacre

IN THE EARLY EVENING OF DECEMBER 6, 1989, the last day of the fall term, a young man entered the building of École Polytechnique, one of Canada's premier engineering schools, on the grounds of the University of Montreal. An hour later fourteen women lay murdered, ten more women and four men were injured, and the gunman was dead from suicide. Until 2020 the Montreal Massacre, as it came to be known, was the single most destructive mass shooting to have occurred on Canadian soil. The gunman had specifically targeted the school and his victims because, as a self-described "anti-feminist," he did not believe that women should pursue careers in engineering, a field of study that he thought should be reserved solely for men. The events of December 6, 1989, ushered in major changes in Canadian society, from stricter gun control to creating a national conversation on misogyny and violence against women.

I

After spending roughly forty minutes in the registrar's office, rummaging through a large plastic bag whose contents he shielded from onlookers, and without so much as a word to anyone in the office, Marc Lépine rose and made his way to École Polytechnique's third floor. Witnesses later recounted how he leaned against a wall, holding the plastic bag, which appeared to have a long object within. As soon became clear, this object was a rifle. He also held a smaller, white plastic bag, which, it was later revealed, concealed a hunting knife. At 5:10 p.m., armed with the rifle and hunting knife, the killer went from the third floor to the second and entered room C-230.4, where a class in mechanical engineering was taking place with about sixty students.[1] He moved to the front of the room, clutching the rifle in both hands, and interrupted a student who was giving a final presentation. Approaching the student he shouted, "Everybody stop everything." To get their attention, he fired a rifle shot into the ceiling and told the students to separate themselves into two groups, motioning that young women should move to the left of the room and young men to the right. After telling the men that they were free to leave, he approached the group of nine young women, who were now at the front of the room, as far as possible from the classroom door.

According to the *Report of the Coroner's Investigation*, he then said to the group, "Do you know why you are here?" One of the girls nervously answered, "No," to which he replied, "I am fighting feminism." The student who had spoken then said, "We are not feminists, I have never fought against men." Rather than hear her out—his mind having been made up in the days, months, or even years before—he started firing into the group, from left to right. Six of the nine young women were murdered in cold blood, with the others surviving only by pretending that they too were dead. Back in the corridor, walking methodically and slowly down the hallway, the killer shot randomly at people, injuring several more, before reloading his rifle in a stairwell. Returning to the corridor, he approached another door. When he tried to force his way in, the woman inside quickly locked the door, but as she tried to flee, the gunman shot her through the glass, killing her instantly.

The killer next took the escalator down to the cafeteria on the first floor. At the entrance, he aimed and fired at another young woman who was near the wall by the kitchen, killing her. He walked through the cafeteria, firing randomly, until he reached the other end, whereupon he shot and killed two female students, both of whom were trying to escape. He then went back up to the third floor, shooting indiscriminately at students and faculty. He entered another classroom, B-311, and after telling some students to "Get out!" he fired, killing three female students. Proceeding to the front of the class, where an injured young woman pleaded with him for help, he took out the hunting knife and stabbed her three times, killing her.

He next put the knife on the instructor's desk, along with his cap and two boxes, each filled with twenty bullets. He took off his coat, put it around the barrel of his rifle, and muttered under his breath, "Oh merde," before killing himself by firing the last bullet in the magazine into his head. Police later reported that they had found another full box of twenty bullets on a chair at the front of the classroom near the entrance door.

This was the first large-scale massacre in modern Canadian history,[2] and the fact that women had been singled out to be murdered made it all the more horrifying. It was not a random attack, but a deliberate and politically motivated one.

Though police were blamed for their inaction as they waited outside the building while an active shooter rampaged inside, they had very little precedent to guide them, as school shootings were nearly unheard of in 1989. Many of the witnesses and survivors tell how, initially, they had thought they were part of some elaborate prank or practical joke, not uncommon among young engineering students.

In the span of nineteen minutes, fourteen women were murdered, and fourteen more people were injured. The names of the victims are

Geneviève Bergeron (born 1968), civil engineering student
Hélène Colgan (born 1966), mechanical engineering student
Nathalie Croteau (born 1966), mechanical engineering student
Barbara Daigneault (born 1967), mechanical engineering student
Anne-Marie Edward (born 1968), chemical engineering student
Maud Haviernick (born 1960), materials engineering student
Barbara Klucznik-Widajewicz (born 1958), nursing student
Maryse Laganière (born 1964), budget clerk in the finance department
Maryse Leclair (born 1966), materials engineering student

Anne-Marie Lemay (born 1967), mechanical engineering student
Sonia Pelletier (born 1961), mechanical engineering student
Michèle Richard (born 1968), materials engineering student
Annie St-Arneault (born 1966), mechanical engineering student
Annie Turcotte (born 1969), materials engineering student[3]

The Quebec government declared three days of provincial mourning. On December 11, 1989, a funeral for nine of the women was held at Montreal's famed Notre-Dame Basilica, attended by Prime Minister Brian Mulroney, Quebec premier Robert Bourassa, and Montreal mayor Jean Doré, in addition to thousands of other mourners.

II

The killer was born Gamil Rodrigue Liass Gharbi, the son of Rachid Gharbi, an Algerian immigrant who had lived through the civil war in that country, and Monique Lépine, a Canadian nurse from Quebec. In an interview with *Maclean's*, years after the shooting, his mother described the relationship between father and son:

> Once, he [Rachid Gharbi] slammed my son's face so hard the marks were there for a week. But mostly it was psychological. He was forbidding me to pick up my child; in his mentality, if a baby was crying, you shouldn't console him. He was very cold, I don't think that he was a father, to tell you the truth. I would never have left the kids with him alone, I didn't trust him. He said himself, very loud, that kids before the age of six were like little dogs you had to train.[4]

When her son was six—and her daughter, Nadia, four—the young nurse left her abusive husband. The two children lived with other families as their mother worked, able to see her only on weekends. His mother described the young boy as very attentive to her, but also as "strategic...and enigmatic." His sister—who died from a drug overdose seven years after the massacre—used to tease him mercilessly, according to his mother, and one day the young boy was so upset that he dug a grave in his backyard and stuck Nadia's picture on a tombstone he had built for the occasion.[5]

As a present for his fourteenth birthday, his mother allowed him to change his name legally. Gamil Gharbi now became Marc Lépine. The reason for the name change was noted as "hatred of his father." His next ten years seem to have been marked by a series of failures, both in school and in life. He applied to join, but was rejected by, the Canadian Forces because, as he mentioned in his suicide note, his behaviour was deemed to be "asocial." He applied to various science and technical programs at local community colleges, but would usually drop out before completion. He was fired from his job at a hospital for his "poor attitude." In the fall of 1986, Lépine applied for admission to the École Polytechnique and was accepted with the caveat that he complete two required courses, which he never did.[6] In 1988 he began a computer programming course, but again abandoned it before completion.

Based on information gathered from interviews with members of his family and an analysis of various documents that he had written (including his suicide note), a forensic psychiatrist concluded that the murderer's multiple homicide/suicide strategy was indicative of people who "may identify a person or group of persons negatively and the collected aggressive emotions experienced may be projected onto [that person or group]."[7]

For the killer, that group—as was clear to the nation within hours of the massacre—was women.

A suicide note was found tucked inside the killer's jacket pocket but was never officially released because authorities said they were worried about copycat murders. Roughly a year later, however, Francine Pelletier, a noted Québécois journalist and feminist, was anonymously sent a copy of the note, which was published in *La Presse* on November 24, 1990. In the note, the murderer explained that his act was "political," designed to "send the feminists, who have always ruined my life, to their Maker."[8] Aware that he might be psychologized as a "mad killer," he wrote, "I consider myself a rational erudite." Next he complained about how "the feminists have always enraged me. They want to keep the advantages of women (e.g. cheaper insurance, extended maternity leave preceded by a preventative leave, etc.) while seizing for themselves those of men." He then went on to list the names of nineteen other women he wanted to kill, including feminist figures (among them Pelletier) and symbolic targets such as the province's first female police officer and firefighter.

III

The fourteen women killed at École Polytechnique were not afforded the same luxury of expression. They were unable to reflect on their dreams and could not reveal their last thoughts and hopes on paper. We get some glimpses, fleeting as they are, in the stories of those women who survived the attack. "They were beautiful girls. They were intelligent girls. They were girls with high potential," said Nathalie Provost, "and it is that way that I will remember them."[9] Provost, a twenty-three-year-old student who was one of three women to survive the initial shooting in room C-230.4, was interviewed by Michael Enright on CBC Radio after she had watched the funeral from her hospital bed.

Provost was the young woman who responded to the killer's charge that they had to die because they were feminists. In an interview with the BBC years later, she said, "I was telling [him] that I was not a feminist, and that we were not feminists. It is so simple: it is because we had all the opportunities that the guys of our age had. So, for me, I did not have to fight to be where I was so I was not able to claim anything as a feminist."[10] However, on the twenty-fifth anniversary of the massacre, she did admit that she now considers herself to be a feminist. "I'm much more aware that in my daily behaviour, I uphold feminist values," she said, listing setbacks for women around the globe, including millions of girls denied the right to an education.[11]

Although the group of nine women, scared for their lives and huddled in a corner, tried to convince the killer that they were not feminists, they were feminists. All were working to overcome, in their own ways, barriers that prevented gender equality. By virtue of wanting to be engineers, they sought to change the world for the better by entering a field that was hitherto predominantly male. While they certainly comprised a visible minority in the École Polytechnique on that cold December afternoon in 1989, today the number of women in STEM (science, technology, engineering, and mathematics) programs in Canada has increased dramatically. In 2019, Statistics Canada released a study using data from the Education and Labour Market Longitudinal Platform that showed women make up 44 per cent of first-year STEM students, and women tend to graduate faster than men from all STEM programs.[12] The young women who were murdered in cold blood in 1989, and those who survived their injuries, helped pave the way for all those who came after them.

Though she did not see herself as a feminist in 1989, Provost welcomed the new commemorative plaque installed at the memorial to the victims in Place du 6-Décembre-1989 on the thirty-year anniversary of the massacre.[13] The earlier plaque had simply referred to "the tragic event," stating that the site aims to "promote the values of respect and non-violence," but the city of Montreal decided to change the wording to more accurately reflect the crime. The plaque now reads (in English translation):

> This park is named in memory of the 14 women assassinated in an anti-feminist attack at the École Polytechnique on December 6, 1989. It serves to recall the fundamental values of respect and equality, and condemns all forms of violence against women.[14]

Other victims have subsequently opened up about their feelings and inner experiences of dealing with the Montreal Massacre. Heidi Rathjen, who survived by hiding in a darkened room that the killer did not enter, decided to leave a promising engineering position to devote herself to working full-time for stricter gun control. I shall discuss the impact that the massacre had on gun control in later sections; suffice it to say now that Rathjen, and those like her, sought to memorialize the deaths of their fellow students by working to stop such tragedies from ever happening again.

Michèle Thibodeau-DeGuire, director of public relations at the Polytechnique and the first female civil engineer to graduate from the 141-year-old engineering school, took shelter under her desk when the shots rang out. While some saw the killer's action as a symptom of systemic misogynistic forces, Thibodeau-DeGuire is convinced that it was the isolated act of a sick individual: "Some people say it was a madman, that it wasn't the problem of society—it was the problem of one person. I tend to think that makes sense."[15]

Benoît Laganière, a twenty-one-year-old male engineering student, fled from the school's cafeteria. Some people publicly accused the male students of not doing enough to stop the killer, but Laganière says that the events happened so quickly and it was not at all clear at the time that the gunman was only targeting female students. The tragedy inspired Laganière to devote his life to working for gender equality, and he subsequently worked as an employment counsellor in the engineering department of Université Laval in Quebec City. "People are with us, they support our struggle," he said, and "all I want, all my actions, are to achieve a safer society, so that no one else will have to live through this. That is my deepest wish."[16]

Others were not so lucky. Feelings of guilt and remorse were widespread among survivors, with several students later committing suicide. Sarto Blais, for example, hanged himself eight months after the massacre, saying in his suicide note he was torn apart by guilt that he did not stop the killer.[17] The following year his parents also committed suicide, mourning the loss of their only son.[18]

Diane Riopel, who taught engineering at the school at the time, had decided to head home early on that fateful December day. While the massacre "is part of our history," she says, "it is not our only history." She continues by stating: "Now we [also] talk about what we've done," including producing thousands of female graduates.[19] When CBC host Michael Enright asked Nathalie Provost what her dream was in the aftermath of the massacre, she replied, "I dream of a better world, I dream of a world where respect of humanity and life is big."[20]

IV

The Montreal Massacre reframed the conversation over gun control in the minds of many Canadians. The murders shifted the focus to show some of the deep-rooted connections between firearms and violence against women, including but not limited to intimate partner abuse. It is no coincidence that the majority of the mass murders that occurred in the years after the École Polytechnique event—such as the vehicle homicide attack of a so-called incel ("involuntary celibate") on April 23, 2018, or the April 18–19, 2020, rampage in Nova Scotia, which would become Canada's deadliest, both to be discussed briefly below—also had their origins in misogyny and domestic violence.[21]

At the time of the massacre, Canadians owned sixteen million unregistered rifles and shotguns, with 1,400 people a year dying from gun-related injuries.[22] The anti-feminist murders at École Polytechnique created a national momentum for stricter gun-control laws. Many of the survivors and relatives of victims became vocal advocates for restricting access to guns, including the type of firearm used by the killer. Heidi Rathjen, the student mentioned above who was in one of the classrooms that the killer did not enter, organized the Coalition for Gun Control with Wendy Cukier.[23] In the days immediately after the massacre, they started a petition for gun control, which eventually grew to over 560,000 signatures, the largest in Canada's history at the time. Suzanne Laplante-Edward and Jim Edward, the parents of Anne-Marie Edward, one of the victims, have also worked tirelessly for stricter gun-control laws and a comprehensive registry of firearms. "There's no question that my beautiful daughter would still be alive today," said Laplante-Edward, "if better gun control laws had existed back then."[24]

Since gun-control laws had not been updated since the 1960s, some were surprised at what the existing laws allowed. For example, they had allowed the killer—a mentally disturbed man who had been rejected by the Canadian military due to his anti-social tendencies—to buy an assault-type rifle with ease, along with two thirty-shot magazines. The tireless work of the survivors and the families of victims to prevent such purchases provided some comfort that the tragedy had not been in vain.

Their activities, along with those of other gun-control advocates, led to the passage by the federal Progressive Conservative government of Bill C-17 in 1992, which introduced new, tighter regulations for firearm purchases, storage, and use, and also prohibited purchase of some firearms. In 1995, the Liberals amended the Criminal Code to include Bill C-68, the Firearms Act. The latter bill, which passed nearly six years to the day after the massacre at École Polytechnique, provided the strictest gun-control legislation in Canadian history. It ushered in a set of new regulations that included requirements on how gun owners were to be trained, a screening of firearm applicants, a twenty-eight-day waiting period on new applicants, rules concerning gun and ammunition storage, and magazine capacity restrictions. Most important was the registration of all firearms. The so-called long-gun registry required owners of all restricted and prohibited firearms to register their guns.

Opposition to the registry, particularly outside Canada's major cities, was immediate, setting the stage for what would become a highly politicized debate that exposed an urban/rural divide in the country. Gun owners argued that their right to legal recreation was unjustly restricted, claiming that the majority of gun owners were law-abiding citizens who used their firearms for hunting and other recreational activities. Provincial governments—especially in Alberta, Ontario, and Nova Scotia—argued that the registry exceeded the federal government's mandate and that it was also too expensive to run effectively. A group of Inuit in Nunavut filed a lawsuit against the federal government, arguing that the gun registry went against an understanding that the Inuit—like other Indigenous communities—could hunt, trap, and fish without licensing or fees.

The first steps toward a long-gun registry began under Kim Campbell's federal Progressive Conservative government in the immediate aftermath of the Montreal Massacre, before the new law and the registry were ushered in by Jean Chrétien's Liberals. When the new Conservative Party of Canada gained power in 2006, under the leadership of Stephen Harper, the party was vehemently opposed to such measures. Though Conservative opposition was couched in economic terms, with claims that the registry had become too expensive, it was also politically motivated, since the majority of support for the Conservatives came from more rural populations. The Harper government repealed the part of the registry tracking non-restricted firearms in 2012,[25] much to the chagrin of the survivors and the families of victims of the rampage in Montreal.[26]

In response, the Quebec government challenged the repeal in the courts, but in 2015 the Supreme Court ruled against Quebec, allowing the federal government to destroy non-restricted registry records. The government of Quebec then created a provincial firearms registry.

On the thirty-year anniversary of the Montreal Massacre, the Ruger Mini-14 semi-automatic rifle that the killer used was still available for purchase in Canada. Moreover, on January 29, 2017, a man who killed six worshippers at a Quebec City mosque and seriously injured five others had been able to buy, with apparent ease, large-quantity magazines to increase the damage that he inflicted.[27]

"On this 30th anniversary, I feel very old in this battle," said Nathalie Provost, one of the École Polytechnique survivors, in December 2019. "After 30 years, we're still repeating the same things. Even though there's a consensus, the majority of Canadians want better gun control."[28] Indeed, an Angus Reid poll released five months later, on May 1, 2020, in the aftermath of a murderous rampage in Nova Scotia that killed twenty-two individuals, certainly seemed to back up Provost's statement. It revealed that an overwhelming majority—nearly four in five Canadians—support a complete prohibition on civilian possession of the types of weapons used in the Montreal and Nova Scotia Massacres. It also showed that two-thirds (65 per cent) of Canadians *strongly* support such a move.[29]

V

While the killer's actions are clear enough, a continuous and perhaps surprising debate has circulated concerning his motivations. Some, including the first female graduate from École Polytechnique mentioned above, insist that it was the work of a lone and crazed gunman. More cynical are commentators like conservative columnist Barbara Kay. Writing in the *National Post* on the sixteenth anniversary of the tragedy, she went so far as to claim that

> from this human tragedy of no inherent political significance, a political industry emerged, which produced in the massacre's name: gun control laws, lavish public spending on women's causes, feminist-guided school curricula and a high tolerance for overt misandry.[30]

Such a position is clearly and perhaps purposely overstated for political purposes.

In contrast, the majority of Canadians believe that the attack was clearly informed by the killer's misogyny, something that was much larger than he was, and there can be little doubt that the massacre clearly exposed some of the systemic sexism in Canadian society, which has always granted men institutional power and privilege over women and women's bodies. December 6, 1989, thus functioned as an important catalyst for the Canadian feminist movement. Just six months before the massacre, Chantal Daigle, a young woman from Quebec, had successfully overturned an injunction at the Supreme Court that had been obtained by her violent ex-partner and which had prevented her from terminating her pregnancy. More than ten thousand women demonstrated in the streets of Montreal in her support.[31] There was a growing awareness, in other words, of some of the legal problems that beset women in Canada, and a growing desire to take action to correct such systemic problems.

Because the police had initially refused to release the killer's suicide note, some activists thought they were trying to downplay his true motives. Francine Pelletier, the journalist mentioned earlier in this chapter, spent a year trying to get hold of the note before receiving a copy from an anonymous source through the mail.[32] Given the contents of the suicide note and the fact that all of the immediate victims were young women, there can be little doubt that it was an anti-feminist attack.

In response to the killings, the House of Commons created a subcommittee on the Status of Women. In June 1991 it released a report, *The War Against Women*, which described the Montreal Massacre as "a dramatic expression of male rage" and "an extreme form of violence that women confront regularly in their lives."[33] The subcommittee went on to recommend a set of legal reforms, a requirement for gender sensitivity training for police and judges, stable funding for women's groups, a national policy on housing, and a national education strategy. The full Standing Committee on Health, Welfare and Social Affairs refused to endorse *The War Against Women* report because of its "extreme" language and its deployment of the "war" metaphor. Nevertheless, following its recommendations, the federal government did establish the Canadian Panel on Violence Against Women in August 1991.[34] The mandate of the panel was "to heighten public awareness of the problem, and enable participants to seek solutions for the root causes of 'violence against women' and focus on preventative measures."[35] While some feminist groups heralded the panel, others saw it as a token response to a much larger and systemic problem.

Regardless of the nature of the response, the reality of violence against women is an unfortunate reality in Canadian society, which was exposed to the clear light of day by the Montreal Massacre. In 1993, Statistics Canada released the findings of a national survey on violence against women conducted between February and June of that year. The results of the survey further revealed the widespread nature of violence against women. Almost half of all Canadian women had experienced at least one incident of violence since the age of sixteen. Half reported violence by men known to them and a quarter reported violence by a stranger. In terms of domestic violence, roughly 25 per cent of Canadian women had experienced violence at the hands of a current or past marital partner.[36]

In 1991, Dawn Black, an NDP MP from British Columbia, introduced a private members bill to declare December 6 the Day of Remembrance and Action on Violence Against Women. The bill received all-party support, and now commemorative demonstrations are held across the country each year on the day of the tragedy to honour the memory of the murdered women. According to Status of Women Canada, the day is

> also an opportunity to consider the women and girls for whom violence is a daily reality, and to remember those who have died as a result of gender-based violence. And finally, it is a day on which communities can consider concrete actions to eliminate all forms of violence against women and girls.[37]

VI

If December 6, 1989, drew attention to violence against women, what was missing—as is so often the case in national conversations in Canada—were Indigenous voices. As previously mentioned several times already, though Canada prides itself on being the end result of three founding peoples—French, English, and Indigenous—the overwhelming needs of the first two have always superseded those of the third. Recall, for example, that initial conversations over patriation of the Constitution completely overlooked the voices and concerns of Canada's First Peoples.

Indigenous communities have been marginalized by Canadian structures of power, and Indigenous women have been marginalized to an even greater degree. They have been subjected to both misogynistic and racial violence. Indigenous women and communities, in addition to non-Indigenous women's groups and international organizations, had long called for action to investigate and address the disproportionate rates of violence and the high numbers of missing and murdered Indigenous women and girls in Canada. Such lobbying, however, tended to go unnoticed.

As early as October 2004, for example, Amnesty International released a report called *Stolen Sisters: A Human Rights Response to Discrimination and Violence Against Indigenous Women in Canada*.[38] Statistics confirm that Indigenous women and girls suffer higher rates of violence and homicide than non-Indigenous women and girls. In 2015, for example, a Statistics Canada report revealed that Indigenous women—making up 2.5 per cent of the population—experienced violence at a rate 2.7 times higher than non-Indigenous females.[39] Moreover, a 2015 RCMP report, *Missing and Murdered Aboriginal Women*, showed that Indigenous women represent 10 per cent of the total population of missing women in Canada. The same report also revealed that, between 1980 and 2014, 16 per cent of female homicides involved Indigenous women.[40]

In order to address this discrepancy, on September 1, 2016, Prime Minister Justin Trudeau established the National Inquiry into Missing and Murdered Indigenous Women and Girls (MMIWG). The inquiry heard testimony from hundreds of witnesses and families of missing women across the country, with the aim of investigating the root causes of the violence. The final report, released to great fanfare on June 3, 2019, made headlines around the world when it accused Canada of genocide:[41]

> While the Canadian genocide targets all Indigenous Peoples, Indigenous women, girls and 2SLGBTQQIA people are particularly targeted.[42] Statistics consistently show that rates of violence against Métis, Inuit, and First Nations women, girls, and 2SLGBTQQIA people are much higher than for non-Indigenous women in Canada, even when all over differentiating factors are accounted for. Perpetrators of violence include Indigenous and non-Indigenous family members and partners, casual acquaintances, and serial killers.[43]

Though there were some discrepancies in and misuse of statistics by the inquiry,[44] it nevertheless revealed a disturbing portrait of violence, marginalization, silence, and inaction within the political structures of Canada and its judicial system. The report made 231 recommendations—including changes to police practices and the criminal justice system—that the Liberal government of Justin Trudeau promised to act on. Despite this, Indigenous leaders remained suspicious, echoing the language of the report that "this genocide has been empowered by colonial structures."[45]

Some critics of the report argued that the language was too harsh or that it was politically motivated.[46] Quebec premier François Legault remarked, "A genocide is when one wants, systematically, to make a nation disappear. I don't think that is what we're talking about, but we're talking about something very serious." Bernard Valcourt, the former Conservative minister of Aboriginal Affairs under Stephen Harper, tweeted that to call this genocide was a "thunderous silly conclusion."[47] Despite such claims by critics, there can be little doubt that anglophones and francophones have committed genocide on Indigenous populations. One only need point to the notorious government-sponsored residential school system, in which tens of thousands of young Indigenous boys and girls were abused—physically, sexually, emotionally—for decades. In this regard the MMIWG report further echoed the 2015 Truth and Reconciliation Commission (TRC) report that acknowledged "cultural genocide" (see chapter 8).

VII

On April 18 and 19, 2020, a murderer went on a rampage in rural Nova Scotia, killing twenty-two people and injuring three others before he was shot and killed by the RCMP. The attacks became the deadliest rampage in Canadian history, exceeding the massacre at École Polytechnique. Significantly, not unlike the Montreal perpetrator, the killer in Nova Scotia also had a history of misogyny.[48] On the evening the rampage began, for example, he had quarrelled with his long-time girlfriend before assaulting her and tying her up. She escaped and told the police what had happened, informing them that her attacker was in possession of a mock police uniform and a mock police cruiser. After the killings, a former neighbour described how she and her husband had decided to move from their house because they were afraid the future killer was "a dangerous man who beat his girlfriend and kept a cache of weapons in his home."[49]

In 2013, Statistic Canada released a profile of family violence in Canada and noted that intimate partner violence accounts for one-quarter of all police-reported violent crimes.[50] In another report, Statistics Canada found that in 2014 approximately every six days a woman in Canada was killed by her intimate partner.[51] While not everyone who commits domestic violence will go on to be a mass murderer, the chances of a mass murderer having imagined or committed actual violence against women has been noted.[52] In the aftermath of the Nova Scotia attack, experts in intimate partner violence in Canada have encouraged the passage of legislation on "coercive control," which would make it unlawful to socially isolate and psychologically intimidate one's partner.[53] Such legislation has existed in the United Kingdom since 2015.

Amanda Dale, a member of the advisory panel for the Canadian Femicide Observatory for Justice and Accountability, remarked that the details of the Nova Scotia massacre were "terrifyingly affirming of a pattern that we've seen in Canada."[54] Indeed they were. Many of the most infamous murders and massacres in modern Canada have misogyny at their root.[55] To cite three examples, notorious serial killer Robert Pickton murdered sex workers at his farm in Port Coquitlam, British Columbia, between 1983 and 2002. From 1986 to 1992, serial rapist Paul Bernardo attacked and raped numerous women; between 1990 and 1992, with his wife Karla Homolka, he raped and killed three young women. Bernardo was known to be abusive to both his mother and girlfriends, and his father had molested Bernardo's sister.[56] And on April 23, 2018, an "incel" drove a rented van onto a sidewalk in downtown Toronto, killing ten people and injuring sixteen.[57] The murderer in that case admitted to police that he was a violent misogynist who had been radicalized online. He said that he was a virgin who had never had a girlfriend, and that the rampage was motivated by his own sexual frustration and hatred of women.[58] He also confided to police that he was part of a much larger online community and that he drew inspiration from other men who had committed violence in retribution for not being able to attract women.

What connects all these heinous crimes is misogyny, the motivating force behind the Montreal Massacre. In the immediate aftermath of that tragedy, Canadians—as symbolized by the message on the initial commemorative plaque in Place du 6-Décembre-1989—were unable to admit publicly, even if they knew privately, the root cause of the murder. The new plaque unveiled thirty years later did note that the victims were "assassinated in an anti-feminist attack." This switch of language indicated a transformation of the larger conversation. Though it has not ended violence against women, that fateful December day in 1989 disclosed, as few other events could, the gender-based problems inherent to Canadian society and, just as importantly, the growing need to address them.

VIII

On the eve of the thirty-year anniversary of the Montreal Massacre, Alain Perreault, one of the male survivors of the attack, and president of the student association at École Polytechnique at the time, remarked,

> I think it probably has helped us as a society in Quebec and Canada. To have such an awful thing happen raised the debate about the place of women in society. In a professional way as well: what is the role of women in non-traditional roles. What can we do with, for example, access to firearms, and so these two topics were useful for us as a society to address.[59]

If all of the dates recounted in this book function as mirrors which give Canada—and, by extension, Canadians—glimpses of itself, sometimes we do not like what we see. December 6, 1989, is such a date. Reflected in it, we see clearly the problem of gender imbalance endemic to Canadian society. The Montreal Massacre shows just how such imbalances are created by misogyny and, in turn, how the imbalance further powers misogyny in a vicious circle. Despite important advances in gender equality since that date, however, gaps remain. In 2016, for example, fewer than one in five leadership roles were held by women.[60] In 2018, female employees between the ages of 25 and 54 earned $4.13 (or 13.3 per cent) less per hour than their male counterparts, meaning that for every dollar earned by men, women earned $0.87.[61]

Despite the fact that December 6, 1989, was responsible for introducing some of the most restrictive gun legislation in Canadian history, it has not ended violence against women. This is probably because such violence is structural, which means it is, in many ways, just as dangerous with or without the availability of guns. In this respect, while some high-powered guns may be banned in Canada, neither the misogyny nor the anti-feminism that produced the Montreal Massacre has disappeared. Gender-based violence continues to be an ongoing threat to women in Canada, just as it is to women around the globe. It continues to function as a catalyst for large massacres. Even with stricter gun-control laws, such as those ushered in by Bill C-68, the Nova Scotia killer was able to obtain the weapons he used to carry out his crimes, many of them banned, by illegal means.

Moreover, the targeting of a particular group to demonize and subsequently terrorize has expanded to include others, particularly Muslims in the post 9/11 world. As Mélissa Blais, author of *"I Hate Feminists!" December 6, 1989 and Its Aftermath*, has argued, there are striking similarities between the attack at École Polytechnique in 1989 and the terrorist attack—committed by another disaffected youth who blamed others for his problems—at a mosque in Quebec City in 2017.[62] That killer held far-right, white nationalist, and anti-Muslim views, with the internet functioning as an incubator for his radicalization.[63] According to some reports, he also espoused anti-feminist views, describing feminist groups as "feminazis."[64]

The Montreal Massacre, nonetheless, has made Canadians aware of the triangulation between misogynistic violence, gender stereotypes, and the political structures that make them possible. December 6, 1989, is a date, etched in the minds of many, that forced uncomfortable questions, ones that linger into the present. It is a day that made Canadians, from all branches of the government to society in general, think about what kind of country they wanted Canada to be. The date made Canadians of all stripes and political orientations confront the nature of gun ownership and gun violence, and at the same time encouraged them to think about the place of women in the workforce and in society. That fateful day in December, like all the days examined in this book, quickly took on a significance beyond the events that actually happened.

On December 6, 2019, at 5:10 p.m., thirty years to the day and minute after the Montreal Massacre began, two current École Polytechnique students read aloud the names of the fourteen women killed as fourteen beams of light lit up the Montreal sky. Speaking at the ceremony, Catherine Bergeron, whose sister Geneviève was killed in the massacre, said, "These fourteen beams of light let us know where we are and, above all, help guide us [to] where we want to be. The lights that shine over Canada today are lit for you, in your names and your memory. We will love you forever."

SUGGESTIONS FOR FURTHER READING

Mélissa Blais. "*I Hate Feminists!*" *December 6, 1989 and Its Aftermath*. Translated by Phyllis Aronoff and Howard Scott. Winnipeg: Fernwood Press, 2014.

R. Blake Brown. *Arming and Disarming: A History of Gun Control in Canada*. Toronto: University of Toronto Press, 2012

Peter Eglin and Stephen Hester. *The Montreal Massacre: A Story of Membership Categorization Analysis*. Waterloo, ON: Wilfrid Laurier University Press, 2003.

Monique Lépine and Harold Gagné. *Aftermath*. Translated by Diana Halfpenny. Toronto: Viking Canada, 2008.

Louise Malette and Marie Chalouh, eds. *The Montreal Massacre*. Translated by Marlene Wildeman. Charlottetown: Gynergy Books, 1991.

Heidi Rathjen and Charles Montpetite. *December 6: From the Montreal Massacre to Gun Control*. Toronto: McClelland and Stewart, 1999.

SUGGESTIONS FOR FURTHER VIEWING

Nick Printup. *Our Sisters in Spirit*. 2015. Accessible on YouTube at www.youtube.com/watch?v=zdzM6krfaKY.

Gary Rodgers. *After the Montreal Massacre*. National Film Board of Canada, 1990.

Denis Villeneuve. *Polytechnique*. Remstar Productions, 2009. (This movie is a fictional portrayal of the Montreal Massacre.)

6

MAY 25 1995

Egan v. Canada

"THERE IS NO PLACE FOR THE STATE in the bedrooms of the nation," Pierre Trudeau once famously remarked, adding further that "what's done in private between adults doesn't concern the Criminal Code." While true to an extent, such statements thinly and conveniently paper over the fact that social and legal protections have always tended to privilege the relationships of heterosexual couples at the expense of same-sex ones. In other words, though the state may well have remained outside the nation's bedrooms, it did not necessarily treat all those bedrooms equally. Though change had been in the air prior to May 25, 1995, the day the Supreme Court of Canada ruled on *Egan v. Canada*, I have opted to choose this day because it, more than any other day or court case before it, cleared the space for a redefinition of marriage and, in the process, opened up new ways to think about the constitution of a family. While the present chapter deals with the changing role of same-sex relationships and marriage, which is the way the media often frames the issue, it is important to remember that *Egan v. Canada* is fundamentally about the issue of equality before the law for *all* Canadians. It is a human rights issue, as defined by the Charter, and not simply a partisan one.

Since its inception in 1982, the Charter of Rights and Freedoms had granted certain protections and equalities, thereby setting in motion a number of forces that, in time, created the conditions whereby gay and lesbian Canadians—and their domestic partnerships—could attain full equality before the law. The desire for equality was not driven simply by the need for symbolic recognition, however. Much more concretely, legal equality would grant same-sex couples access to the basic benefits enjoyed by heterosexual couples, such as bereavement leave, access to spousal pensions, and marriage. While this chapter is in many ways more legalistic than previous ones, it also shows more clearly the fundamental role the Charter played in the country's evolution.

I

On March 22, 1960, Everett George Klippert was arrested in Calgary on charges that he had committed "indecent assault" on seventeen young men. Though gay sex was illegal and thus had no age of consent, it is worth noting that later court proceedings found no problem with the age of his "victims." The fact that the charge initially implied he had "assaulted" boys or young men only fed into societal stereotypes of the day that gay men were "perverts" and preyed on the young. The charges were ultimately changed to "gross indecency," and Klippert was jailed for four years. After serving his time, he moved to the Northwest Territories, but was charged with similar crimes the following year, at which point he was again jailed. Given the fact that it was his second conviction, he was now declared a "dangerous sexual offender."[1] An appeal to the Supreme Court upheld the initial ruling, with three justices stating that Klippert had "shown a failure to control sexual impulses and that he was likely to commit further sexual offences of the same kind."[2]

The Court's ruling created a ripple effect with unintended consequences. In Parliament on November 8, 1967, the day immediately after the Supreme Court decision had upheld Klippert's conviction and status as a dangerous sexual offender, Tommy Douglas, leader of the NDP, stood up and asked the prime minister, Lester B. Pearson, a question:

Mr. Speaker, my question is for the right hon. Prime Minster. In view of the decision of the Supreme Court yesterday confirming the sentence of indefinite preventative detention of George Klippert, and since most authorities are now agreed that homosexuality is a social and psychiatric problem rather than a criminal one, I should like to ask the government whether it will consider setting up a commission similar to the Wolfenden Commission in Great Britain which brought in such enlightened and human recommendations for coping with this problem.[3]

Pearson replied, "I will be very glad to consider that matter." When Douglas asked whether any government departments were actively looking into the issue, Pierre Trudeau, the minister of justice, said, "One aspect of this matter is being looked at in the context of another law."

Six weeks later, Trudeau introduced Bill C-150, the Criminal Law Amendment Act, which decriminalized homosexual acts between consenting adults, in addition to legalizing contraception, abortion, and breathalyzer tests to be used on suspected drunk drivers. It was in this context that Trudeau uttered his famous words about the state having no place in the bedrooms of the nation. Despite the change in law, however, Klippert remained in jail until July 1971, at which point he, the last person to be charged with "homosexual acts" on Canadian soil, was released.[4]

These events were just the beginning of a long series of legal rulings in Canada that led to a dramatic shift in thinking about homosexuality and same-sex partnerships. What this chapter shows is how a gradual chipping away at what was assumed to be the natural order of things created a set of profound changes in Canadian law and society more broadly. This chipping away took on much greater momentum after the Charter's enactment in 1982, but there were several precursors. It began with the Criminal Law Amendment Act, introduced in 1967 and passed in 1969. In 1977, Quebec included sexual orientation in its provincial Human Rights Code, making it the first province in Canada to pass a civil rights law that made it illegal to discriminate against gays in housing, public accommodation, and employment. And in 1978, homosexuals were removed from the list of "inadmissible classes" in the Immigration Act.

Such positive momentum for equality in the courts met its fair share of challenges. In 1980, Bill C-242, which had sought to add sexual orientation as a prohibited grounds of discrimination in the Canadian Human Rights Act, failed to pass first reading in the House of Commons. NDP MP Svend Robinson, who in 1988 came out as the first openly gay MP, tried to introduce similar bills several times over the next decade, with all meeting the same fate. "Sexual orientation" was finally added to the act only in 1996. In 1991, Robinson also tried to get the definition of "spouse" in the Income Tax Act and Canada Pension Plan Act expanded to include the phrase "of the same sex." Again, to no avail.

Also in 1991, King's College, a Christian college in Edmonton, fired Delvin Vriend, a gay man, from his job. I discussed *Vriend v. Alberta* briefly in chapter 3. It's enough to say here that the Supreme Court ruled in this case that sexual orientation was a characteristic protected from discrimination, even though it was not specifically included in the Charter, and that provincial governments could not exclude protection of individuals from provincial human rights legislation on the basis of sexual orientation.

II

When the father of Brian Mossop's partner passed away in 1985, Mossop asked his employer—the federal government's Translation Bureau—for a bereavement leave to attend the funeral. The agreement between the government and the union provided for up to four days of bereavement leave on the death of a member of an employee's immediate family. Mossop's request was denied because his partner, gay activist Ken Popert, was not deemed to be "immediate family." While this term could be, and was, interpreted to refer to a common-law spouse, the government refused to allow the term—and thus the leave—to refer to same-sex partners.

Mossop decided to take his employer, the Canadian government, to the Canadian Human Rights Commission. Since discrimination based on sexual orientation had not yet been added to the Canadian Human Rights Act, he argued that he had been discriminated against based on family status. Though the Commission ruled in his favour, the government appealed to the Federal Court of Appeal, which overturned the initial ruling. The latter court argued that "family status" could not refer to homosexual relationships. Mossop next appealed to the Supreme Court, which upheld the Appeal Court's ruling.

Two important items emerged from *Canada v. Mossop*. First, it was the first time the Supreme Court heard a case that involved equality rights of gays. Second, in her dissenting opinion, Supreme Court Justice Claire L'Heureux-Dubé argued that the term "family status" could be interpreted broadly enough to include same-sex couples living together in a long-term relationship. She wrote:

> The family is not merely a creation of law, and while law may affect the ways in which families behave or structure themselves, the changing nature of family relationships also has an impact on the law. It is clear that many Canadians do not live within traditional families. In defining the scope of the protection for "family status," the Tribunal thought it essential not only to look at families in the traditional sense, but also to consider the values that lie at the base of our support for families. It found that these values are not exclusive to the traditional family and can be advanced in other types of families. On the evidence before it and in the context of the Act, the Tribunal concluded that the potential scope of the term "family status" is broad enough that it does not *prima facie* exclude same-sex couples.[5]

Despite the fact that Mossop lost, the case succeeded in starting a national conversation. L'Heureux-Dubé's dissenting opinion was also significant in the sense that it recognized "the changing nature of family relationships." And in its ruling against Mossop, the Supreme Court noted that he might want to reformulate his case to argue that section 15 of the Charter of Rights and Freedoms rendered the Human Rights Act's exclusion of sexual orientation to be unconstitutional.[6] However, he decided not to pursue this.

All of this set the stage for *Egan v. Canada*. James Egan (1921–2000) was a prominent LGBT activist. Since he was self-employed, he was able to speak out in ways that many others were not able to at the time for fear of losing their jobs.[7] Beginning in his early twenties, Egan had written hundreds of letters, articles, and op-eds to Canadian and US magazines and newspapers, in which he tried to correct negative stereotypes about gay people and also called for equality before the law. He often published under the pseudonym "Leo Engle" (the name of his grandfather) or "J.L.E." At a time when mainstream media outlets portrayed gay men as "sexual deviants" or "criminals," Egan offered a welcome alternative. With titles such as "I am a Homosexual" and "Reader Defends Homos, Says They're Inverts," Egan's articles, not surprisingly, caused considerable commotion in certain circles.[8]

When Egan and his long-term partner, John Norris Nesbit, reached retirement age, Egan decided to apply for spousal benefits for Nesbitt. According to the Old Age Security Act, the spouse of a pensioner may receive a spousal allowance should their combined income fall below a certain amount. Though the couple would have come out ahead financially if they had collected separate individual pensions, they chose to go the spousal benefit route in order to challenge the law and make a case for the legal rights of same-sex couples.[9] Needless to say, the couple was refused because section 2 of the Old Age Security Act defined "spouse" strictly as a member of the opposite sex.

The couple decided to mount a legal challenge to fight the ruling. Picking up a thread from the ruling in *Canada v. Mossop*, they argued that the Old Age Security Act's definition of "spouse" infringed on their Charter rights. According to section 15(1),

> Every individual is equal before and under the law and has the right to the equal protection and equal benefit of the law without discrimination and, in particular, without discrimination based on race, national or ethnic origin, colour, religion, sex, age or mental or physical disability.

In Federal Court, the judge ruled that the language of the Old Age Security Act created a distinction between "spouses" and "non-spouses" (e.g., siblings), with the latter not being eligible for benefits. This judge seemed to want to equate a same-sex partner to a sibling, which interestingly would have allowed Mossop to receive a bereavement leave to attend the funeral of his partner's father. Invoking *Mossop* here may well be apropos of nothing, but it does show how ambiguous and even contradictory the law can be, and demonstrates the wide range of interpretations that can be applied to it. Or perhaps more to the point: the law should have been clear—especially in light of section 15 of the Charter—but the various levels of government were unable or unwilling to act.

Egan and Nesbitt's case was dismissed. They appealed to the Federal Court of Appeal, which upheld the initial ruling.

The couple next took their case to the Supreme Court, which sided with the original judge in a fairly close decision (4–1–4). The majority opinion, articulated by Justice Gérard La Forest, claimed that

> marriage has from time immemorial been firmly grounded in our legal tradition, one that is itself a reflection of long-standing philosophical and religious traditions. But its ultimate *raison d'être* transcends all of these and is firmly anchored in the biological and social realities that heterosexual couples have the unique ability to procreate, that most children are the product of these relationships, and that they are generally cared for and nurtured by those who live in that relationship. In this sense, marriage is by nature heterosexual. It would be possible to legally define marriage to include homosexual couples, but this would not change the biological and social realities that underlie the traditional marriage.[10]

The appeals to tradition, religion, biology, and society were well rehearsed and part of the discourse at the time. Once again, Justice L'Heureux-Dubé disagreed with her colleagues. In her dissenting opinion she wrote:

> Although the claimants cannot be said to suffer any economic prejudice from the distinction since they are each entitled as individuals to a certain minimum income level, it cannot be overlooked that the rights claimants have been directly and completely excluded, *as a couple*, from any entitlement to a basic *shared* standard of living for elderly persons cohabiting in a relationship analogous to marriage. This interest is an important facet of full and equal membership in Canadian society.[11]

For her, the deprivation of a basic standard of living for all couples, whether or not they happened to be married, was discriminatory and prevented, in her own words, "full and equal membership in Canadian society." She concluded her dissent by arguing that,

> given the marginalized position of homosexuals in society, the metamessage that flows almost inevitably from excluding same-sex couples from such an important social institution is essentially that society considers such relationships to be less worthy of respect, concern and consideration than relationships involving members of the opposite sex. This fundamental interest is therefore severely and palpably affected by the impugned distinction.[12]

Despite the fact that Egan and Nesbitt lost their case, the consequences were huge. The Court unanimously held that sexual orientation was an analogous ground under section 15 of the Charter and therefore had to be a prohibited ground of discrimination. Justice La Forest, in the majority opinion, observed:

> I have no difficulty accepting the appellants' contention that whether or not sexual orientation is based on biological or physiological factors, which may be a matter of some controversy, it is a deeply personal characteristic that is either unchangeable or changeable only at unacceptable personal costs, and so falls within the ambit of s. 15 protection as being analogous to the enumerated grounds.[13]

With this, we see an acknowledgement that sexual orientation is now a protected ground that cannot be discriminated against, and an acknowledgement that this protection extends to same-sex partnerships. It was no longer a matter of *if* the definition of "spouse" could be changed or *if* same-sex couples had the same rights as heterosexual ones, but only a matter of *when*.

III

The ramifications were massive and soon became apparent in the world outside the courts. The same month the verdict was announced in *Egan v. Canada*, an Ontario Court judge—also basing his judgment on section 15 of the Charter—ruled that the Child and Family Services Act of Ontario could no longer prevent same-sex couples from adopting children. This made Ontario the first province to make it legal for same-sex couples to adopt. British Columbia, Alberta, and Nova Scotia quickly followed suit.[14]

The main issue of *Egan v. Canada*—namely, a same-sex partner being able to claim benefits that had traditionally gone to those of the opposite sex—was revisited by the Supreme Court of Canada almost four years to the day later in M. *v.* H. In that case, two women who had lived together for more than a decade—Joanne Mitchell ("M") and Lorraine McFarland ("H")—broke up in 1992. M sued H for spousal support under Ontario's Family Law Act. That act defined "spouse" as either a person who was married or "either of a man and woman who are not married to each other and have cohabited...continuously for a period of not less than three years." Cohabiting was defined as "to live together in a conjugal relationship, whether within or outside marriage."

In M. *v.* H., the Court ruled that same-sex couples should have the same benefits and obligations as heterosexual common-law couples, including equal access to benefits from social programs to which they had contributed. The majority ruling, again based on the Charter of Rights and Freedoms, declared:

> The exclusion of same-sex partners from the benefits of s. 29 [of the Family Law Act of Ontario] promotes the view that M., and individuals in same-sex relationships generally, are less worthy of recognition and protection. It implies that they are judged to be incapable of forming intimate relationships of economic interdependence as compared to opposite-sex couples, without regard to their actual circumstances. Such exclusion perpetuates the disadvantages suffered by individuals in samesex relationships and contributes to the erasure of their existence.[15]

The Supreme Court ruled that the words "a man and woman" in the definition of "spouse" should be replaced with the phrase "two persons." The Court also ruled that the Ontario Family Law Act's definition of "spouse" as a person of the opposite sex was unconstitutional, as indeed were any provincial laws that denied equal benefits to same-sex couples. Ontario was given six months to amend the act.[16]

The M. *v.* H. ruling did not affect the legal definition of marriage, which was still stated in heterosexual terms. It applied solely to same-sex couples, and gave them equality with common-law couples—who often had significantly fewer rights than married spouses.

In many ways, the Supreme Court was moving much more quickly on issues of equality than the federal government. Perhaps in response to M. *v.* H., the next month the federal government voted 216 to 55 in favour of enshrining the traditional definition of "marriage" as the union between a man and a woman. Anne McLellan—justice minister in the Chrétien government—declared that the traditional definition of marriage was clear and that the government had "no intention of changing the definition of marriage or legislating same-sex marriage."[17]

The following year, on April 11, 2000, Jean Chrétien's Liberals introduced Bill C-23, the Modernization of Benefits and Obligations Act, which would give same-sex couples who had lived together for more than a year the same benefits and obligations as common-law couples. It passed by a vote of 174 to 72. The act also included a definition of marriage as "the lawful union of one man and one woman to the exclusion of all others." While the definitions of "marriage" and "spouse" remained in the traditional sense of the term, the definition of "common-law relationship" was expanded to include same-sex couples.

Perhaps seeing the writing on the wall, in May 2000 the Government of Alberta passed legislation stating that, should a court at some point in the future redefine marriage to include anything other than that between a man and a woman, the province would invoke the notwithstanding clause. It thus became the first and only provincial government to define marriage as solely between a man and a woman.

That same month the City of Toronto announced that it was seeking legal guidance to determine whether Canada's ban on same-sex marriages was constitutional. In July 2000, Andrew Petter, BC's attorney general, stated that his province would do the same.

All these legal decisions were pushed forward on a more practical level when, on December 10, 2000, Rev. Brent Hawkes of the Metropolitan Community Church in Toronto announced that he intended to marry two same-sex couples. Hawkes had decided to take advantage of a legal loophole by using the ancient Christian tradition of publishing the "banns of marriage." Despite the fact that same-sex couples could not obtain marriage licences, the Ontario Marriage Act allowed couples to be granted a licence if their names were published and read out at church for three Sundays in a row.[18] On January 14, 2001, Hawkes—wearing a bullet-proof vest and with police officers guarding the church—married the two couples, making them the first legal same-sex marriages in Canada and, by extension, the world.[19]

The province of Ontario announced that it had no intention of recognizing the marriages because they flouted federal law, which defined marriage as the union between a man and a woman to the exclusion of all others.[20] In spite of such objections, the following summer the Ontario Superior Court ruled that prohibiting gay couples from marrying was unconstitutional and was in clear violation of section 15 of the Charter of Rights and Freedoms. The court gave Ontario two years to extend marriage rights to same-sex couples. This ruling was also significant because it represented the first time that a Canadian court had ruled in favour of recognizing same-sex marriages under the law. As a direct result of the Ontario ruling, Alberta's provincial government passed a bill that would ban same-sex marriages and define marriage as exclusively between a man and a woman.

Then on June 17, 2003, Prime Minister Jean Chrétien announced that his government would introduce legislation to make same-sex marriage legal. Though a devout Catholic, he stated, "There is an evolution in society." Even so, the new law was carefully worded to allow churches and other religious groups to "sanctify marriage as they see it." That is, if a specific church or denomination decided it did not want to perform same-sex marriages, it could not be forced to. A draft of the bill was sent to the Supreme Court to confirm its constitutionality. The Court ruled that the federal government could change the definition of marriage to include same-sex couples, and reaffirmed the notion that religious leaders could not be compelled to perform same-sex marriages.

Finally, on June 28, 2005, Bill C-38, the Civil Marriage Act, passed in the House of Commons with a 158–133 vote, supported by most members of the Liberals, the NDP, and the Bloc Québécois, and opposed by the majority of Conservatives. It became law on July 20, 2005, making Canada the fourth country in the world—after the Netherlands, Belgium, and Spain—to officially recognize same-sex marriage, though it is worth reiterating that Canada was the first country in the world to have a legal same-sex marriage in 2001. And by the time the Civil Marriage Act passed, same-sex marriage was already legal in eight provinces and one territory.

IV

The changes in law recounted in the previous section were largely made possible because of the Charter of Rights and Freedoms. Every court case that helped to make all Canadians equal, and in the process redefined marriage, referred to section 15 of the document. In this respect, to return briefly to the subject matter of chapter 3, the Charter achieved its aim of evolving as Canadian society did. The Charter, in other words, was a document, as Pierre Trudeau had foreseen, that would change as Canada changed and, in the process, force Canada to make certain changes even if it did not want to.

The move to equality was not necessarily a smooth one, however. While in retrospect the journey from *Egan v. Canada* in 1995 to the Civil Marriage Act in 2005 can be measured by a relatively short span of ten years, the changes to Canadian society were momentous. And these changes were not without critics, often very vocal ones.

Such momentous changes over a relatively short period were bound to meet with resistance. This came from many directions, but particularly from religiously and socially conservative groups who objected to equality of gays and lesbians, same-sex unions, and ultimately same-sex marriage, regardless of what the Charter had to say about the issue of equality for all Canadians. There were the usual religious objections and denouncements. "They could go to hell when they die," opined the outspoken Roman Catholic bishop Fred Henry of Calgary.[21] Such opposition was not confined to the Catholic Church, but was also shared by some Muslim and Jewish groups. Evangelical churches added their voices to the protest. "With the legalization of gay marriage, faith has been violated and we've been forced to respond," said Charles McVety, president of the Canada Christian College in Toronto and a leader of several evangelical Christian organizations that formed in opposition to gay marriage.[22] McVety went so far as to approach the Rev. Jerry Falwell and other American evangelical leaders for their advice on how to build a right-wing religious movement in Canada.[23]

Canada's new legislation had ripples on the other side of the border as well. Peter Sprigg of the Family Research Council, a right-wing lobby group in the United States, commented on the situation in Canada: "The [Canadian] government has simply caved in to the demands of the pro-homosexual activists, whereas in the United States, we're actively resisting any redefinition of marriage."[24]

Being a religious believer did not have to render one an opponent to such legislation. Delegates from the United Church of Canada voted to consecrate same-sex marriages, but that decision, at least initially, caused deep divisions within the church.[25] Mirroring Canada, the United Church of Canada at the time it was established in 1925 had considered homosexuality to be a sin, but by the late 1970s was urging Ottawa to amend human rights laws to protect gays and lesbians from discrimination. As early as 1988, the United Church created a task force that produced a document titled *Gift, Dilemma, and Promise: A Report and Affirmations of Human Sexuality*, which concluded that "all human beings, regardless of sexual orientation, are persons made in the image of God." Not only did it recommend that the United Church welcome sexually active gay men, lesbians, and bisexuals into all aspects of the church, including the ministry, but also that the church develop liturgies to recognize gay and lesbian relationships.[26] The church ordained its first gay minister, Tim Stevenson, in 1992.

The issue of same-sex marriage was much more complicated for some politicians. Both Prime Minister Jean Chrétien and his successor, Paul Martin, for example, were devout Catholics. Even though the Catholic Church was firmly opposed to such unions, both leaders were well aware of the need to keep religion out of the decision-making process and enact legislation for all Canadians, not just Catholics, in order to maintain the separation between church and state. Though Martin admitted that he had wrestled with his conscience over the question of gay marriage, he told reporters that his duties and responsibilities as a politician "must take a wider perspective" than his faith.[27] It was also clear to both prime ministers that the Supreme Court was unlikely to overturn its decisions in cases like *Egan v. Canada* or M. *v.* H.

Interestingly, and despite the harsh musings of Calgary's Bishop Henry, a poll at the time revealed that 56 per cent of Canada's twelve million Roman Catholics favoured same-sex unions, compared to around 38 per cent of Protestants.[28] Writing in the *New York Times*, op-ed columnist Frank Bruni noted that countries with Catholic majorities made up half of the twenty-some countries that had legalized same-sex marriage, shattering the myth that Catholics could not embrace the idea of same-sex marriage.[28]

And even though the real issue behind the aforementioned Supreme Court cases was equality, in the minds of most Canadians it transformed into an acceptance (or rejection) of gay marriage. A 2003 survey by the NFO CF group found support for same-sex marriage stood at 46 per cent, while 46 per cent were opposed.[30] A virtual deadlock. However, a closer look at the numbers is revealing, if not surprising. Roughly 70 per cent of Canadians between the ages of eighteen and thirty-four accepted same-sex marriage; men tended to be evenly divided, but women were more likely to approve than disapprove. In terms of regions, same-sex marriage had greater support in Quebec and Atlantic Canada, and less support in Saskatchewan and Alberta. Opposition to same-sex marriage stood at 55 per cent among those who said that church attendance was important, but dropped to 28 per cent among those who attached little or no importance to church attendance.[31]

V

Opposition to equality for all Canadians did not just come from conservative religious groups. It also received a great deal of political opposition, especially from provincial legislatures in Alberta and Saskatchewan. As early as 2000, Alberta, as mentioned, became the only province to pass legislation defining marriage in exclusively heterosexual terms. Premier Ralph Klein had said in the leadup to 2004's provincial election that his government would use "whatever legal means are at our disposal to make sure the solemnization of marriage, which is a provincial matter, remains between a man and a woman."[32]

After the Supreme Court's landmark opinion on the Liberals' draft bill, Alberta was the only province to keep fighting the legalization of same-sex marriage.[33] The province's justice minister, Ron Stevens, told reporters that Alberta was a "just and tolerant province," and its opposition to same-sex marriage was only about "upholding the definition of marriage, as it is traditionally understood by society."[34] Despite the fact that the federal government made same-sex marriage legal in 2005, meaning that the province could not refuse to issue marriage licences to same-sex couples, Alberta's Marriage Act was not officially updated until 2014.[35]

At the federal level, there was also considerable opposition to the new legislation. In 2002, when Stephen Harper became the leader of the Canadian Alliance and leader of the Official Opposition, he had to fire his family issues critic, Larry Spencer, an MP from Saskatchewan. Spencer, a former Baptist pastor, had commented publicly to reporters about "a conspiracy to seduce and recruit young boys in playgrounds and locker rooms," and had claimed that homosexuals were infiltrating the North American judiciary, schools, religious community, and entertainment industry. Spencer laid the blame for all of this at the feet of former prime minister Pierre Trudeau when he legalized homosexuality in 1969.[36] Spencer then went on to ruminate publicly that the legalization of same-sex marriage would inevitably lead to the legalization of pedophilia and polygamy.

Even after Harper removed Spencer from his portfolio, the social conservativism of the Reform Party lingered in the new Canadian Alliance, and remained when the Alliance merged with the Progressive Conservative Party in 2003 to "unite the right" and form the Conservative Party of Canada.[37]

There was opposition within the Liberal Party as well. When it came time to vote on the Civil Marriage Act, Prime Minister Paul Martin had said that while backbench Liberals could vote as they wished, he expected his cabinet ministers to vote for the bill.[38] In response, cabinet minister Joe Comuzzi said that he would resign from cabinet so he could vote against the bill. Several other Liberals voted against the bill, but the Bloc Québécois and all but one NDP MP voted in favour to ensure it passed.

After its passage, Stephen Harper noted that should his party form the next government it would revisit the question of same-sex marriage. Harper, an evangelical Christian who would frequently end his speeches with the phrase "God bless Canada,"[39] told reporters that the bill lacked legitimacy because it had only passed due to the support of the Bloc, a non-federalist party.[40] While Conservatives conceded that they did not have the numbers to block the same-sex marriage bill, they claimed to have tabled a number of amendments intended to preserve marriage as the exclusive union of a man and a woman.[41]

In the 2006 federal election, same-sex marriage was one of several key issues, in addition to the long-gun registry (see chapter 5) and the simmering sponsorship scandal that had seen the federal Liberals misdirect public funds for government advertising in Quebec. During the campaign, Harper, who believed that same-sex couples should be recognized through civil unions, promised to preserve the gay marriages already performed across Canada.[42] His Conservative Party was able to form a minority government, and on December 7, 2006, they tabled a motion in the House of Commons to reopen the same-sex marriage debate and introduce legislation to restore the traditional definition of marriage without affecting civil unions and while respecting existing same-sex marriages. It was, however, fairly easily defeated by a vote of 175–123, with twelve Conservatives—including five cabinet ministers—breaking from party lines and voting against the motion, and thirteen Liberals supporting it.[43]

Harper had said that a free vote would settle the matter, and he subsequently told reporters that the vote should put an end to parliamentary wrangling about same-sex marriage.[44] Despite this, the issue was raised briefly in the 2019 federal election when Conservative leader Andrew Scheer refused to clarify his own position on same-sex marriage or explain his opposition to the 2005 Civil Marriage Act when, as a young MP, he declared same-sex marriage to be a "contradiction in terms," since marriage was designed for the "natural procreation" of children, something that a marriage of two men or two women could not achieve.[45] Scheer was also the only federal leader who refused to march in Pride parades.[46]

VI

In 1985, ten years prior to *Egan v. Canada*, a Parliamentary Committee on Equality Rights released a report titled *Equality for All*.[47] The report recounted the widespread level of discriminatory treatment directed against homosexuals in Canada, documenting the harassment, violence, physical abuse, psychological oppression, and hate propaganda directed at gay Canadians. The committee recommended that the Canadian Human Rights Act be amended to make it illegal to discriminate based on sexual orientation, something that left-leaning politicians such as Svend Robinson had been calling on the government to do for years.

The following year, the federal government responded to the report with a document titled *Toward Equality*. In terms of protections and safeguards for sexual orientation, it said, "Though fully cognizant of the social dilemmas that the issue raises, the Government is committed to the principle that all Canadians have an equal opportunity to participate as fully as they can in our society." It continued:

> The Government believes that one's sexual orientation is irrelevant to whether one can perform a job or use a service or facility. The Department of Justice is of the view that the courts will find that sexual orientation is encompassed by the guarantees in section 15 of the Charter. The Government will take whatever measures are necessary to ensure that sexual orientation is a prohibited ground of discrimination in relation to all areas of federal jurisdiction.[48]

The fact that the government's response mentioned that it was "fully cognizant of the social dilemmas" of sexual orientation perhaps needlessly politicized the debate, one that still continues in certain conservative political and religious circles in Canada.[49] And though the response invokes section 15 of the Charter, which guarantees equality rights for all Canadians, the federal government surprisingly waited another ten years to add "sexual orientation" as a protected characteristic under the Canadian Human Rights Act.

There are a number of ways to interpret this action. The first is to say that the federal government only took action on the issue of sexual orientation—and subsequently same-sex marriage—after the Supreme Court victories surveyed in this chapter. A related interpretation is that the Charter of Rights and Freedoms worked exactly as it was intended to: it simultaneously changed, and then responded to the changes in, Canadian society. In this latter case, we should remember that only four years separated the enshrinement of the Charter in the Canadian Constitution and the federal government's response to the *Equality for All* report.

A lot changed in those four years. Even more changes would be ushered in by *Canada v. Mossop*, *Egan v. Canada*, and M. *v.* H. The story of sexual orientation in Canada is, in many ways, the story of modern Canada. From the criminalization of homosexuality in 1969 to gays and lesbians achieving full legal equality and the right to marry in 2005 represents a sea change in Canadian society. While that change might have happened too quickly for many Canadians, it clearly showed that, to reiterate, the Charter did what it was supposed to do. This perspective is certainly not meant to ignore or downplay the suffering of those same-sex couples who, at the time, were not able to collect the same benefits as heterosexual married couples, nor is it meant to ignore the violence—past, present, and future—directed at LGBTQ2S individuals and groups.

But the issue of same-sex marriage, in the final analysis, is not simply a gay or lesbian issue. It is a human rights issue, one that had a tremendous effect on the type of country that Canada aspired to be. In this context, one cannot discount the sheer force that the Charter of Rights and Freedoms has had in the development of the nation.

Significantly, though, while gay marriage has been decided in the courts and cannot be reversed, the issue of intolerance toward LGBTQ2S individuals and groups has morphed in more conservative parts of the country, where it tends to focus on other aspects, such as "gay-straight alliances" (GSAs). Such groups are formed to provide a safe space at local schools, respect diversity, and foster a sense of belonging. GSAs thus seek to create a nurturing environment where students, regardless of sexual orientation or gender identity, can meet to socialize, engage in activities, and support one another in an inclusive way. Students often form and participate in GSAs without the knowledge of their parents. While such groups exist throughout Canada, they have caused considerable controversy in Alberta. When Jason Kenney's United Conservative Party was elected in 2019, for example, it wanted to revisit legislation that allowed GSAs and threatened to notify parents should their children join a GSA.[50] So even though the Supreme Court and the federal government have ruled on the issue of equality of all Canadians, religious and social conservatives still find ways to circumvent that law.

VII

In 2002, CBC commissioned an Ekos poll to take the nation's temperature when it came to the issue of same-sex relationships. In response to the question "The federal government is considering changing the definition of marriage—from a union of a man and a woman to one that could include same-sex couples. If a referendum was held on this issue, how would you vote?" 45 per cent of Canadians said they would vote "yes" to change the definition, whereas 47 per cent said they would vote "no."[51]

Seventeen years after the release of that poll, and fourteen years after the passage of the Civil Marriage Act that legalized full marriage rights for same-sex couples, a new poll found that 75 per cent of Canadians supported same-sex marriage. Interestingly, the poll found a wide cultural divide among Canadians over the issues, with 71 per cent of respondents of so-called European descent backing same-sex marriage compared to 44 per cent support from respondents of East Asian backgrounds and 42 per cent support from respondents of South Asian descent.[52]

Egan v. Canada was a monumental day in modern Canadian history. Though James Egan and John Norris Nesbitt ultimately lost their case for spousal access to retirement benefits, the Court agreed that sexual orientation was a protected ground by virtue of section 15 of the Charter. All the changes that followed flowed from that decision. Like so many of the days that shaped modern Canada, few knew the exact ramifications of the decision on May 25, 1995. In hindsight, however, we can see it ushered in a set of further rulings and court cases that would make all couples and, by extension, all Canadians equal before the law. While violence against the LGBTQ2S community has certainly not ended in certain corners of the country, discrimination on the basis of sexual orientation is now illegal, meaning that no one will again meet the unfortunate fate of George Klippert.

SUGGESTIONS FOR FURTHER READING

James Egan. *Challenging the Conspiracy of Silence: My Life as a Canadian Gay Activist*. Edited by Donald W. McLeod. The ArQuives / Homewood Books, 1998.

Peter W. Hogg. "Canada: The Constitution and Same-Sex Marriage." *International Journal of Constitutional Law* 4.4 (2006): 712–21.

Kathleen E. Hull. *Same-Sex Marriage: The Cultural Politics of Love and Law*. Cambridge: Cambridge University Press, 2006.

Sylvain Larocque. *Gay Marriage: The Story of a Canadian Social Revolution*. Translated by Robert Chodos, Louisa Blair, and Benjamin Waterhouse. Toronto: Lorimer, 2006.

Miriam Catherine Smith. *Lesbian and Gay Rights in Canada: Social Movements and Equality-Seeking, 1971–1995*. Toronto: University of Toronto Press, 1999.

SUGGESTIONS FOR FURTHER VIEWING

Clint Alberta. *Deep Inside Clint Star*. National Film Board of Canada, 1999.

Sharon A. Desjarlais. *First Stories—Two Spirited*. National Film Board of Canada, 2007.

Laurent Gagliardi. *When Love is Gay*. National Film Board of Canada, 2007.

7

OCTOBER 30 1995

The Quebec Referendum

ON OCTOBER 27, 1995—three days before Quebecers were to vote on the future of their relationship to Canada—tens of thousands of Canadians, at the urging of federal politicians, converged on Place du Canada in downtown Montreal. The so-called Unity Rally was an orchestrated attempt to demonstrate fondness for Quebec and Quebecers, and to let them know that their rightful place was within Confederation. Even Air Canada went so far as to offer special reduced fares to Montreal for the occasion, something that Quebec's electoral office later declared was an attempt to "undermine democracy." Regardless, the die was cast for what would be a nail-biting end to an often vitriolic and emotionally charged campaign.

While 1995 ushered in a rethinking of marriage and the family in Canada, it also brought the country to the precipice of a full-blown constitutional crisis that had been years in the making. Three years after the failure of the Charlottetown Accord, Quebecers went to the polls again to vote in a referendum on the fate of Quebec. This time it was a provincial referendum, not a national one. On October 30, 1995, they were asked—in rather awkward fashion—whether the province should leave Canada and become a sovereign nation. Though the No side eventually carried the day, winning by the slimmest of margins (50.58 per cent to 49.42 per cent), the referendum once again exposed the tensions that had been simmering under the surface since 1867, if not before.

I

October 30, 1995, was, in many ways, the culmination of a journey that several previous days had set in motion. On November 15, 1976, for example, the separatist Parti Québécois, a provincial party committed to Quebec sovereignty, took power for the first time. Though their victory was, in large part, based on a mandate of good governance from Quebecers who were tired of the numerous scandals of Robert Bourassa's Liberals, it also fanned the flames of nationalist hopes and aspirations. And the historic victory reminded anglophone Canadians of the need to accommodate Quebec, something they had become all too familiar with during the October Crisis in 1970. The Parti Québécois victory led directly to March 20, 1980, the day the first Quebec referendum on sovereignty was held. On that occasion the No (or "remain") vote also carried the day, but by a much larger margin (59.56 per cent as opposed to 40.44 per cent who voted to leave).

Six days before that first referendum, Prime Minister Pierre Trudeau had addressed a large crowd at the Paul Sauvé Arena. In remarks that reached out to Quebecers while also trying to allay the fears of all Canadians, he challenged English Canada by stating that things would have to change. A No vote in the upcoming referendum, he warned, could not be interpreted as a simple endorsement of the status quo. In a deft move, and reading the mood of the crowd, Trudeau next appealed to emotions—a tactic that was not foreign to the sovereignty/federalist debate. A few days earlier, Quebec premier René Lévesque had insulted Trudeau's middle name, "Elliott," saying it was not authentically French. In response, Trudeau now recounted the story of his parents. He told his audience that his name was both Québécois and Canadian, and that one should not have to choose. The terms of the debate did not have to be either/or. He went on to criticize Lévesque for threatening to tear apart Quebec families, in addition to breaking up

Canada. Even Trudeau's critics praised the speech, noting in retrospect that it helped to secure a victory for the No side. Though, of course, one should not lose sight in Trudeau's rhetoric of the issues that were at stake for many Quebecers. All of the grievances and fault lines described in earlier chapters remained. No political speech could paper over the growing chasm separating Canadian federalists from Quebec nationalists.

Appearing on the same stage immediately after the referendum, with tears in his eyes, Lévesque said that the fight for Quebec sovereignty was not over and that they should "wait until next time."

Though Trudeau had successfully prevented the country's demise, he now worked to create a new federalism based on a strong central government and the creation of a strong Canadian identity—two items that would certainly not be congenial to nor win the favour of Quebec nationalists. Trudeau's desire informed the patriation of the Constitution in 1982 and the establishment of the Charter of Rights and Freedoms. Yet, as seen in chapter 3, everything did not go to plan. If the patriation of the Constitution was a seminal day in the shaping of modern Canada, it was also made significant by Quebec's unwillingness to take part. Nowhere was this on clearer display than in Lévesque's decision to fly the Quebec flag at half-mast throughout the province.

By 1995, Lévesque's "next time" was here, though he and Trudeau were no longer the major players in the debate. Between 1985 and 1994, the more amicable relationship between Robert Bourassa's provincial Liberals and Brian Mulroney's federal Progressive Conservatives had shown, at least initially, positive momentum for the integration of Quebec into the constitutional fold. That momentum was slowed considerably, however, by the failure of provincial governments—specifically Newfoundland and Manitoba—to amend the Constitution with the proposed Meech Lake Accord. Meech Lake, it will be recalled, would have acknowledged Quebec as a "distinct society." This was followed two years later by anglophone Canada's refusal to support the Charlottetown Accord in a national referendum. Many Quebecers viewed the failure of these two accords as tantamount to an anglophone rejection of Quebec. What had been a set of honest attempts to smooth over ill-will between anglophone and francophone Canada only succeeded in exacerbating old tensions and contributed to renewed separatist sentiment in Quebec.

II

Though the issues in 1995 were familiar, the actors were new. However, those new actors played their parts in much the same way their predecessors had for decades. After nine years of Liberal rule, which had witnessed the unlikely political rebirth of Robert Bourassa, the 1994 provincial election returned the Parti Québécois (PQ) to power. One of leader Jacques Parizeau's campaign promises was to hold a referendum on Quebec sovereignty within a year of his election.[1]

The Montreal-born Parizeau, who was educated in Paris and received his PhD in economics from the London School of Economics, had played a large role in the "quiet revolution," which had been responsible for the modernization of Quebec. A firm proponent of economic interventionism, he was instrumental in nationalizing Hydro-Québec and the Asbestos Corporation mines. He joined the Parti Québécois in 1969, but broke with it when Lévesque signalled a willingness to work with federalists. He rejoined the PQ as leader in 1988, making independence a top priority and working on the assumption that Canada could not possibly have strong Quebec and Canadian governments at the same time.

Though familiar, there were some changes. On the scene now was a new federal party, the Bloc Québécois, paradoxically committed to Quebec sovereignty. The Bloc thus possesses the same mandate at the federal level as the PQ does at the provincial. Formed in 1991, the Bloc was the outgrowth of disaffected former Liberal and Progressive Conservative francophone politicians who had been disillusioned by the collapse of the Meech Lake Accord. Its first leader was Lucien Bouchard, who had been a cabinet minister in the Mulroney government.[2] During the leadup to the 1995 referendum the Bloc—which runs candidates only in Quebec—also functioned as the Official Opposition in Ottawa. Though the Bloc and the PQ have strong informal ties, they are not linked organizationally.

Another actor in the run-up to the referendum was Jean Chrétien, the prime minister. He had been the federal justice minister in 1982 and prepared the way for the patriation of the Constitution, which Quebec had refused to endorse. A major player in the "night of the long knives," Chrétien had echoed the retired Trudeau's opposition to the Meech Lake Accord. This made him unpopular in Quebec, especially among moderate francophone voters, federalist and separatist alike, who made up the swing vote.[3]

The 1995 referendum thus had two parties actively working for Quebec's separation from Canada, and a prime minister unpopular in Quebec. However, Chrétien was not particularly interested in having a national crisis on his hands. Indeed, a major element of the Liberals' successful 1993 election platform had been to redirect the country's attention from precisely the type of constitutional debate that was now engulfing Quebec and increasingly, as the referendum date approached, the rest of Canada.

The nationalist movement in Quebec, as seen in chapter 1, never spoke with a unified voice. Some wanted peaceful negotiations, while others employed violence to achieve their goals. Increasingly the debate was about the terms for sovereignty that would be put before the electorate. Parizeau, for example, was opposed to the traditional PQ desire to develop a close economic relationship with the rest of Canada after separation. Such a relationship, he feared, would encourage the Canadian government to drag its feet and perhaps refuse to negotiate. Given the emotional circumstances of separation on the one hand, and the promise of free trade agreements with other nations on the other, he maintained that an economic partnership with Canada was unnecessary.

In contrast to Parizeau's view, Lucien Bouchard was concerned that a proposal which lacked the promise of such a partnership with the rest of Canada would not appeal to moderate or "soft" nationalists, who would be worried about the economic consequences of separation. Joining Bouchard in this regard was Mario Dumont, leader of the recently formed Action démocratique du Québec. Afraid that the hesitancy of Bouchard and Dumont would weaken the case for sovereignty, Parizeau agreed to negotiate his position with them. In June, the three separatist leaders agreed to an accord that would include an economic partnership with Canada after a positive vote. The three leaders also agreed that a declaration of sovereignty would occur after a period of one year, whether or not an agreement had been reached with the federal government.[4]

On October 7, almost three weeks before the vote, Parizeau announced that he would appoint Bouchard to be the new nation's "chief negotiator" for partnership talks with Canada. The move came as a dramatic surprise to the campaign. With the announcement, the popular Bouchard now became the public face of the Yes campaign, with some speculation that he had won some internal power struggle with the more hardline Parizeau, though others claimed that Parizeau was in fact using the popular Bouchard for his own ends.[5] The latter seems more likely given the fact that the announcement would have appealed to undecided voters by implying that there would be a partnership with Canada in the post-separation era.

Bouchard's moderate approach and his intimate involvement at Meech Lake made him virtually untouchable among his detractors or critics. As well, in December 1994, nearly a year before the referendum, Bouchard came close to death after contracting necrotizing fasciitis. With his left leg amputated and appearing publicly on crutches, his capital with voters only increased. The charismatic Bouchard now provided an emotional and symbolic rallying point for the Yes side, increasingly drawing even moderate sovereigntists and the undecided. Only a vote for sovereignty, he argued, would put an end to Canada's long-standing constitutional issues—on full display with the failure of the Meech Lake and Charlottetown Accords—and create the conditions for a new partnership with English Canada.

III

Despite initial predictions of a heavy sovereigntist defeat, an eventful and highly emotional campaign ensued. If the Yes side picked up immediate momentum with the appointment of Bouchard, the No campaign lacked such a commanding figure. Its primary leader was Daniel Johnson, the provincial Liberal leader and former premier of Quebec, who had been defeated by the PQ in the 1994 election. With the Yes side leading in the polls, Johnson was worried that federal politicians, not used to the political culture of Quebec, might inadvertently make mistakes. He thus limited the appearance of federal politicians, including Prime Minister Jean Chrétien, in the province. Also prominent in the No campaign was Jean Charest, the federal Progressive Conservative leader (and future Liberal premier of Quebec).

The campaign officially began on October 2, 1995, with a televised address by both leaders. The two sides immediately staked out familiar positions. Parizeau emphasized that this might well be the last opportunity for the foreseeable future for Quebecers to gain sovereignty. If he appealed to the heart, Johnson sought to engage reason. He argued that a Yes vote would lead to worries among businesses and investors, thereby creating economic uncertainty.[6] Regardless, the process was set in motion, with each side now doing its best to convince the undecided. Under Quebec's referendum law, both sides presented their messages in a brochure to be sent to every resident of the province. Each side was given a $5-million budget; receiving additional money or contributions from persons or institutions was illegal.[7]

As part of its strategy to increase support for sovereignty, the Quebec government also mailed to every household in the province a draft of the Bill Respecting the Future of Quebec. Attached to the draft was a letter from Parizeau himself, wherein he wrote:

> As you will notice, there is a blank page in the document you have just received. It is the preamble which has intentionally been left unwritten. This preamble will eventually become the Declaration of Sovereignty of Quebec. It must describe who we are as a people and who we wish to become. As such, it must be a vivid reflection of our values and our hopes, our traditions and our ambitions. This blank page calls out to all of us. We must devise it together, participate and contribute the best of ourselves.[8]

He then symbolically closed the letter "Jacques PARIZEAU, Prime Minister." Though the preamble page was intentionally left blank, the draft bill laid out the process for independence, arguing in its preamble that what followed "will set forth the fundamental values and main objectives the Quebec nation wishes to make its own once it has acquired the exclusive power to make all its laws, collect all its taxes and conclude all its treaties."[9] Though the draft said the new constitution would "guarantee the English-speaking community that its identity and institutions will be preserved," and that it would recognize "the right of Aboriginal nations to self-government on lands over which they have full ownership," it added that "such guarantee and such recognition shall be exercised in a manner consistent with the territorial integrity of Quebec."

To appeal to the undecided, the draft bill maintained that the new nation would maintain "an economic association with Canada" in order "to preserve and further develop the free circulation of goods and services," in addition to remaining within the North American Free Trade Agreement and retaining the Canadian dollar as Quebec's legal currency.

"I think we'll make it," Parizeau told journalists on the eve of the campaign. "I think we'll have a country very soon, and yes, it is exciting." Johnson, on the contrary, decried Parizeau's vision as "a gigantic joke." He remarked, "We haven't been oppressed or exploited. We helped build this country, and without Quebec, Canada will no longer exist."[10]

As in any referendum—where politicians abdicate the decision-making process, pushing it back onto the electorate with a simplistic and binary yes/no vote on what is often a very complex and intricate set of issues—each side appealed to the hearts and fears of voters. Business leaders warned of the risks of independence, noting that major firms—such as Bombardier and Standard Life—had both threatened to leave Quebec in the event of a Yes vote. Paul Martin, the federal finance minister, went so far as to warn that independence would likely cost the province one million jobs.

IV

On October 30, 1995, Quebecers went to the polls. They had to answer yes/no or oui/non to the following question:

> Do you agree that Quebec should become sovereign after having made a formal offer to Canada for a new economic and political partnership within the scope of the bill respecting the future of Quebec and of the agreement signed on June 12, 1995?
> (French: *Acceptez-vous que le Québec devienne souverain, après avoir offert formellement au Canada un nouveau partenariat économique et politique, dans le cadre du projet de loi sur l'avenir du Québec et de l'entente signée le 12 juin 1995?*)

The wording of every referendum question has its detractors.[11] This one was no different. When Parizeau unveiled the question in the middle of September, he boldly declared, "A sovereign Quebec is a country. And if we choose a sovereign Quebec as our country, that means we are not choosing Canada as our country."[12] While his intentions were certainly clear, the wording of the actual question was anything but.

Clocking in at forty-three words in English (forty-one in French) the language was surprisingly ambiguous. There was no mention of a "country" nor even the idea of an actual secession from the rest of Canada. As if to appeal to the undecided—after all, there was no need to convince those who had already made up their mind—the language was deliberately imprecise and non-threatening. The language of a "new economic and political partnership" with Canada implies a continuation. This despite the fact that a Yes vote would have broken up the country. There would be, contrary to the tenor of the question, no business as usual.

Even more strange is the reference to the June 12 agreement. This agreement—sometimes referred to as the Tripartite Agreement—was the understanding between Parizeau, Bouchard, and Dumont that they would enter into an economic partnership with Canada should there be a Yes vote.[13] Yet no federal leader had ever agreed to it. In fact, quite the opposite. Few politicians outside Quebec—one exception was Ontario premier Mike Harris—had shown any interest in negotiating a possible partnership agreement with an independent Quebec. Provincial Liberal leader Daniel Johnson complained that the language was an attempt to trick voters by pretending that they were not being asked to endorse the "irrevocable separation of Quebec from Canada." Several premiers, including New Brunswick's Frank McKenna and Saskatchewan's Roy Romanow, warned that Quebecers should not expect a special deal with Canada if they voted Yes.[14]

After the provincial government released the wording of the official referendum question, *Le Journal de Montréal* and the *Globe and Mail* conducted a poll through the group Léger & Léger. They found 50.2 per cent support for the Yes side compared with 49.8 per cent for the No side, with a margin of error of plus or minus 3.2 percentage points. It was, in sum, a virtual dead heat.

As Canadians watched anxiously, Quebecers headed to the polls. Turnout was more than 94 per cent of the population. As predicted, the race was so tight that a victor was impossible to declare until virtually every vote had been counted. The No side carried the day, though just barely, with 50.58 per cent of the vote, compared to 49.42 per cent for the Yes side. The country breathed a tremendous sigh of relief.

In his concession speech, Jacques Parizeau was both angry and shocked at the result. Some said he had not bothered to write a concession speech, so assured was he of victory. He stood before a crowd of his supporters and said that Quebecers had not really lost the referendum because more than 60 per cent of francophones had voted for independence. He referred to this group as "nous" (we). Since every "we" needs a "they," the latter group became for him, in his own words, "l'argent et des votes ethniques" (money and ethnic votes).[15] He then promised to "exact revenge" for the loss by never abandoning the dream of a francophone nation in Quebec.

Though some sovereigntist leaders had sought to create an inclusive Quebec, Parizeau's words exposed the elephant in the room. He had reverted, once again, to an ethno-nationalism that many sovereigntists had sought to leave behind. The response to his remarks was swift. Bob Rae, Ontario's NDP leader, said in response to reporters' questions that it was the most "disgraceful speech" he had ever heard from a premier. He also suggested, as several others did, that alcohol might have been a factor. The old and well-established Jewish community in Montreal took Parizeau's "money" comments to refer to them. The League for B'nai Brith issued a statement saying: "We hope he will retract this statement after he's had the opportunity to speak with his advisers and to reflect on the damage he has caused to the feelings of people who reside in his province."[16]

Parizeau resigned the following day. Given the offence of his comments, there was really no choice. Speaking to the *New York Times*, Alain Noel, a pro-sovereigntist political scientist at the Université du Montreal, explained that Parizeau "clearly misrepresented" the position of the Yes vote. "The modern sovereignty movement is broad, territorial, liberal, pluralistic and multicultural. It is definitely not anti-ethnic."[17] In January 1996, Lucien Bouchard replaced Parizeau as leader of the PQ.

In a short address to the nation immediately after the referendum, Prime Minister Chrétien spoke of the need for reconciliation. He said Canadians had heard the message from Quebec, and he pledged to work with Quebecers for change. Chrétien had said little during the campaign leading up to the referendum and had largely dismissed the possibility of a Yes victory. Indeed, the only federal leader on the No side who spent a great deal of time in the province was Jean Charest, leader of the Progressive Conservatives. A month after the referendum, Chrétien offered Quebec significant concessions, including recognition that the French-speaking province was indeed a "distinct society," something that neither the Meech Lake nor Charlottetown Accords had been able to achieve.[18] Though such a status would not—contrary to the desire of many Quebecers—be enshrined in the Constitution, it would nevertheless be enacted as law by the House of Commons. This meant that no federal law could be passed that would compromise Quebec's distinct culture. Chrétien also granted the province a veto over constitutional changes.

These post-referendum developments are significant for at least two reasons. First, despite the failure of the Charlottetown Accord with voters, several of its key elements were now adopted, albeit non-constitutionally. Second, and related, in the aftermath of the Charlottetown Accord and Quebec referendums, we now begin to witness a growing trend toward non-constitutional reform. This is largely the result of the sheer logistical difficulty of enacting broad constitutional amendments, which demand unanimous approval at both the federal and provincial level. Non-constitutional reforms, on the contrary, often focus on a single issue and require only the passage of federal legislation.

As is typical in Canada, however, whenever one province or region receives—or is perceived to receive—special treatment, protests are immediately set off in the others. When Quebec is given certain privileges, western provinces necessarily complain. "How in heaven's name [Chrétien] thinks you can unify the country by giving a constitutional veto to people who want to break it up," said the Reform Party leader Preston Manning. "That's not just bizarre, that's crazy."[19] For Manning, the Charlottetown Accord, like all of the constitutional wrangling that went on before it, focused everyone's energies on Quebec and its constitutional interests without even thinking about the western provinces, which also had real grievances. Manning and the Reform Party ran on the principles of fiscal responsibility and governmental reform, particularly the replacement of the traditional patronage system that benefited the East's interests with an elected Senate that would have to answer to voters and be more representative of interests other than those of Quebec and Ontario. Unlike western separatists before and after him, who sought to leave Canada, Manning's goal was to reconfigure political power with the aim of meeting the demands of what was referred to as the "New West." Manning's vision was to promote the West's interests while working with and remaining in a federal framework.

Reform's main appeal was to a growing sense of western alienation from the rest of the country, and especially from Ontario and Quebec.

In their 1991 book *Deconfederation: Canada Without Quebec*, University of Calgary historian David Bercuson and political scientist Barry Cooper argued that Quebec should leave and that Canada would be better off after the departure, since the fixation on Quebec had created a national paralysis.[20] With an independent Quebec, for example, Manning's Reform Party would have formed the Official Opposition. Such voices clearly demonstrate that not everyone wanted Quebec to stay. They also show how many Canadians were beginning to get fed up with the time and energy devoted to dealing with the "Quebec problem."

V

The morning after came quickly enough. The first casualty, as seen, was Jacques Parizeau. Despite the closeness of the vote, and the palpable emotional disappointment on the part of the Yes side, there was a remarkably quick acceptance of the results. There were, for example, no immediate calls for recounts in the manner that would plague the American election five years later. Neither was there threat of legal action from the losing side. Instead, business quickly returned to normal. At least on the surface. There were certainly complaints, though. The No side, for example, pointed to voting irregularities, arguing that there was an unusually high number of spoiled ballots, particularly in those areas that were expected to produce high No votes.[21] Not to be outdone, the Yes side complained that the federal government was processing too many citizenship application requests—approving roughly a quarter of a year's applications in the month before the referendum.[22] The Yes side assumed, probably with good reason, that new immigrants would vote against the referendum's proposal. Despite such mild complaints, the Directeur générale des élections, the provincial equivalent of the Electoral Commission, noted neither irregularity nor impropriety. The fact that the losing side accepted the result, and did so quickly, meant that there was the perception all around that the process had been fair, or at least as fair as possible.

Accepting the result, but maintaining the PQ position that Quebec had always been treated unfairly by anglophone Canada, Lucien Bouchard promised not to hold another referendum until all of the conditions were in place to ensure a victory. These included no fiscal deficit, high levels of employment, a popular leader, and a clear lead in the polls. With this in mind, the PQ won another majority government in 1998, even though they received less of the popular vote than the Liberals, now led by Jean Charest.[23] Despite Bouchard's desire to have another vote when these conditions had been met, no further referendum has been held in Quebec.[24] In many respects, the separatist movement went quiet in the years following the 1995 referendum. Today, the overwhelming majority of Quebecers do not support sovereignty, certainly not enough to warrant another referendum according to Bouchard's criteria.[25]

While the momentum for independence has slowed, the nationalist sentiment that fuelled it has remained consistent. The 2018 election, for example, saw the right-leaning Coalition Avenir Québec (CAQ)—led by François Legault, a former champion of independence—take the province's reins. The CAQ maintains that the debate over sovereignty has harmed Quebec by limiting its economic and political progress. While the party does not support independence—with Legault going so far as to declare the CAQ would never hold a referendum—it does identify itself as nationalist.[26] The CAQ further affirms that Quebec can thrive in Canada, but that to do so it needs more power from Ottawa. Significantly, in the same 2018 provincial election, the Parti Québécois was reduced to only ten seats, with 17 per cent of the popular vote, not enough to grant it official party status.[27]

There was a different reaction at the federal level. The 2019 election saw the Bloc Québécois increase its tally from ten to thirty-two seats in Parliament, with 32.5 per cent of the popular vote in Quebec (compared to 19.3 per cent in the previous election). This helped to deprive the Liberals of a majority government.[28] On the eve of the election, the Bloc leader, Yves-François Blanchet, again brought up the issue of Quebec's independence: "We can once again tell our Scottish and Catalan friends that in the struggle for self-determination, Quebec is back on Monday."[29] Despite tipping his hat to the Scots and Catalans, Blanchet, like Quebec sovereigntists before him, played on the insecurities of a majority francophone province surrounded not just by English Canada, but also by a much larger English North America. This insecurity was increased by the rise of primarily English-language social media sites and English-dominated Netflix.[30]

However, like Legault, Blanchet sought to tap into the nationalist aspirations of Quebecers without necessarily appealing to their sovereigntist ones. "Both Blanchet and Legault," said Gérard Bouchard (of the

Bouchard-Taylor commission, mentioned in chapter 4, which described Quebec's interculturalism) when interviewed by the *New York Times*, "are reaffirming a type of nationalism that had been dormant for decades but is coming back."[31] Jean-Marc Léger, the chief executive of the Léger polling firm, also remarked on the victories of the CAQ and Bloc: "Identity politics are still fertile ground in Quebec. A majority of Quebecers aren't satisfied with Quebec's constitutional relationship with Canada and they want more economic and provincial powers. But they don't want independence."[32]

The Canadian government, in contrast, had a different solution in mind in the years immediately following the referendum. In 1996, Jean Chrétien's Liberals asked the Supreme Court for an advisory opinion on whether it would be possible for any province to secede, unilaterally, from the rest of Canada. Responding to the request, the Court opined that while there was nothing in international or domestic law preventing a province from seceding unilaterally, both sides would have to negotiate with one another in good faith should a clear majority of a province's citizens vote for independence in response to a clear question.[33] The latter implied, among other things, that the question in the 1995 referendum was anything but clear. The Supreme Court also found that international law declares there is no right to unilateral secession except for colonies and oppressed people, which the Court said did not apply to Quebec. The Court also warned that if Quebec tried to secede outside of the Canadian constitutional framework, which Parizeau had certainly intended, other countries would reject the action as illegal or illegitimate.[34]

In response to the Supreme Court's ruling, the federal government passed the Clarity Act in 2000, setting out the terms and conditions for any future referendum on independence. Though in theory the terms were for any province wishing to leave Canada, it was clear that passage of the act was a direct response to recent events in Quebec. It states that any referendum about sovereignty must refer directly to independence and not to any other constitutional arrangement. The latter, it will be recalled, was implied in the 1995 referendum question. The act also stipulated that such a referendum would need to be won by a clear majority, which has been interpreted to mean 60 per cent support and not just 50 per cent plus one vote. Finally, a Yes vote would necessitate an amendment to the Constitution, which would mean all the provinces would need to be included in the eventual negotiations.

Canadians had other ideas, and their reactions were less clear. In the days immediately after the referendum, Angus Reid/Southam News released the results of a national poll, showing the response to a series of questions they had asked all Canadians, not just people in Quebec. Asked how satisfied they were with the narrow No victory, roughly half of all Canadians (49 per cent) indicated they were very or somewhat satisfied with the result, while 48 per cent said they were very or somewhat dissatisfied with the outcome.[35] The mood in Canada, in other words, was little different from that in Quebec. The poll also revealed how Canadians outside Quebec struggled to make sense of what had just happened: 35 per cent said the result was a victory for the Yes side, while 40 per cent viewed it as a defeat, with 21 per cent believing it was neither. The poll also found that a majority of English-speaking Canadians (61 per cent) were "prepared to see some concessions made to keep Quebec in Canada" compared to 32 per cent who would "rather see Quebec leave than make any concessions."

Perhaps most tellingly, the same poll found significant consensus both within and outside Quebec that "it is now time to make some substantial changes to the way Canada works"; 78 per cent of Quebecers and 66 per cent of those in the rest of Canada agreed with this statement. In contrast, only 21 per cent of Quebecers and 32 per cent of those living elsewhere said they were "more or less satisfied with the way things work now." Clearly a referendum that revolved around the Constitution had once again exhausted Canadians.

VI

The overwhelming majority of Quebec's native francophones had voted Yes, but virtually all of the province's non-native French speakers had voted resoundingly for the No side. When Jacques Parizeau took the stage in the election's immediate aftermath, he noted that 60 per cent of francophones had voted Yes. When he blamed the loss on "money and the ethnic vote," these non-native French speakers were some of whom he had in mind as the ethnic vote. With this phrase, he articulated clearly an undercurrent that had always existed within the sovereigntist movement. His comments—including his call for "revenge"—were shocking and xenophobic. They were widely criticized in the media, both at home and abroad.[36]

They also flew in the face of the Yes side's campaign, where both Parizeau and Lucien Bouchard had carefully sought to cast the sovereigntist movement in the image of liberal nationalism. André Bourbeau, a Liberal member of the National Assembly (Quebec's provincial legislature) and a former finance minister, perhaps summed up the situation best when he said, "I'm surprised to hear Mr. Parizeau lose his good judgment. We

live in a democracy, a vote is a vote. We're all Quebecers, wherever we come from."[37]

"Ours is not an ethnic nationalism," Lucien Bouchard constantly affirmed throughout the campaign, "for it recognizes that the 'nation quebecoise' is constituted by the people as a whole who inhabit Quebec."[38] What was supposed to be an inclusive nationalism, one that reflected and celebrated a multiethnic and multilingual Quebec, where the rights of all minorities would be protected, fizzled with Parizeau's unfortunate word choice. Though, to be sure, there were signs of such resentment before. In the week before the referendum, Bouchard had remarked to reporters, "Do you think it makes sense that we have so few children in Quebec? We're one of the white races that has the least children. That doesn't make sense."[39]

Parizeau's draft bill for independence—sent to every household in Quebec—included absolutely no provisions pertaining to the French language or culture. Indeed, the only time the word "French" appears in the document is completely innocuous: "Quebec shall take the necessary steps to remain a member of the Commonwealth, the French-speaking community, the North Atlantic Treaty Organization, the North American Aerospace Defense Command, the North American Free Trade Agreement and the General Agreement on Tariffs and Trade." Despite the fact that Parizeau was on the record saying that a sovereign Quebec would be both multicultural and multilingual—presumably a way to differentiate his vision from previous iterations of Quebec nationalism—his rant erased all the hard work that both he and Bouchard had done.

What, many asked themselves, was the place of minorities in the province? If the Yes vote had carried the day, would they still have been welcome? And if they were welcome, would they possess the same rights and freedoms as francophones? In light of Parizeau's comments, many wondered if the Yes side had simply used the inclusive rhetoric to curry favour with non-francophones. All these questions, and others, swirled in the minds of many. Even the referendum question—given a charitable reading—could support a liberal nationalist reading. It did not ask outright "Do you want to leave Canada?" Instead, as critics of its wording duly noted, it attempted to emphasize a set of values held in common with the country the Yes side sought to leave behind. These included citizenship, institutions, economic partnerships, and even currency.

A liberal nationalism was supposed to have replaced an ethnic nationalism. But writing in the *New York Times*, University of Toronto political scientist Andrew Stark said, "Mr. Parizeau's comments after the referendum, so out of step with the rest of the campaign, show that his approach to liberal nationalism was ultimately a cynical one: How can we fine-tune the message, making it tribalistic enough to appeal to the majority but not so obstreperous as to alarm the minority? Obviously, he never hit the right note."[40]

Parizeau's remarks also produced a good deal of surprise and anger among those who had voted Yes. It's possible his words upset so many—supporter and foe alike—that they defused what could have been an awkward aftermath with potential for recriminations and perhaps even violence. Still, it is a shame to have one's entire political life defined, or remembered, by two unfortunate sentences.

October 30, 1995, also reminds us of the relationship—often tense—between nationalism and immigration. In this context, the Quebec referendum revealed just how problematic it is to weigh one against the other. It forces us to ask the difficult question, can there ever be such a thing as an inclusive nationalism? Does nationalism, in other words, exclude by its very definition? An editorial in the *Globe and Mail*, for example, titled "Mr. Bouchard's Ethnic Nationalism," pointed out the uncomfortable truth that, despite the rhetoric, Quebec separatism was ultimately "rooted in ethnic rather than civic nationalism. Blood is more important than citizenship."[41]

VII

Canada is a country historically composed of two major groups, anglophones and francophones. It is also a country that has severely marginalized a third group: Indigenous populations. If the first two groups demand—and receive—the greatest attention, the latter, unfortunately, is often simply ignored in the context of national conversations. The land upon which Quebecers went to the polls on October 30, 1995—the day that almost ripped Canada apart—was ultimately stolen from its original inhabitants. The descendants of those inhabitants were not consulted about the referendum and potential separation from Canada to the extent they should have been. No one, for example, bothered to ask Quebec's Indigenous leaders what they wanted. The decision had been made for them. The only time Indigenous voices were brought into the debate was to score symbolic points for the federalist side.

The PQ's position, since the time of René Lévesque, had always been to recognize the rights of Indigenous peoples to self-determination. However, Quebec would do so only to the extent that such self-determination did not infringe on the territorial integrity of Quebec. Such a statement is rather ambiguous. What, for example, does infringing on Quebec's "territorial integrity" mean? Surely every piece of land within the province or future nation is imagined to be fundamental or integral to sovereigntists.

As a result, Indigenous leaders in Quebec have tended not to support sovereignty because of their own territorial land claims, which include their desire for autonomy. In the context of the 1995 referendum, this meant that two groups—both the Yes side and Indigenous leaders—were fighting over self-determination on the same piece of land. Both wanted to be able to determine their own futures on their own territory. Of course, it was never framed this way in the media or in the political debates between the Yes and No sides.

Northern Quebec, for example, has a large Cree and Inuit population, and their land claims comprise roughly two-thirds of Quebec's landmass. During the leadup to the referendum, both the Cree and Inuit argued that their territory should remain under Canadian jurisdiction. Their leaders also demanded that Indigenous groups be full participants in any new constitutional negotiations resulting from the referendum.[42] If Quebec has the right to leave Canada, they reasoned, then the Cree and Inuit peoples have the right to keep their territory in Canada, as defined by the 1975 James Bay and Northern Quebec Agreement.[43] Why, they asked, should Quebec sovereignty come at the expense of the original inhabitants of the land?

One of the most vocal Indigenous leaders was Grand Chief Matthew Coon Come of the Grand Council of the Crees in northern Quebec. A lawyer by training, Coon Come issued a legal paper titled *Sovereign Injustice*, which made the case for Cree self-determination within the larger context of Canada. He wrote: "The James Bay Crees and other Aboriginal peoples in Canada are not seeking to secede from Canada. However, they are seeking clear and unequivocal confirmation of their right to self-determination. Faced with the threat of a unilateral declaration of independence by Québec, Aboriginal peoples seek to exercise their right to choose to remain in Canada."[44]

Coon Come also reasoned that the desire on the part of sovereigntists to see themselves as unique and culturally distinct, but not to acknowledge the same criteria for Indigenous populations was tantamount to racism. On October 24, 1995, one week before the provincial referendum, the Cree organized their own referendum, wherein they posed the question "Do you consent, as a people, that the Government of Quebec separate the James Bay Crees and Cree traditional territory from Canada in the event of a Yes vote in the Quebec referendum?" Of those who voted, 96.3 per cent wanted to remain in Canada.[45] The Inuit of northern Quebec also held their own referendum, asking the question "Do you agree that Quebec should become sovereign?" 96 per cent voted "no."[46]

All of this, of course, is a matter of whose voices matter. Given the history of Canada, it is no surprise that anglophone and francophone voices have always taken precedence. Though symbolic, the Indigenous referendums nevertheless revealed a major tension in both Québécois and Canadian society: namely, the shameful treatment of Indigenous populations. The Quebec referendum only reinforced this. Needless to say, no one paid much attention to the results of the Cree and Inuit referendums, mirroring the larger attitude of Canadian society toward Indigenous peoples.

In 2014, Ghislain Picard, Chief of the Assembly of First Nations Quebec–Labrador, reminded Quebecers that First Nations have as much right as they do to determine their own future. Should another referendum be held, he said, Indigenous populations in Quebec will not be bound by it.[47] "The Government of Quebec, in defending the territorial integrity of Quebec by denying our aboriginal and treaty rights, our Indigenous title and our political sovereignty, is blatantly ignorant," he said, adding, "Must we remind you again that this 'territory' is still unceded indigenous land? It is not up to anyone but ourselves to decide our future. We will never accept that our self-determination be subordinated to that of another nation."[48]

Indigenous leaders now possess what they lacked in 1995: the United Nations Declaration on the Rights of Indigenous Peoples, adopted by the UN General Assembly in 2007 and endorsed by Canada in 2016. Article 3 of that document states that "Indigenous peoples have the right to self-determination. By virtue of that right they freely determine their political status and freely pursue their economic, social and cultural development."[49] Any future talk of separation in Quebec—or, more recently, in Alberta—will have to take into consideration Indigenous communities.[50] One province cannot simply walk away from Confederation and not reckon with the complex issue of Indigenous land claims and treaty rights.

VIII

The narrow defeat of the Yes side in the referendum led to a near consensus among Canada's provincial, territorial, and federal governments that something had to be done to demonstrate to Quebecers that a renewed federalism remained a viable option to sovereignty. On September 14, 1997, provincial and territorial premiers met in Calgary to attempt to solve, once and for all, the long-standing constitutional problems so Quebec would sign on and a united Canada could move into the future.

There was, however, one holdout who was not at the Calgary meeting. Lucien Bouchard, now the premier of Quebec, had refused to attend. He had been invited, according to Franck McKenna, premier of New Brunswick, but had declined, saying that "there was nothing that could be done that would satisfy him."[51] Plus ça change, as the French saying goes, plus c'est la même chose. The more things change, the more they stay the same.

The result of the meeting was the so-called Calgary Declaration, which contained the following seven points:

1. All Canadians are equal and have rights protected by law.
2. All provinces, while diverse in their characteristics, have equality of status.
3. Canada is graced by a diversity, tolerance, compassion and an equality of opportunity that is without rival in the world.

4. Canada's gift of diversity includes Aboriginal peoples and cultures, the vitality of the English and French languages and a multicultural citizenry drawn from all parts of the world.
5. In Canada's federal system, where respect for diversity and equality underlies unity, the unique character of Quebec society, including its French speaking majority, its culture and its tradition of civil law, is fundamental to the well-being of Canada. Consequently, the legislature and Government of Quebec have a role to protect and develop the unique character of Quebec society within Canada.
6. If any future constitutional amendment confers powers on one province, these powers must be available to all provinces.
7. Canada is a federal system where federal, provincial, and territorial governments work in partnership while respecting each other's jurisdictions. Canadians want their governments to work cooperatively and with flexibility to ensure the efficiency and effectiveness of the federation. Canadians want their governments to work together particularly in the delivery of their social programs. Provinces and territories renew their commitment to work in partnership with the Government of Canada to best serve the needs of Canadians.[52]

On one level, the Calgary Declaration was able to do what neither the Meech Lake nor Charlottetown Accords had done—namely, recognize the unique character of Quebec society, including its language, culture, and civil law. In so doing, though, it added the stipulation that all provinces were equally diverse.

The idea was that after the unofficial adoption of the Declaration, all premiers would take the document back to their provincial or territorial constituencies for public consultation, with the understanding that "each province and territory is free to decide on the range or scope of consultation as well as the most appropriate mechanism for consultation." All eleven signatories subsequently initiated some form of public consultation, and six eventually went on to ratify the Declaration in their provincial legislatures.

Though the Declaration was meant to give federalists in Quebec a "new offer," the PQ returned to power in the 1998 provincial election, and the Declaration was all but abandoned. Writing in the *National Post* in 2006, incoming federal Liberal leader Stéphane Dion claimed that the Declaration had failed in Quebec because it "had no teeth" and because, ultimately, "the premiers of other provinces tried to define, for us Quebecers, the type of recognition we wanted."[53]

IX

In the aftermath of the referendum, it turned out that, contrary to his rhetoric, Parizeau had intended to unilaterally declare Quebec's independence if the Yes side had achieved a majority of 50 per cent plus one vote. It also turned out that, should there have been a Yes victory, Ottawa would have refused to negotiate. Both sides had kept their cards close to their chests.

So where do matters stand on the sovereignty issue in today's Quebec? In 2005 the Centre for Research and Information in Canada conducted a poll that revealed 40 per cent of Quebecers favoured sovereignty. This number may well be misleading, however, especially when we remember that six months prior to the 1995 referendum, only 39 per cent favoured a Yes vote.[54] It was only after the entry of the charismatic Bouchard into the race that the Yes side began to pick up positive momentum.

While both the CAQ and the Bloc have stressed they are more interested in economic matters, both continue to emphasize the importance of civic nationalism. While such a nationalism is meant to be secular and inclusive, it always risks transforming into a form of ethnic nationalism, something that has the potential to define one group—in this case white francophones—as dominant to others. Aware of this, former premier Lucien Bouchard accused the PQ in 2010 of largely failing immigrants and cultural minorities.[55] This trend has continued in recent years, with PQ, Liberal, and CAQ governments proposing or passing provincial legislation directed at religious minorities, particularly Muslims.[56] Only by taking these groups into account, Bouchard warned, would it be possible to create winning conditions for the Yes side in the future.

Plus ça change, plus c'est la même chose.

SUGGESTIONS FOR FURTHER READING

Mario Cardinal. *Breaking Point Quebec/Canada: The 1995 Referendum*. Montreal: Bayard, 2005.

Jean Chrétien. *My Years as Prime Minister*. Toronto: Vintage Canada, 2007.

Chantal Hébert with Jean Lapierre. *The Morning After: The 1995 Referendum and the Day That Almost Was*. Toronto: Knopf Canada, 2014.

Robert A. Young. *The Secession of Quebec and the Future of Canada*. Revised and expanded edition. Montreal and Kingston: McGill-Queen's University Press, 1998.

SUGGESTIONS FOR FURTHER VIEWING

Jackie Corkery. *Breaking Point* (French: *Point de rupture*). CBC Television/Radio-Canada, 2005.

Stéphane Drolet. *Referendum: Take Two*. National Film Board of Canada, 1996.

Paul Jay. *Never-Endum Referendum*. High Road Productions in association with the National Film Board of Canada and Baton Broadcasting Incorporated. On YouTube at: www.youtube.com/watch?v=rHAOpGv-NQ8.

8

JUNE 2 2015

The Release of the Executive Summary of the Truth and Reconciliation Commission

SOME DAYS ARE YEARS IN THE MAKING. So momentous and full of symbolism, though, they risk being subsumed by their own hype. One such day is July 2, 2015, the day that the Executive Summary of the Truth and Reconciliation Commission's Final Report was released to great fanfare in Ottawa. Few Canadians would argue with the fact that First Nations, Inuit, and Métis people have been poorly and unjustly treated. Perhaps a bigger surprise is that it took the Canadian government until 2015 to acknowledge this to the extent that it did. Indeed, the fact that it took so long for a prime minster to apologize, publicly and officially, for the horrors inflicted on Indigenous communities—as Stephen Harper did in 2008—might also appear to be too little, too late.

If all of the previous dates in this book had fairly clear, if often rather complicated, afterlives, the full fallout of July 2, 2015 remains to be seen. Not just because it was so recent, but also because it brings the

country to a proverbial crossroads. Either Canada's relationship with its Indigenous communities will stay the same, in which case this day will represent one more empty promise and betrayal. Or the TRC report can usher in a massive rethinking of this relationship, which would mean this day has the potential to be remembered as one of the most momentous in modern Canadian history.

Truth and Reconciliation Commissions (TRCs), after all, solve very little themselves. TRCs work on the assumption that something traumatic has happened within a country and that it is necessary to confront it. By virtue of their rawness, including the potential for reliving the events in question, they desire to address wrongs committed in the past. They most frequently arise when a government seeks to uncover past abuses, often after periods of intense internal strife (e.g., South Africa) or a civil war (e.g., The Congo), or in the aftermath of a dictatorship (e.g., Chile after Pinochet).

TRCs are symbolic, only commencing when all the parties are ready to cooperate. They often begin after an acknowledgement of guilt, something that lays down the conditions for an apology. A simple and heartfelt "We are sorry" subsequently and ideally signals a desire to move forward. However—and this is a very big however—deeds must follow words and promises must be backed by action.

Many of the previous days discussed have tangentially involved Canada's Indigenous populations. Indigenous concerns, however, have usually been confined to the margins, as Indigenous people have been forced to play supporting roles in a never-ending drama that has largely starred white Canadians, be they anglophone or francophone. June 2, 2015, is a day that will hopefully put Indigenous issues front and centre in a set of national conversations.

I

We must never lose sight of the fact that what ultimately became Canada had its origins as a colonial state. Like any such state, local inhabitants were seen as uncivilized and barbaric and, because of this, not eligible for the same rights and protections as the colonizers. Neither European nor Christian, Indigenous populations were thought to be savages and heathens, in dire need of improvement and education. The colonial power thus saw one of its jobs as "reforming" them so they could be transformed into useful citizens. Rather than accept alternative religious and cultural traditions, including diverse social patterns, Europeans sought to force their own ways upon Indigenous groups. That which did not conform had to be excised. Though it is important to note that many people today argue that the creation of residential schools was motivated by prejudice with the larger aim of cultural assimilation, the TRC found and stated explicitly that residential schooling was primarily about dispossessing Indigenous nations of land and sovereignty and was, thus, also an attempt by Canada to evade its treaty obligations.

In 1876, nine years after Confederation, the Government of Canada passed the Indian Act (French: Loi sur les Indiens). It was—indeed, still is—a wide-ranging act covering governance, land use, healthcare, and education, as well as determining who is (and is not) eligible for what became known as "Indian status." The purpose of the act was rather paradoxical. While imagining the category "Indian," it simultaneously sought to erase it. The Indian Act administered all affairs of Indigenous people with the hope that they would eventually renounce traditional ways in order to partake of Canadian civilization, imagined as white and Christian. We see this in the language of a report issued by the Department of the Interior, which was responsible for "Indian Affairs." It states,

> Our Indian legislation generally rests on the principle, that the aborigines are to be kept in a condition of tutelage and treated as wards or children of the State.... The true interests of the aborigines and of the State alike require that every effort should be made to aid the Red man in lifting himself out of his condition of tutelage and dependence, and that is clearly our wisdom and our duty, through education and

> every other means, to prepare him for a higher civilization by encouraging him to assume the privileges and responsibilities of full citizenship.[1]

This sentiment is further echoed in the words of John A. Macdonald—Canada's first prime minister, and minister of the Interior from 1878 to 1888—who proclaimed in 1887 that "the great aim of our legislation has been to do away with the tribal system and assimilate the Indian people in all respects with the other inhabitants of the Dominion as speedily as they are fit to change." While presumably nobly intended, such comments strike us today as hopelessly paternalistic and, with the hindsight of history, hopelessly problematic. Indeed, as we shall see in chapter 10, a statue of Macdonald was recently decapitated precisely because of his involvement in what are now seen as racist activities.

Ever since its implementation, the Indian Act has shaped, controlled, and defined the lives of Indigenous communities. It has meant that bureaucrats in Ottawa—particularly within the Department of Indian Affairs and Northern Development (now called Indigenous Services Canada)—are the ones ultimately responsible for defining who is a status or registered Indian, and who is not. To be recognized by the government as an "Indian" is to have what is for all intents and purposes a foreign category bestowed on one from the outside. Politicians and bureaucrats, in other words, are the ones in charge of determining whose names get added to the "Indian register."[2]

If the Indian Act defined (and defines) who exactly an "Indian" was, it also sought to dismantle the definition through the concept of "enfranchisement." As individual Indigenous people—not tribes or groups—were deemed to become "civilized," bureaucrats decided for them that they would lose their status and become a "productive member" of Canadian society.[3] Until that happened, however, they were required to stay on lands that were "reserved" for them. These reserves, held "in trust" for Indigenous peoples by the federal government and not to be confused with ancestral land claims, were the places where Indigenous populations were supposed to live until they were able to prove to the state that they were sufficiently "civilized" to enter mainstream Canadian society. Those who lived and, indeed, those who continue to live on reserves do not own their land or even their houses, both of which are administered under the auspices of the federal government. To get a sense of the numbers, according to Statistics Canada's National Household Survey in 2011, there are more than 600 First Nations/Indian bands in Canada and 3,100 reserves across the country.[4] Roughly half of Canada's 637,660 "status Indians"—a number that does not include Inuit or Métis—continue to live on a reserve.[5] Who gets to be defined or classified as a "status Indian" is also not particularly clear. Nor has it always been transparent who gets to keep one's status or who can pass status (and, of course, the associated rights that go with it) on to one's offspring. Historically, for example, if someone with Indian status served in the armed forces, obtained a university degree, or took up a profession (e.g., lawyer, doctor), they automatically lost their status because they were then deemed to be sufficiently "Canadian" and, by extension, sufficiently "non-Indian." Until as late as 1960, Indigenous people could only vote in federal elections if they first renounced their "Indian status."[6] An Indigenous woman with status could lose it upon marrying a non-status (read: white) man. It was only in 1985 and the passage of Bill C-31—a bill to bring the Indian Act into line with gender equality as defined by the Charter of Rights and Freedoms[7]—that many Indigenous people had their status restored. If Bill C-31 clarified some things, it also complicated others. Individuals are now no longer either simply status or non-status, but are referred to as either "6(1)" or "6(2)." Those under subsection "6(2)" are those who had their status reinstated because of Bill C-31. Should a status Indian under subsection 6(2) have children with a non-status person, their children are ineligible for Indian status (the "second-generation cut-off"). If two "6(2)" people marry, then their children revert to "6(1)." Once again, it is the federal government in Ottawa determining who is or is not a (particular type of) status Indian.

Such examples contradict the perspective of many non-Indigenous popular commentators who tend to see injustices as either past events or as residues or "legacies" from the past that we are now called to deal with. Critical Indigenous commentators, however, see such injustice as something that continues to be actively perpetuated by the state in the present through, for example, child welfare policies, rates of over-incarceration, resource extraction on Indigenous territories, and other matters. We would do well to note, then, that policies of assimilation and dispossession have not vanished, despite the removal of certain clauses from the Indian Act.

Some 140 years after its initial creation, the act continues to be controversial.[8] The federal government still uses it as the primary legislation to administer everything from laws to membership and elections in First Nation communities. Many non-Indigenous Canadians think that it bestows a set of privileges on First Nations, Inuit, and Métis people—like tax-free status, free university, monthly cheques—not available to the rest of the country. Such a view is not only unfortunate but also inaccurate, as these benefits are only available to some First Nation people with very specific restrictions. This view also overlooks the great social and cultural tragedy that the Indian Act has imposed on Canada's Indigenous communities. This tragedy, and its inherited trauma, continues to have a negative impact on communities, families, and individuals.

Many Indigenous leaders regard the act as a racist and paternalistic piece of legislation, grounded in Canada's colonialist past. "Once the Indian Act is done away with," says Grand Chief Derek Nepinak, head of the Assembly of Manitoba Chiefs, "only then will First Nations have control of our own destiny to become self-sufficient and self-governing."[9] Leaders such as Nepinak regard the Indian Act as ultimately responsible for many of the social problems—including high rates of alcoholism, substance abuse, and suicide—facing today's Indigenous communities.[10]

Though it has been amended several times over the years, one cannot deny the fact the Indian Act has sought to control the lives of Indigenous people ever since Canada's formation as a country. It has forced—at great personal and communal cost—Indigenous communities to try to fit into a society that that did not want them and into which many did not want to assimilate. It restricted their movement, made them change their names, and made it illegal to speak their languages and practise their customs.

One of the catalysts for this cultural genocide was the notorious residential school system.

II

Residential schools provided an elaborate institutional infrastructure set up across the length and breadth of Canada with the explicit intention of removing all traces of "Indian-ness" from Indigenous children. Funded by the Canadian government and run by Christian churches, the aim of the system was to educate Indigenous youth by converting them to Christianity and assimilating them into Canadian society. Though predating Confederation, such schools became much more active with the creation of the Indian Act. An 1894 amendment to the act made it mandatory for Indigenous children to attend these schools. Since many communities did not have schools nearby, the idea was that children would leave their communities and stay at residential schools in order to comply with the new law. Rather than put schools on reserves, the government and churches intentionally built them far away in order to minimize contact between families and their children. Since Indigenous individuals needed passes to leave their reserves, access to their children was made even more difficult.

Addressing the House of Commons in 1883, John A. Macdonald extolled the virtues of this system:

> When the school is on the reserve the child lives with its parents, who are savages; he is surrounded by savages, and though he may learn to read and write his habits, and training and mode of thought are Indian. He is simply a savage who can read and write. It has been strongly pressed on myself, as the head of the Department, that Indian children should be withdrawn as much as possible from the parental influence, and the only way to do that would be to put them in central training industrial schools where they will acquire the habits and modes of thought of white men.[11]

Residential schools existed in all of the provinces, with the exception of Prince Edward Island and New Brunswick.[12] The last such school—Gordon's Indian Residential School in Punnichy, Saskatchewan—closed its doors only in 1996. Over the course of the system's more than hundred-year existence about 30 per cent of Indigenous children were placed in these residential schools. The federal government calculates the number to be around 150,000 children.[13]

The residential school system did irreparable harm to both the children and the larger cultural frameworks of which they were a part. Students were not only removed from their families but also subjected to great physical and emotional abuse.[14] It is clear from Survivor testimony and subsequent records that there was rampant sexual abuse in these schools, though this was something that was denied by the churches at the time.

Despite the purported goal of assimilation, those who graduated from these schools were then unable to fit into either their own communities or mainstream Canadian society. They were, literally, ghosts, several generations of whom had been betrayed by both the federal government and Canada's mainline churches.

The entire system was predicated on the assumption that European civilization and Christian religion were superior to Indigenous culture, which was seen as savage and brutal. Students were forbidden, on threat of corporal punishment, from speaking their traditional languages and were instead forced to speak English or French. They were also prohibited from performing their traditional spiritual and religious practices.[15] This meant that the federal government, along with Christian churches—the Catholic Church, in particular—were complicit in the systematic disruption of the transmission of Indigenous practices, customs, languages, and beliefs to subsequent generations. These practices and customs had defined Indigenous life for centuries, if not millennia, and were now forcibly halted. The higher than average rates of post-traumatic stress disorder (PTSD), alcoholism, substance abuse, and suicide among Indigenous communities continue to tell the tale of this disruption.

The number of school-related deaths remains unknown owing to a lack of records.[16] Though the Truth and Reconciliation Commission report put the number at 3,200, it also duly noted that the number was probably much higher, and surely warranted further investigation.

Others died by suicide, in fires, or by freezing to death while trying to escape. One of the last projects of the late Gord Downie, lead singer for The Tragically Hip (see chapter 9), was *Secret Path*, a multimedia project that recounted the story of Chanie Wenjack, a young Anishinaabe boy from the Marten Falls First Nation, who died trying to return home after escaping from the Cecilia Jeffrey Indian Residential School in 1966.[17] Wenjack's death led to an inquiry at the time that brought national attention to the plight of Indigenous students at residential schools.[18] But the abuse largely continued unabated.

In 1986, the United Church of Canada was the first church to apologize for its role in the residential school system.[19] The apology reads, in part: "We tried to make you be like us and in so doing we helped to destroy the vision that made you what you were. As a result, you, and we, are poorer and the image of the Creator in us is twisted, blurred, and we are not what we are meant by God to be." The Presbyterian Church issued an apology in 1994,[20] and the Anglican Church did so in 1993. In 2019, the Anglican Church also issued a more general apology for the spiritual harm of colonization.[21]

One of the 94 Calls to Action of the TRC—to be examined shortly—called specifically on the pope "to issue an apology to Survivors, their families, and communities for the Roman Catholic Church's role in the spiritual, cultural, emotional, physical, and sexual abuse of First Nations, Inuit, and Métis children in Catholic-run residential schools."[22] Despite this, and even after personal appeals by Prime Minister Justin Trudeau and the Government of Canada,[23] the Catholic Church long neglected to offer such an apology. It took a group of Indigenous delegates travelling to the Vatican for an audience with the pope before an apology was finally be issued. On April 1, 2022, Pope Francis apologized for the Catholic Church's role in the Canadian residential school system.[24]

III

On June 11, 2008, Prime Minister Stephen Harper stood up in the House of Commons and made his own historic apology on behalf of the Government of Canada, and all Canadians, for the existence of the residential school system. Immediately in front of him was a circle of eleven chairs reserved for five Indigenous leaders and six residential school Survivors. He spoke from a prepared statement, which, in part, read as follows:

> The government recognizes that the absence of an apology has been an impediment to healing and reconciliation. Therefore, on behalf of the Government of Canada and all Canadians, I stand before you, in this Chamber so central to our life as a country, to apologize to Aboriginal peoples for Canada's role in the Indian Residential Schools system.
>
> To the approximately 80,000 living former students, and all family members and communities, the Government of Canada now recognizes that it was wrong to forcibly remove children from their homes and we apologize for having done this. We now recognize that it was wrong to separate children from rich and vibrant cultures and

> traditions, that it created a void in many lives and communities, and we apologize for having done this.[25]

Harper's apology was followed by remarks from Stéphane Dion, the Liberal leader, who acknowledged his party's complicity in the residential schools policy (the Liberals had governed Canada for over eighty years since Confederation). Following this, Gilles Duceppe of the Bloc Québécois and the NDP's Jack Layton reflected on the apology, while also criticizing the Harper government for failing to endorse the United Nations Declaration on the Rights of Indigenous People. From the circle of chairs, Phil Fontaine, National Chief of the Assembly of First Nations, responded to the apology: "Never again will we be the 'Indian problem.' Today is the result of the righteousness of our struggle."[26]

In the speech, Harper also announced the Truth and Reconciliation Commission, although it is important to note that Harper and his government did not create the TRC. Instead, it was established as part of an out-of-court settlement reached with former residential school students in 2005. In effect, the courts imposed it on his government. In his announcement, Harper stated that:

> It [the TRC] will be a positive step in forging a new relationship between Aboriginal peoples and other Canadians, a relationship based on the knowledge of our shared history, a respect for each other and a desire to move forward together with a renewed understanding that strong families, strong communities and vibrant cultures and traditions will contribute to a stronger Canada for all of us.

Despite the historic nature of the apology, it did not ring true for many. Leo Ashamock, who had been the subject of sexual and physical abuse (including being put in an electric chair) at the notorious St. Anne's Residential School in Fort Albany, Ontario, was not ready to forgive. "Reconciliation is between two parties," he said in a 2018 CBC interview, "and it has to be honest. But the way I feel about it now, it doesn't live up to its name about being truthful, and reconciling. I think the words that came out of the prime minister, when he did the apology, I didn't feel it—when I was watching it on TV. I think it was just words coming out, and no feeling. So I didn't feel there was anything reconciliatory about that."[27]

Others agree, saying that while an apology is one thing, it has to be accompanied by certain tangible actions. National Chief Shawn Atleo of the Assembly of First Nations, speaking four years after the official apology, declared, "We're faced with a real moment of reckoning here," but quickly added that "the rate and pace of change is too slow."[28] Atleo noted that at the same time the federal government was issuing its apology and patting itself on the back, it was also actively fighting First Nations organizations in court in a bid to quash their demands to fund Indigenous child welfare at the same levels as provincial welfare programs. Indeed, in 2014 Atleo went so far as to resign his position as National Chief in order to oppose the Harper government's overhaul of Indigenous education.[29]

Harper's apology was not unexpected. Nor did it come from nowhere. Rather, it was the end result of a much lengthier process that grew out of the Indian Residential Schools Settlement Agreement (IRSSA). The IRSSA was an agreement between the Government of Canada and 86,000 Indigenous individuals who had been enrolled in residential schools. Formed in 2005 as a response to the largest class-action lawsuit in Canadian history, the IRSSA acknowledged the pain and distress caused by the residential school system. Just as importantly, it established a $1.9-billion compensation package called the Common Experience Payment (CEP) for all former students.

The average lump-sum payment through the CEP to Survivors was $28,000. According to Bernard Valcourt, the minister of Aboriginal and Northern Development in Harper's cabinet, by December 31, 2012, a total of $1.62 billion had been paid to "78,750 recipients, representing 98% of the 80,000 estimated eligible former students."[30] In addition to the CEP, there also existed an Independent Assessment Process (IAP) for those students who had experienced sexual and serious physical abuse. The maximum payment from the IAP was $275,000, but an additional $250,000 could be awarded in cases where income loss occurred. This process, of course, required victims of sexual violence to present their claims, talking about events that had happened to them, often in private, thereby putting the onus of responsibility on victims. Many of the claims were denied for technical reasons, further traumatizing victims and their families.[31]

The IRSSA also allocated $60 million for the Truth and Reconciliation Commission (TRC). The commission's explicit aim was to document and preserve the experiences of Survivors from the residential schools. Originally launched in June 2008 with Justice Harry LaForme, a member of the Mississaugas of the Credit First Nation, as chair, the commission nearly fell apart several months later when LaForme stepped down, claiming an "incurable problem" since the other two commissioners refused to accept his authority. The TRC was relaunched the following year under the leadership of Justice Murray Sinclair, an Ojibway judge.[32]

To achieve its goal of documentation and preservation, the TRC was given a seven-year (2008–2015) mandate to provide residential school Survivors with an opportunity to share their experiences during public and private meetings that were held across the country. The TRC was also charged with preserving records that documented the residential school system and to set up a national research centre to permanently house the documents. This led to the creation of the National Centre for Truth and Reconciliation, which opened its doors in November 2015 at the University of Manitoba. One of the stipulations of the IRSSA was that all those religious and government bodies involved in the operations of the residential schools were legally obliged to submit all relevant residential school records to the TRC. The centre thus functions as an archival repository for the documents, including church and government records, residential school photographs, other relevant items—and the statements of over seven thousand Survivors that were collected during the course of the TRC investigations.[33]

IV

With great fanfare a four-day event was held in Ottawa from May 31 to June 3, 2015, to coincide with the release of the TRC's Executive Summary. The event began with a Walk for Reconciliation on Sunday, May 31, and culminated with closing ceremonies held on Wednesday, June 3. The event, as Justice Sinclair remarked, was meant for all Canadians and not just Indigenous people. The focal point occurred on June 2, with the public release of the Executive Summary, including its 94 Calls to Actions.[34] It was an event like no other, with Survivors, politicians, and representatives from churches in attendance, packed into a room in Ottawa. Hope and anger mingled, along with reflections on injustice, and fear that federal and provincial lethargy would soon set in. As Survivors wiped away tears and comforted one another, others were much more skeptical, and some expressed anger at the Aboriginal Affairs minister, whose government had refused to adopt the United Nations Declaration on the Rights of Indigenous Peoples. In an interview with the CBC News outside the event, Vivian Ketchum, who had attended the Cecilia Jeffrey Indian Residential School in northern Ontario, remarked, "I don't expect much to happen after. This is just going to be one final hurrah for us and we're just going to be placed aside. I think that's the reality for us [Survivors]."[35]

The 94 Calls to Action recommended, among other things, that the government work to reduce the number of Indigenous children in foster care (#1), fund Indigenous language protection (#15), provide sensitivity training for judges and others involved with enforcing the law (#27), and implement Aboriginal justice systems (#42). In terms of reconciliation, it recommended all branches of Canadian government fully adopt and implement the Declaration on the Rights of Indigenous Peoples (#43–44), demand a public apology from the pope (#58), provide funding to integrate Indigenous issues into the Canadian education curriculum at all levels (#62), fund the National Centre for Truth and Reconciliation (#78), and educate new immigrants to Canada on the history and plight of Indigenous peoples (#93). The 94th, and final, Call to Action was to amend the Oath of Citizenship to read:

> I swear (or affirm) that I will be faithful and bear true allegiance to Her Majesty Queen Elizabeth II, Queen of Canada, Her Heirs and Successors, and that I will faithfully observe the laws of Canada including Treaties with Indigenous Peoples, and fulfill my duties as a Canadian citizen.

The Calls to Action thus urged all levels of government, including Indigenous, to work together for the common cause of repairing the harm done and to move toward reconciliation.

At the time of the Executive Summary's release, Prime Minister Harper said that, of the 94 Calls to Action, he would be amenable only to the creation of the National Centre for Truth and Reconciliation, and would wait for the final report before responding further. Indeed, on the same day that the Executive Summary was released, he refused to say that what the residential school system had done led to the "cultural genocide" of Indigenous communities. He also said that his government would not implement the United Nations Declaration on the Rights of Indigenous People, despite the TRC's recommendation.[36]

However, by the time the final report was released in December 2015, an October federal election had brought an end to Conservative rule and saw Justin Trudeau's Liberals form a majority government. Unlike Harper, Trudeau was on the record stating that his government was in favour of implementing all 94 recommendations from the Truth and Reconciliation Commission, including the creation of a public inquiry into missing and murdered Indigenous women and girls.[37]

Despite the promises, Trudeau has come under strong criticism from Indigenous leaders.[38] Although he constantly states that "there remains no more important relationship to me and to Canada than the one with Indigenous peoples," some have begun to question his commitment to addressing issues facing Indigenous communities.[39] Despite Trudeau's expressions of goodwill, many problems with truth and reconciliation remain. Perhaps most pertinent today are issues surrounding the application and use of pipelines on Indigenous lands. In February 2020, for example, protesters from the Wet'suwet'en First Nation objected to the construction of the Coastal GasLink Pipeline on their unceded lands in northern British Columbia.[40] The protest quickly spread across the country, with other protesters offering their support and solidarity, while also drawing attention to Indigenous land claims, police brutality against Indigenous peoples, and other outstanding issues.[41] Such solidarity protests led to railway blockades that halted, among other things, traffic along a major Canadian National Railway line between Toronto and Montreal, and a shutdown of passenger rail service and rail freight operations in much of Canada.

V

Data from the 2011 National Household Survey reveals that 4.3 per cent of the total Canadian population identified as Indigenous—once again, a generic rubric that includes First Nations, Inuit, and Métis—equivalent to roughly 1.4 million Canadians.[42] The survey also showed that 85 per cent of

First Nations people were registered—that is, in possession of status. While the survey also found that the Indigenous population was increasing at a faster rate than non-Indigenous, it noted that almost half (48.1 per cent) of all children aged 14 and under in foster care were Indigenous. Nearly 4 per cent of Indigenous children, in other words, were foster children compared to 0.3 per cent among non-Indigenous.[43]

As noted earlier in this chapter, the National Household Survey found that of the 637,660 First Nations individuals who reported being "status Indians," nearly half continued to live on a reserve. Citing the 2011 census, the Executive Summary of the TRC noted that "only 8.7% of First Nations people, 5.1% of Inuit, and 11.7% of Métis have a university degree."[44]

This last set of statistics is disconcerting, since access to and completion of post-secondary education is beneficial to changing the structures of power. While some think the system is beyond repair, and thus desire to stay outside of its structures, it is surely necessary that there be more Indigenous lawyers, politicians, and constitutional experts. Legal and political activism will be one of the major ways to dismantle some of the institutional, legal, economic, and social forces that have been so detrimental to Indigenous communities over the years.

In terms of social forces, one only needs to look at the loss of Indigenous languages and the cultures they supported. Access to and preservation of culture and language are specifically mentioned in the United Nations Declaration on the Rights of Indigenous Peoples. According to Article 8:1 of that document, "Indigenous peoples and individuals have the right not to be subjected to forced assimilation or destruction of their culture." Article 8:2(d) stipulates that "states shall provide effective mechanisms for prevention of, and redress for...any form of forced assimilation or integration."[45]

The problem, of course, is that once one has to preserve a language, it is already at the risk of extinction. Indeed, the TRC Executive Summary is full of harrowing stories about children punished, both physically and sexually, for speaking their native language. This was in addition to the emotional trauma they suffered from accusations of being different or uncivilized. Mary Courchene, formerly a student at the residential schools at Fort Alexander in Manitoba and Lebret in Saskatchewan, described how this trauma affected her relationship with her family and, by extension, her culture:

> And I looked at my dad, I looked at my mom, I looked at my dad again. You know what? I hated them. I just absolutely hated my own parents. Not because I thought they abandoned me; I hated their brown faces. I hated them because they were Indians...So I, I looked at my dad and I challenged him and I said, "From now on we speak only English in this house," I said to my dad. And you know when we, when, in a traditional home where I was raised, the first thing that we all were always taught was to respect your Elders and never to, you know, to challenge them. And here I was, eleven years old, and I challenged...my dad looked at me and I, and I thought he was going to cry. In fact his eyes filled up with tears. He turned to my mom and he says..."Then I guess we'll never speak to this little girl again. I don't know her."[46]

Cases like this are what the TRC sought to draw attention to and document for future generations. Such disturbing stories also reveal the extent to which the powerless absorbed the critiques of the powerful, and why Indigenous individuals and communities have so much mistrust when it comes to participating in or relying on the larger Canadian society.

VI

In 1973, while the residential school system was still in operation, the federal government began to recognize Indigenous land claims. This came on the heels of a set of demands from First Nations, Inuit, and Métis peoples to have their land rights and Aboriginal title both acknowledged and respected. If residential schools and the other structures put in place by the Indian Act have defined Indigenous and non-Indigenous relations in the past, what will increasingly define these relations in the future are land claims. Like so much in the past, however, it is once again the system of the colonizer—in this case the law and its structures—that defines what is and is not Indigenous land.

Land claims tend to be divided into two types, comprehensive and specific. Comprehensive claims deal with those communities that did not sign treaties with the Government of Canada, whereas specific claims relate explicitly to the administration of the numbered treaties signed between

1871 and 1921 and other agreements, with specific terms designated for each treaty. Indigenous leaders today state that many of these lands, which they refer to as unceded, were taken from them unjustly, whether to expand Canada in the years immediately after Confederation or to allow access to mineral and other resources.

Land claims are among the most symbolically important issues facing federal and provincial governments, on one hand, and Indigenous populations, on the other. Many of these claims are also economically consequential, involving vast amounts of land, sometimes in resource-rich territories. For example, various Algonquin groups have laid claim to an area of land that involves 8.9 million acres of the Ottawa watershed, including ground upon which both the Parliament Buildings and the Supreme Court sit.[47]

An example of a successful land claim agreement is the Nisga'a Final Agreement, signed between the Nisga'a First Nation, the Government of British Columbia, and the Government of Canada on May 27, 1998, which came into effect on May 11, 2000. The agreement—signed ten years before Harper's official apology and seventeen years before the release of the TRC report—granted the Nisga'a close to 2,000 square kilometres of land, giving them full control over it, including all forestry and fishing resources contained within. The agreement was the first in the country to incorporate inherent self-government directly in the treaty. Also significant was the fact that it meant the Nisga'a First Nation was no longer under the jurisdiction of the Indian Act, meaning, among other things, that the Nisga'a could run their own health services and schools.[48] The settlement represented the first modern-day comprehensive treaty in the province, and the first agreement signed by a First Nation in British Columbia since Treaty 8 in 1899. British Columbia is an interesting case because, unlike the rest of Canada, where Indigenous people signed treaties with the Crown in exchange for reserves and other promises, only a few nations in northeastern British Columbia signed treaties.

All treaties signed after the Nisga'a Final Agreement have included the notion of self-government.[49] Moreover, a Supreme Court ruling in 2014 gave Indigenous peoples expanded access to land beyond the borders of reserves. In that judgment, the Court ruled unanimously in favour of a land claim by the Tsilhqot'in First Nation in the British Columbia interior. This ruling came after the province granted a logging licence on land that had served as the Tsilhqot'in Nation's traditional hunting grounds but was outside the boundaries of its reserve. The Tsilhqot'in took the province to court, with lower courts disagreeing on whether the semi-nomadic Tsilhqot'in Nation, a group of six Indigenous bands, had title to the lands. The Supreme Court said the Tsilhqot'in did have title and laid out for the first time the mechanism whereby a First Nation could prove its title.[50] Even without a declared land title, the Supreme Court ruled, the province must consult with Indigenous groups about uses of the land in dispute and accommodate their interests.

The victory was important for First Nations in British Columbia because there are literally hundreds of Indigenous groups across the province with unresolved land claims. James O'Reilly, a veteran Indigenous rights lawyer, told CBC News that the Supreme Court's ruling could also be applied to 40 per cent of Quebec's territory.[51] This, of course, has tremendous implications—as witnessed in chapter 7—for that province's sovereignty movement.

Another example of a modern treaty is that of the Tla'amin First Nation near Powell River on the British Columbia coast. After twenty-two years of talks between Tla'amin leaders, the Government of British Columbia, and the federal government, a final agreement was reached, and on April 5, 2016, the Tla'amin became a self-governing nation, possessing ownership of about 21,000 acres. The agreement also included upfront payments of $42 million and annual compensation of more than $700,000 dollars for resources, like lumber, that had already been harvested.

However, this case is noteworthy for the criticism that arose after the treaty was signed. Those members of the Tla'amin opposed to the agreement argued that it gave the nation less than 5 per cent of its traditional land and would extinguish the nation's rights and title to traditional territory for the future. In a referendum, only 57.5 per cent of the community voted for the agreement, with claims from the "no" side that there had been voting irregularities.[52] Elder Doreen Point, a critic of the deal, was worried about how the new autonomous nation would address social issues such as poor infrastructure and high unemployment. "We're not ready for self-government," she said. "Maybe the people benefitting from this are ready, but the community isn't...We are not a reserve that generates revenue—there's nothing for us to fall back on. We may have forestry, but when it comes to the benefit of the community how far does $250 per person take you? Not very far."[53]

Land claims, in other words, can come with their own set of social problems. For example, they give some Indigenous groups the ability to engage in resource extraction and exploitation that had previously been undertaken almost exclusively by white Canadians. While some Indigenous governments are happy about the new economic opportunities such activities bring, other members of their nations are opposed to it. For example, the Trans Mountain Pipeline has carried crude and refined oil from Alberta to the British Columbia coast since the 1950s. In 2013, the Trans Mountain Expansion Project was proposed, which would involve building a second pipeline between Edmonton, Alberta, and Burnaby, British Columbia, to move close to 600,000 more barrels of diluted bitumen a day. Controversy arose when environmental and First Nations groups opposed to the expansion project mounted legal challenges and protests to impede construction. Other First Nations were working with Trans Mountain to secure employment for their members and to mitigate the environmental impact of the pipeline. After five Secwepemc activists were arrested for blocking the pipeline, Rosanne Casimir, Chief of the Tk'emlups te Secwepemc, said she and her band council did not support the protesters. "We have participated in the decision-making matters that affected our rights and as previously stated, we are VERY proud to have made an impact and changes to the environmental process."[54] In contrast, protester Kanahus Manuel said, "When we're saying that the Canadian government, the Trudeau government, did not get the free, prior and informed consent of the Secwepemc people collectively, it's important for us to continue to say that this is a collective right...It's a collective right with all 10,000 Secwepemc that are within the Secwepemc Nation. [If] one child stands up and says no, that's our law. That's our law as Secwepemc people."[55]

In August 2018, the Federal Court of Appeal ruled that the federal government had not sufficiently consulted First Nations in the area. After the government consulted with these groups and again approved the pipeline in June 2019, the Supreme Court dismissed further court challenges on July 2, 2020.[56] Clearly, despite the Supreme Court's ruling, these challenges and protests are far from over.

VII

On January 21, 2020, the Correctional Investigator of Canada issued a news release stating that more than 30 per cent of prison inmates in Canada are Indigenous.[57] When broken down by region, Indigenous individuals in Alberta, Saskatchewan, and Manitoba make up 54 per cent of the entire prison population. For a group that comprises just under 5 per cent of the country's population, this number is staggering.[58] The rate of incarceration among Indigenous people is rising at the same time that the number of federally incarcerated non-Indigenous prisoners has been declining. Indeed, the number of Indigenous individuals incarcerated rose from 17.59 per cent of the total incarcerated population in 2001 to the 2020 number. Indigenous women, moreover, account for 42 per cent of the total female inmate population in Canada. Dr. Ivan Zinger, the Correctional Investigator of Canada, said such high numbers represent the "Indigenization" of Canada's correctional system. According to Zinger,

> On this trajectory, the pace is now set for Indigenous people to comprise 33% of the total federal inmate population in the next three years. Over the longer term, and for the better part of three decades now, despite findings of Royal Commissions and National Inquiries, intervention of the courts, promises and commitments of previous and current political leaders, no government of any stripe has managed to reverse the trend of Indigenous over-representation in Canadian jails and prisons. The Indigenization of Canada's prison population is nothing short of a national travesty.[59]

Zinger also documented how Indigenous inmates are disproportionately placed in maximum security institutions, over-represented in use of force incidents, and, historically, more likely to be placed and held longer in solitary confinement. When compared with non-Aboriginal inmates, they serve a higher proportion of their sentence behind bars before being granted parole.[60] A recent study of recidivism rates revealed that Indigenous people reoffend or are returned to custody at much higher levels than non-Indigenous—as high as 70 per cent for Indigenous men, especially in the Prairie provinces.[61]

Such numbers once again reveal the structural problems inherent in a Canadian society that has long overlooked its most marginalized. The poverty rates among Indigenous communities, when combined with racism in policing, create a system that has been lethal. Many of these problems are the direct result of the Indian Act, which in its attempt to erase the presence of Indigenous languages and cultures actually succeeded in worsening the plight of Indigenous people, tearing apart families and depriving children of culture and community that would give them stability. This is why the final report of the National Inquiry into Missing and Murdered Indigenous Women and Girls described what is happening to Indigenous peoples as a "genocide" that "has been empowered by colonial structures."[62]

In 2017, the Liberal minister of Indigenous Services, Jane Philpott, remarked to the CBC that the disproportionate number of Indigenous children caught in Canada's child welfare system was tantamount to a "humanitarian crisis," which she compared to the horrors of the residential school system.[63] To this list of problems one could also add the fact that many reserves lack access to clean drinking water and proper sanitation.[64]

While much of the present chapter has focused on communities on reserves, we must not lose sight of all those individuals in cities, far removed from their bands and their families, who live in poverty. Indigenous individuals, for instance, are much more likely to sleep on the street than are non-Indigenous individuals. A 2014 study showed that more than half of all homeless people in Thunder Bay were Indigenous.[65]

The majority of the statistics included in this section were gathered either right before or immediately after the release of the final report of the Truth and Reconciliation Commission. They all raise a set of uncomfortable questions. Is there the political will to address the issues that the TRC documented? To what extent, in other words, is Canada, and all Canadians, prepared to change to remedy the problems that Indigenous individuals and communities face? The TRC brought the documentary evidence to the forefront; it remains to be seen what will be done with it. It can either remain in the archives on the campus of the University of Manitoba or become the pathway to meaningful structural changes in Canadian society.

Exactly one year and one day after the release of the final report of the Inquiry into Missing and Murdered Indigenous Women and Girls (MMIWG), Chantal Moore, a young woman from the Tla-o-qui-aht First Nation in British Columbia, was killed by police during a welfare check in Edmunston, New Brunswick.[66] Eight days after her death, police in New Brunswick shot and killed Rodney Levi, a Mi'kmaq man with mental health issues. These are but two names in what has been a long list of murdered individuals.

To rectify violence within Indigenous communities, some leaders have called for the creation of Indigenous courts that would mete out punishment and justice in accord with traditional values. This, they argue, would coincide with the use of Indigenous justice centres, and the creation of justice-oriented diversion programs that would provide alternatives to incarceration.[67] Such institutions, presumably funded by the federal government, would not just punish offenders but would also seek to uncover the underlying social causes of Indigenous crime.

Many of these initiatives were laid out in the MMIWG final report. That report also called for a national protocol to set basic standards for all police investigations of serious violent crimes against Indigenous people,[68] in addition to the establishment of a national Indigenous-led police oversight body. To date, little has changed in the wake of the MMIWG report. In this, as many Indigenous leaders might say, its fate has been not unlike the TRC report.

VIII

In an interview on the eve of Canada Day 2020, former Progressive Conservative prime minister Brian Mulroney mused about life in a post-COVID-19 Canada. He immediately brought up the issue of the country's Indigenous populations. "I consider the aboriginal situation, the Indigenous situation in Canada to be the single greatest blight on our citizenship," he said. "We can't move ahead with a new agenda for Canada if we don't deal with the Indigenous people and systemic racism."[69]

While many of the stories about the days featured in this volume discuss how the events that happened on the day had major ramifications in shaping modern Canada, the day recounted here is, as mentioned in the chapter's opening, slightly different. June 2, 2015, is, at least at the moment, more about its potential than about what the events of the day have actually accomplished. The worry is that it might change very little. But even if that is the case, this day brings with it the recognition of the trauma that has been inflicted within the country. Though Indigenous communities were on the receiving end of this, the trauma—and the TRC clearly showed this—is ultimately shared by the entire nation.

June 2, 2015, is also symbolic. It is about what kind of nation Canada is to become. The history of Canada has been a series of betrayals of First Nations, Inuit, and Métis peoples, so many Indigenous leaders are justifiably dubious. Given the history, it is easy to sympathize with them. But if Canada is to be an egalitarian society, where everyone is treated equally before the law and is involved in the political process—and not just talked about in such a manner—then much hard work remains to integrate these groups successfully into the framework of Canada.

Such an integration, however, cannot involve—as the Indian Act and the residential school system maintained—assimilation. On the contrary, it must involve processes of truth and reconciliation between two parties—Indigenous and non-Indigenous—that recognize the harm, pain, and genocide committed by the latter against the former. In this respect, June 2, 2015, is about what might happen next, and not simply about what did happen. A ceremony in Ottawa and talk of truth and reconciliation can only be fulfilled with deeds and actions that recognize and atone for these past traumas.

SUGGESTIONS FOR FURTHER READING

Mark Abley. *Conversations with a Dead Man: The Legacy of Duncan Campbell Scott.* Madeira Park, BC: Douglas & McIntyre, 2013.

Christopher Alcantara. *Negotiating the Deal: Comprehensive Land Claims Agreements in Canada.* Toronto: University of Toronto Press, 2013.

Lynn Gehl. *Claiming Anishinaabe: Decolonizing the Human Spirit.* Regina: University of Regina Press, 2017.

Bob Joseph. *21 Things You May Not Know About the Indian Act: Helping Canadians Make Reconciliation with Indigenous Peoples a Reality.* Port Coquitlam, BC: Indigenous Relations Press, 2018.

Thomas King. *The Inconvenient Indian: A Curious Account of Native Peoples in North America.* Toronto: Penguin Random House Canada, 2013.

Bev Sellars. *Price Paid: The Fight for First Nations Survival.* Vancouver: TalonBooks, 2016.

Truth and Reconciliation Commission of Canada. *Honouring the Truth, Reconciling for the Future: Summary of the Final Report of the Truth and Reconciliation Commission of Canada.* The document may be found online at www.trc.ca/assets/pdf/Honouring_the_Truth_Reconciling_for_the_Future_July_23_2015.pdf.

SUGGESTIONS FOR FURTHER VIEWING

Howard Adler. *Status.* www.youtube.com/watch?v=y4IMXLYMQ3U&t=13s.

Marie Clements. *The Road Forward.* National Film Board of Canada, 2017.

Alanis Obomsawin. *Trick or Treaty?* National Film Board of Canada, 2014.

Tim Wolochatiuk. *We Were Children.* National Film Board of Canada, 2012.

9

AUGUST 20 2016

The Tragically Hip's Final Concert

"IF YOU'RE A MUSICIAN AND YOU'RE BORN IN CANADA it's in your DNA to like The Tragically Hip" according to songwriter and musician Dallas Green, who records under the name City and Colour.[1] If we distinguish between musicians who, by accident of birth, happen to be Canadian and Canadian musicians, we can safely put The Hip in the latter category. Their songs, replete with references to Canadian events and themes, have formed the soundtrack for a generation of Canadians. While The Hip is not the first band to sing about Canada, the enigmatic quality of their lyrics and their haunting melodies convey something different, something deeper. Their music, neither jingoistic nor nationalistic, gets to the heart of being a country that is constantly at risk of being subsumed by the cultural and artistic productions of a much stronger and boisterous neighbour.

On the morning of May 24, 2016, The Tragically Hip announced on their webpage that lead singer Gord Downie had been diagnosed with glioblastoma, an aggressive and terminal brain cancer. A country mourned. Despite the diagnosis, band members subsequently announced they were preparing to go back on the road one more time, with the full realization that it would probably be their last opportunity to perform together.

After thirty-three years together, thirteen studio albums,[2] and millions of records sold, the band informed fans—again on their website—that they were going "to dig deep, and try to make this our best tour yet. This feels like the right thing to do now, for Gord, and for all of us." In June 2016 the band released their final studio album, *Man Machine Poem*. While the tour was meant to showcase the album, it soon took on a much larger momentum. Their concerts, including setlists, were covered in national newspapers, and even those who had never really liked their music became fans. Through July and August, The Hip and Downie crossed the country, saying goodbye to their fans, and vice versa. On Saturday, August 20, 2016, The Tragically Hip took to the stage for their final concert in their hometown of Kingston, Ontario, in front of a live audience that included Prime Minister Justin Trudeau and his wife, Sophie Grégoire Trudeau. The concert was televised and livestreamed, with millions tuning in either at home or in thousands of makeshift viewing parties that sprang up around the country.

On that night the country was able to say a final goodbye to what had been its most treasured band, fronted by a poet who made a country proud, patriotic, and fiercely grateful for the music. The Hip, after all, were the first act to show that one did not have to make it in the United States to become Canadian superstars.

I

The Tragically Hip, often simply known as The Hip, formed in Kingston in 1984. The members were Gord Downie (vocals), Paul Langlois and Rob Baker (guitars), Gord Sinclair (bass), and Johnny Fay (drums). The band's idiosyncratic name is derived from *Elephant Parts*, a collection of comedy skits and music videos made in 1981 by ex-Monkee Michael Nesmith. One of the clips in the collection asks for contributions to "the Foundation for

The Tragically Hip," an institution for "poor, afflicted people in need of Jacuzzis, Lamborghinis and cocaine."[3] To quote the band, "people either like the name, think it's clever and funny, or think it's really pretentious."

After several years of playing bars and cover songs around Ontario, they met the man who became their manager, Jake Gold, and in 1987 they produced their first EP, self-titled, with the help of Red Rider's Ken Greer. Although the album was given national distribution, it largely passed—like so many first albums—under the radar. They became better known when Bruce Dickinson, the president of MCA records, saw them perform at Toronto's famed Horseshoe Tavern. He offered the band a long-term record deal, and two years later The Hip produced their first full-length album, *Up To Here*, which featured their first two hit singles, "Blow At High Dough" and "New Orleans Is Sinking."

A BBC feature article characterized their music as "a combination of bar bands from the 1960s, stadium rock from the 1970s, and college rock of the 1980s."[4] While not far from the truth, that description tells but part of the story. If anything, the band's style constantly changed over the years, with each album evoking a different set of sound structures as the band explored new styles of expression. If earlier albums were inspired by the blues and classic rock, later albums were more enigmatic, revolving around Downie's unique voice.

In 1990 they received a Juno for Most Promising Group of the Year, the first of what would turn out to be sixteen Junos over their thirty-three-year career. In 1996 they released their sixth studio album, *Trouble at the Henhouse*, which included the song "Ahead by a Century," their most successful single in Canada, and also the last song that the band performed together at their final concert. The album received a Juno for Album of the Year in 1997, and the song was nominated for Song of the Year, but lost out to Alanis Morissette's "Ironic." In 2017, The Jerry Cans, a folk-rock band from Nunavut, created an Inuttitut version of the song, which incorporated traditional Inuit throat-singing.

The Tragically Hip was not just a band. It also figured prominently in Canadian popular culture. In 2002, for example, the band made a cameo appearance in the Canadian romantic comedy *Men with Brooms*, playing at a curling rink in Kingston. Two years later they performed the half-time show at the 2004 Grey Cup in Ottawa. The same year they played an unnamed local band rehearsing in Brent's garage on CTV's *Corner Gas*.

In addition, both the band and Gord Downie individually made frequent cameos on *Trailer Park Boys*. On May 12, 2012, they premiered a 90-second clip from their new song, "At Transformation"—from their twelfth studio album *Now For Plan A*—on the iconic program *Hockey Night in Canada*.

The band was thus intimately connected to Canada's artistic and creative life. It was also involved in many environmental causes, especially in Ontario, working, for example, with the Lake Ontario Waterways, an environmental justice advocacy group. Later in his life, Downie became an important advocate for Indigenous rights and national reconciliation between Indigenous and non-Indigenous Canadians. Band members were named to the Order of Canada on June 19, 2017, for "their contribution to Canadian music and for their support of various social and environmental causes."[5] Downie himself was singled out for "promoting dialogue, raising awareness of the history of residential schools and moving the country along the path to reconciliation."[6] Evidence of this may be seen in *Secret Path*, the multimedia project mentioned in chapter 8.

After Downie's death on October 17, 2017, the band announced in July 2018 that The Tragically Hip name would be retired.[7] Though Downie had wanted the band to find a replacement for him so that the others could continue to record and tour together, the remaining members ultimately chose not to.

II

Despite all their achievements at home, success in the massive and lucrative American market proved to be elusive. They signed a deal early in their career with MCA, and after three albums moved to Atlantic Records; both deals saw their albums released south of the border. Though The Hip would go on to sell over a million and a half records in the States, giving the band what would certainly be considered mid-level success, this was nothing compared to the over ten million records sold in Canada. Many of their shows in the United States were well attended, with the band developing a loyal following in Michigan and upstate New York—namely, in places close to the Canadian border. They also regularly attracted thousands to gigs in cities like Boston, Chicago, and Los Angeles. However, The Hip never made the same name for itself south of the border as it did in this country. But it was also never that kind of band, looking for success at any cost. During the tour for *Trouble at the Henhouse* (1996), they recorded their show at Detroit's Cobo Hall Arena for a live album, *Live Between Us* (1997). Though Universal Music Canada, which retains the rights to the band's Canadian catalogue, released the live album in Canada, The Hip, which had just left Atlantic Records, was between deals in the US, so they experimented by selling the record directly to fans over the internet, making them one of the first to engage in this practice. In 1998, Sire Records took over worldwide distribution (outside Canada) of The Hip's entire catalogue.

This is not to say that they were unknown in the United States. They toured there, performing stints as an opening act for Jimmy Page and Robert Plant for thirty shows in 1995 after the release of what critics call one of their best albums, *Day for Night* (1994). They also opened for the Rolling Stones for four European concerts in the same year. On March 25, 1995, they performed on *Saturday Night Live* thanks to an invitation from Dan Aykroyd, a big fan and fellow Kingston native, who also introduced them.[8] This performance represented the band's highest-profile media appearance in the United States. They chose two of their more arty and less accessible songs—"Nautical Disaster" and "Grace, Too"—as opposed to more easily accessible ones, such as "At the Hundredth Meridian" or "Fifty Mission Cap." Despite such exposure, and the fact that their record sales jumped by close to 60 per cent in the two weeks following the broadcast,[9] their career in that country never took off the way it did in Canada. When asked about their lack of commercial success south of the border, Downie once bristled and said to a reporter from the BBC, "You always ask us about our success or lack of success in the States, which I find absurd. While that is a story of the band, there are so many other stories."[10]

The Hip's mid-level success in the US, however, was nothing like their mammoth success and allure in Canada. The Tragically Hip showed that they—and, by extension, the entire country—no longer needed outside validation, whether from Britain or the United States. The Hip thus signalled a certain level of maturity for the still relatively young nation. Traditionally, prominent Canadians—artists and intellectuals—had to leave the country to be truly appreciated at home. Not only did The Hip stay and perform the majority of their gigs at home, but many of their songs explored themes of Canadian geography and history, documenting the country's scenic landscapes and waterways, and telling its stories in new and often highly original ways. The Hip imagined Canada in the same manner that someone like Bob Dylan or Bruce Springsteen engaged with America: as a deep wellspring of poetic inspiration. On news of Downie's death, Prime Minister Justin Trudeau's response to reporters' questions on Parliament Hill was that Downie had truly "uncovered and told the stories of Canada."[11]

And they most certainly did tell the stories of Canada across their diverse discography. Their songs frequently invoke national themes and concerns, often including little-known references. In "Fifty Mission Cap" from 1992's *Fully Completely*, for example, Downie sings about Bill Barilko, the twenty-four-year-old defenceman who scored the Stanley Cup–winning goal for the Toronto Maple Leafs in 1951. Four months later Barilko disappeared in a single-engine aircraft between Rupert House and Timmins, Ontario. The wreckage was only found eleven years later, the same year the Leafs won their next Stanley Cup. Downie described the song as like "an Amelia Earhart story, except everyone's heard of Amelia Earhart."[12]

The song continues to be played in the warm-up playlist at every Leafs home game. Whenever the band played the Air Canada Centre (renamed Scotiabank Arena in 2018) on Toronto's waterfront, Barilko's retired-jersey banner was left in place during the concert, and whenever they played "Fifty Mission Cap" a spotlight would illuminate the banner in the rafters.[13] Upon his death, the Leafs honoured Downie—who, coincidentally, was the godson of Harry Sinden, Team Canada's 1972 Summit Series–winning coach (see chapter 2)—with a moment of silence before their game on October 18, during which Barilko's retired-jersey banner was lowered from the rafters.[14]

Another well-known song, though never released as a single, was "Wheat Kings" from the album *Fully Completely* (1992). The song, which begins with the call of a solitary loon, goes on to recount the story of David Milgaard, who was wrongly imprisoned for twenty-three years for the killing of Gail Miller, a young nursing student in Saskatoon. The lyrics are not meant to provide history lessons to Canadians. On the contrary, they are atmospheric tone poems that revel in ambiguity and find meaning through stream of consciousness. Take "Bobcaygeon," for example, from *Phantom Power* (1998). The song purportedly refers to Toronto's Christie Pits riot of August 16, 1933, when, at the height of the Great Depression, the local Jewish community clashed with the "Swastika Club," which had formed to keep Jews away from the Beaches, a local swimming area. The riot was precipitated by the unfurling of a Nazi flag at a baseball game. This allusion to the riot in "Bobcaygeon" is given a modern context, especially in the video that accompanied the song. It is worth noting, moreover, that the Christie Pits riot had nothing to do with the actual town of Bobcaygeon, Ontario. Downie once admitted that he used the name "Bobcaygeon" because it was the only place name he could find that came close to rhyming with "constellation."[15]

One of the band's best-known songs, "Courage," which also appears on the *Fully Completely* album from 1992, is subtitled "For Hugh MacLennan," a mid-twentieth-century Canadian novelist. The song interweaves, and also quotes directly from, MacLennan's 1958 novel *The Watch That Ends the Night*. The Hip explained that they used the novel as a way to think about trying to be creative when fame demands that one keep doing the same thing one has always done instead of searching for new creative voices and forms of expression. MacLennan "lamented the public's appetite for the familiar over the unique," the band wrote on their website, and "he remarked that at this difficult moment in his life, he felt homesick even at home."[16] The courage the song references, they explain, "is the will to carry on undeterred. To accept our choices, and adapt accordingly when the choices of others affect us. Move forward into the great unknown."

The Hip also performed "Montreal," a song about the École Polytechnique Massacre on December 6, 1989 (see chapter 5), though it did not appear on an album until 2021's *Saskadelphia*, consisting of six previously unreleased songs connected to the recording of *Road Apples* (1991). Speaking on CBC Radio, feminist commentator Andrea Warner argued that, for the most part, Downie's lyrics afford women agency. "That's so important and seemingly simple," she writes, "women get to be people, not just a prop of male fantasy or wish fulfilment."[17]

Their lyrics threw in many terms and place names—the CBC, Jacques Cartier, the "Paris of the Prairies" (i.e., Saskatoon), Millhaven maximum security penitentiary, Algonquin Park, and Mistaken Point, Newfoundland—familiar to most Canadians. What other band in what other country could use the word "deke" in a love song, as in their "Lonely End of the Rink." The themes of hockey and love also appear in their song "Fireworks."

This is what made The Hip unique. While Canada has seen a number of high-profile musicians over the years—perhaps most famously Neil Young, Joni Mitchell, and Leonard Cohen—many chose to leave Canada. None of them became famous by playing sold-out concerts at Centre 200 in Sydney, Nova Scotia, or Regina's Agridome on a freezing and snowy January evening. One had to leave Canada to become famous. There are also a handful of Canadian musicians—Rush, Drake, the Weeknd, and Justin Bieber—who have strong international audiences and retain an allegiance to Canada, or at least the Greater Toronto Area. The Tragically Hip, however, built a huge following of die-hard homegrown fans at the expense of a larger international following. While all of these other Canadians were and are artists, The Hip were truly Canadian artists.[18]

The Hip were not patriotic or nationalist in the sense that, say, Stompin' Tom Connors was. They saw Canada's faults and were frequently critical of the country, including its treatment of Indigenous Canadians and its environmental degradation. They did not try to instill pride in the greatness of Canada. Instead, they teased out universal themes from moments in Canadian history in ways that were enigmatic and frequently dark. The aforementioned "Bobcaygeon," for example, invokes a historical event but interweaves more modern concerns. Dave Kaufman, writing in the *National Post*, proclaimed that "although Downie sings of Canada, his songs are by no means patriotic, or no more than in the way that we're all influenced by where we're from. The band have never been so obvious as to drape themselves in a Canadian flag, but instead, they evoke that shared experience of what it's meant for many of us to grow up in Canada."[19] Their lyrics were not jingoistic, in other words, but retained the same sort of artistic purity as the paintings of Emily Carr or the Group of Seven.

III

There is no denying the fact that the star of the band was Downie, and clearly the final tour was all about him. In the words of Simon Vozick-Levinson in the *New York Times*, "the place of honor that Mr. Downie occupies in Canada's national imagination has no parallel in the United States. Imagine Bruce Springsteen, Bob Dylan and Michael Stipe combined into one sensitive, oblique poet-philosopher, and you're getting close."[20] Downie received a BA in film studies from Queen's University in his hometown. In Queen's May 2016 convocation ceremony, the university bestowed honorary degrees on the entire band, but Downie did not appear at the ceremony. Just days later he announced to the world that he had been diagnosed with glioblastoma, an aggressive form of brain cancer.

The news shocked the country, quickly becoming a national story. When the band announced it would release an album and undertake a national tour that summer, Canadians—even those who had never been huge fans—came out to show their support for both Downie and The Hip. Shows sold out within minutes. I will discuss the final concert in the next section, but for now it's enough to say that the depth of Downie's lyrics and the unique cadences of his voice touched a chord with Canadians from all walks of life.

In addition to his career with The Tragically Hip, Downie released seven solo albums (including one with The Country of Miracles and one with The Sadies). *Coke Machine Glow*, his first solo album, was also the title of his first book of poetry and prose.[21] Downie's poetry echoes his lyrics in its depth and attunement to the natural world. In "Toboggan Hill," for example, we read:

> I'm thinking back to when we were young
> and eating donuts
> with a set of plastic vampire teeth
> that we were passing back and forth.
> We weren't so young as to
> think a dog was a horse.
> Nor were we old enough yet to name
> the cold purpose of musical chairs.
> We were like-minded spirits
> eking out a rhythm
> whispering transmissions
> through wet woollen mittens.
> Growing up on a toboggan hill
> Nothing was material.
>
> I'm thinking back to when we were young
> if only to find out
> forensically
> what it was
> we used to
> want.[22]

In the aftermath of The Hip's final tour, Downie announced the forthcoming release of his fifth solo album *Secret Path*, a multimedia art project, including an album, graphic novel, and animated television program that aired on CBC on October 23, 2016.[23] The work recounts the story of Chanie Wenjack, a young Anishinaabe boy, who died in 1966 after escaping from a residential school in order to return home. Two days prior to the film's release, Downie performed the entire album in a concert at Roy Thomson Hall in Toronto, which turned out to be his final full-concert performance. In attendance at the concert were members of Wenjack's family. The concert was aired by CBC Television after Downie's death. At the 2017 Juno Awards ceremony, the album received two Junos—one for Adult Alternative Album of the Year and one for Recording Package of the Year. In addition, Downie won the Juno for Songwriter of the Year.

In an interview with CBC's Peter Mansbridge on October 13, 2016, Downie talked about how important reconciliation between Indigenous and non-Indigenous Canadians was to him. This concern was shared by the entire band. The Hip, for example, performed in a high school gym at Fort Albany, Ontario, near the Attawapiskat First Nation on James Bay, which at the time (February 2012) was in the news for abysmal housing and the lack of a school.[24] While critical of how relations between the two groups had played out over the previous 150 years, Downie held out great hope for the next 150. He worked tirelessly on reconciliation in the final years of his life, and he created the Gord Downie and Chanie Wenjack Foundation to facilitate this reconciliation.[25] On December 6, 2016, in a tearful ceremony, Assembly of First Nations National Chief Perry Bellegarde honoured Downie with an eagle feather, a symbol of the Creator, for his support of Indigenous peoples in Canada. He also bestowed on the singer an honorary Aboriginal name, Wicapi Omani, Lakota for "man who walks among the stars."[26]

On December 22, 2016, Downie was selected as Canadian Press Canadian Newsmaker of the Year, the first time an entertainer had ever been selected for the honour. He was chosen again for the title in December 2017, posthumously, and in recognition of the public reaction to his death.[27] In September 2017, Downie announced that a solo double album, *Introduce Yerself*, would be forthcoming. It was released posthumously on October 27, 2017, just ten days after his death. 2020 also saw the posthumous release of his final album, *Away is Mine*, recorded three months before he died.

On hearing of Downie's death, Justin Trudeau held a press conference on Parliament Hill and, holding back tears, remembered Downie as "Our buddy Gord, who loved this country with everything he had—and not just loved it in a nebulous, 'Oh, I love Canada' way. He loved every hidden corner, every story, every aspect of this country that he celebrated his whole life."[28]

IV

On the evening of August 2, 2016, The Hip performed their final concert in Kingston's Rogers K-Rock Centre. The show marked the final stop on their *Man Machine Poem* tour. The band donated a portion of the proceeds from the tour to the Sunnybrook Hospital in Toronto. During the tour, both Sunnybrook and the Canadian Cancer Society reported significant increases in direct donations, as fans rallied around the band and its ailing singer.[29] Many of the donations, both the hospital and the society said, came from bake sales, raffles, and concert-viewing parties, in addition to ticket sales from the concerts.

The fifteen-show tour—which included two shows each in Vancouver, Calgary, and Edmonton, and three in Toronto—saw the band perform concerts only every second night so Downie had time to rest between shows. He also travelled with a doctor and a team of other experts to ensure there were no problems on the road.[30] The effects of the glioblastoma and its treatment meant that Downie could not remember the lyrics to the songs he had spent a lifetime writing and needed to have multiple teleprompters on stage to aid him. Though he was exhausted after each performance, the concerts were remarkable successes, and the tour concluded without any major problems.

The Kingston concert was simulcast as a CBC special, *The Tragically Hip: A National Celebration*, which aired on its television, radio, and satellite radio platforms, in addition to its YouTube channel.[31] This was despite the fact that the concert took place on the second-last night of the Summer Olympics in Rio de Janeiro. Ron MacLean, host of the CBC's coverage of the Games, introduced the concert from Rio, where Canadian athletes had a viewing party at the Olympic Village.[32] Turning the proceedings over to Kingston, MacLean, invoking one of The Hip's most popular songs, "Wheat Kings," signed off by saying: "We now go to this late-breaking story on the

CBC." The band had also invited Justin Trudeau and his family to attend.[33] Indeed, aside from the music, the most dramatic moment of the evening was when Downie, from centre stage, personally called out to Trudeau to act on his rhetoric of reconciliation with Indigenous Canadians.

An audience of at least twelve million watched the final concert live. Canadians set up private viewing parties. Cities and towns across the country also held public broadcasts, including one at Kingston's Springer Market Square that was attended by approximately 22,000 people. Another significant viewing party was in Bobcaygeon, the town made famous by The Hip. Even though the band, as noted, never really cracked the international market, the nature of the final tour created considerable buzz in the United States and Europe. Outlets such as the BBC, *The Guardian*, *The New Yorker*, *The New York Times*, and CNN covered the final tour, but especially the last concert date. They were all fascinated by the intimate relationship between the band and the country. These international treatments ran the gamut from the sublime to the ridiculous, as non-Canadian, and even some Canadian, journalists sought to explain the band's success in Canada to non-Canadians. They could be insulting, especially when national stereotypes became the default position. The *New Yorker*'s Edmonton-born Steven Marche, for example resorted to a silly characterization of the audience as "pure Canadiana. The men looked like retired hockey players who had eased themselves into dad bods. The women looked like the daughters of the mothers in Alice Munro stories."[34] Or, they could be more informed and attuned to the pulse of the nation, such as the BBC's portrayal of the band as having, more so than any other Canadian artist, "reflected [on] the sense of what it's like to love and live in a beautiful, overlooked country."[35] That story went so far as to suggest historical reasons for the band's popularity in Canada:

> To understand why the Hip resonates, it's essential to understand Canada's place in the world. From Confederation in 1867 to the end of World War II in 1945, the country lived in the shadow of Great Britain. After the United States became the dominant world power, Canada became dwarfed by America.

Regardless of the international response, the final performance was a purely Canadian affair. Canadians, at home and abroad, long-time fans or the newly converted, watched together as The Hip gave one last live performance. It united the country in ways not seen since the final of the Summit Series in Moscow, when Canadians watched the game—and Henderson's winning goal—on their television sets. Though if the Summit Series was a time of joy and celebration, the concert was one of sadness and uncertainty.

V

It is perhaps telling that Calixa Lavallée (1842–1891), the person who composed the music for "O Canada," the country's national anthem, eventually moved to the United States. Upon his departure he wrote: "When one returns here, one realizes the insignificance of the ideas of our poor country...an artist is not meant to rot in an obscure place and especially in an even more obscure country."[36] After fighting in the American Civil War and marrying a woman from Massachusetts, he died an American citizen.

The late Canadian writer David Rakoff, who lived much of his life in New York City, once remarked that certain things made sense only if you lived your whole life next to a "culturally obliterating behemoth."[37] He was stating what Pierre Elliott Trudeau had said, a little more comically, on March 25, 1969, when, addressing the Press Club in Washington, DC, he spoke of the relationship between the United States and Canada in the following terms: "Living next to [the United States] is in some ways like sleeping with an elephant. No matter how friendly and even-tempered is the beast, if I can call it that, one is affected by every twitch and grunt."

The reasons for the tremendous popularity of The Hip in Canada—not to mention their relative obscurity outside the country—are in many ways obvious. In a country where virtually all of one's popular culture, from music to television, from books to movies, comes from a larger (in terms of population), more arrogant, and much louder neighbour, it is no surprise that Canadians were, and indeed still are, fiercely protective of The Hip.

The fact that they did not make it big in the United States is proof positive of this. Canadians did not need to have American validation to like them. Other artists—perhaps most famously Neil Young—moved down to the US, where they made lives and careers for themselves. When Young finally became an American citizen in 2020, he posted a picture of himself on Instagram saluting next to an American flag and a sign proclaiming "Democrats, register to vote."[38] Though he did not repudiate his Canadian citizenship, when he chastised Donald Trump in an open letter less than a month after he had become an American, he used the phrase "you are a disgrace to *my* country."[39] Canadians might have thought to themselves, "What's wrong with your real country?"

The Hip, however, were different. While they certainly had mid-level success south of the border, they did not care enough to do what they needed to do to gain American fans. Anything that did not conform to American tastes or the so-called American experience, to return to Rakoff's comments, had to be excised. The Hip chose not to. While a band like Rush might release a song with the title "YYZ," it is worth mentioning that it is an instrumental with no lyrics or invocation of Toronto.[40] Unlike other Canadian artists, many of whom moved—and continue to move—to the US because of its huge market and influence, The Hip stayed put. And this only increased their social capital in their own country. Canadians saw in them what Americans did not and could not. The band thus came to symbolize the difference between the two countries in ways that only popular culture or sport can reveal. With the election of Donald Trump to the American presidency less than three months after that final concert in Kingston, these differences grew, as did the tensions between the two countries.

There have been other Canadian bands that never made it big south of the border. Bands like April Wine, Triumph, and Chilliwack, which continue to have large followings in Canada. But The Hip were not like these other bands. Their use of moments, some obscure, from Canadian history, the intellectual inflection of Downie's songwriting, and his charismatic presence on stage set the band apart from these others. This combination of Canadian themes and motifs in their songs and the fact that they refused to change these themes and motifs to appeal to the American market helps to explain The Hip's success at home.

To simply call them a Canadian band—or as they are sometimes called "Canada's band"—is perhaps too neat and tidy. As Michael Barclay has noted, Downie's subject matter was always broader than he was given credit for. He is also correct to note that "this country has dozens of Gord

Downies, all of whom tell Canadian stories in vivid detail, all of whom critically examine the notion of Canada itself."[41]

It is also worth noting that the band's fan base was largely white. A quick look at any concert footage, for example, tends to reveal a sea of white faces. And The Hip's Canada was, by and large, primarily anglophone. Their songs are, for the most part, about English Canadian events. Despite this, The Hip and Gord Downie allowed Canadians to feel like they could lay claim to something in pop culture.

VI

Canadians have a long and complicated relationship with the United States. It is a relationship that The Hip underscores. The United States and Canada share the world's longest international border, at close to 9,000 kilometres in length. This is reflected historically in the high volume of bilateral trade, with nearly US$2 billion per day in goods and services, and roughly 400,000 people per day—at least in the pre-COVID-19 world—crossing between the two countries. Canadian schoolchildren learn about American history at school and are exposed regularly to American popular culture through American television channels and radio stations. The border between the two countries is rather porous, with ideas generally moving in one direction, from south to north.

A poll released by the Pew Research Center in 2015—the year prior to the election of Donald Trump as the American president—found that the majority of Canadians (68 per cent) had a favourable view of the US.[42] There is, however, a sharp partisan divide based on party allegiance: 84 per cent of those who voted for the Conservatives had a positive view of the US; this number dropped to 71 per cent for those who voted for Liberals and only 58 per cent for those who supported the New Democratic Party. Such positive numbers dropped radically in the Trump era. A 2017 Gallup poll found that only 20 per cent of Canadians had a favourable opinion of the American leader.[43] This was even before Trump's dreadful handling of the COVID-19 pandemic. Interestingly, the same poll saw 94 per cent of Americans saying they had a favourable opinion of the Canadian prime minister, Justin Trudeau.

A July 2020 poll, taken during the pandemic by the polling firm Abacus Data, surveyed American perceptions of Canada and Canadians.

The majority of Americans thought that Canada had a better health-care system (60 per cent), more effective measures in place to combat the COVID-19 pandemic (61 per cent), better gun-control measures (56 per cent), a cleaner environment (70 per cent), a better approach to immigration (63 per cent), less racial discrimination (70 per cent), and a better leader (54 per cent).[44] An amazing 53 per cent of Americans aged 18–30 would prefer to live in Canada. The same poll also revealed that 27 per cent of Americans would support US troops being positioned along the border, and 23 per cent of Trump voters thought that the US should invade Canada to take advantage of its resources.[45]

Another Abacus Data poll, this one from June 2020, commissioned by Toronto's Citytv, revealed that Canadians have a much less favourable opinion of Americans, especially when it came to racism. When asked "Do you think President Trump's actions have caused racism against people of colour to increase?" 50 per cent of Canadians said "certainly" and 31 per said "probably." When asked "Do you think discrimination happens in the U.S.A. today?" 66 per cent said "frequently" and 24 per cent said "quite often," while 9 per cent said "from time to time" and 2 per cent said they think discrimination "never" happens in the US.[46] The same poll also found that 61 per cent of Canadians believed that institutional racism exists in Canada.

Misperceptions abound on both sides of the border, and the Trump years have only exacerbated this. If Liberal Americans see Canada as a socialist utopia, they clearly misunderstand the troubles Canada faces. Moreover, if some Canadians think that America is a "land of milk and honey," where taxes are low and opportunities great, they obviously have little idea of the tremendous structural problems inherent in American society. Many of these problems have been exposed by the COVID-19 pandemic.

In an op-ed in the *Globe and Mail*, Laura Dawson, director of the Canada Institute at the Wilson Center in Washington, wrote:

> There is now a growing sense that we've been duped into investing in a relationship that was never as strong as we thought it was. It is dawning on Canadians that Americans—or at least those in charge—don't think much of us or think of us much at all. It is as though Canadians look at Americans

through one end of a telescope—everything looks close up and large—while Americans look at Canadians through the other end of the lens—small, distant and unimportant.[47]

Responding to the "America first" attitude and aggressive protectionism of the Make America Great Again movement, Dawson lamented Trump's on-again, off-again threats of a trade war with Canada. Trump's bargaining technique, she argued, "creates bad faith, and therefore only works in one-time interactions." But when such interactions must be repeated—after all, there is only one Canada, and it lives next door—a sense of commonality based on trust and a set of shared interests ought to carry the day. Even now that Trump is out of office, the tensions remain and do not seem to be going away anytime soon.

The Hip gave Canadians something to hold on to, a lifeline in a storm of American aggression under a fickle leader. It is a coincidence, but nonetheless symbolic, that exactly one month before The Hip's last concert, Donald Trump accepted the Republican nomination at the party's national convention in Cleveland. As America was set on an impending course of divisiveness, its northern neighbour was unifying around a band on its final tour.

VII

When The Hip took to the stage on the evening of August 20, 2016, before a packed arena in Kingston, the country was about to enter a new era. If so much of the Canadian narrative is—and has been—about figuring out its relationship to the United States, often defining itself by what that other country is not, Canada was, unwittingly, on the verge of a new relationship with its neighbour to the south. Interactions between the two nations have usually been cordial—with the occasional blip followed by a quick reconciliation—but the new administration in Washington signalled that things were going to change. In the four years following the concert, Canadians witnessed the US slap punitive duties on their goods, uncomfortable rhetoric threatening placement of the American army along the forty-ninth parallel, and, most recently, closure of the border between the two countries because the US was unable or unwilling to deal adequately with the COVID-19 virus.

When Trump tweeted, upon his departure from Quebec City's G-7 meeting in June 2018, that Trudeau was "very dishonest and weak," most Canadians took exception to the remarks. Two years later, when Trump invited Trudeau and Mexican president Andrés Manuel López Obrador to Washington to a ceremony meant to show solidarity in light of the new United States-Mexico-Canada Agreement, Trudeau politely declined. That the meeting would have taken place during the height of the first wave of the COVID-19 pandemic in the United States—a pandemic that Trump described soon after as like "sniffles"—was the likely reason Trudeau did not attend, though he, diplomatically, said it was the result of scheduling conflicts.[48]

The COVID-19 pandemic has further heightened tensions between the two neighbours. The border between the two countries was closed on May 21, 2020, to all but essential travel. On July 3, 2020, a bipartisan group of twenty-nine members of the US Congress penned an open letter to public safety minister Bill Blair, calling on the Canadian government to plan a phased reopening of the Canada-US border and to consider easing existing measures.[49] Despite the plea, Canadian leaders—with the strong backing of the overwhelming majority of Canadians—steadfastly disagreed with the assessment.[50] It was not until August 2021 that Canada slowly began to reopen the border to non-essential travellers.

It is against this increasingly tortured relationship that we can situate The Tragically Hip. They symbolize, perhaps more than anyone, the sense that Canadians have of their country's place in the world. The relationship between The Hip and Canada—on full display that hot and muggy August night in Kingston—is, in the final analysis, part of the much larger narrative of how Canada perceives itself, often in the light of its unruly neighbour. As Canadians face a constant barrage of cultural imports—in stores, on screens, and on the radio—The Hip offered an alternative. They chose to stay in Canada and perform their beloved songs across its length and breadth, from Toronto's Air Canada Centre to high school gyms in Indigenous communities scattered across the North. Canadians loved them for it. That final concert was an acknowledgement of the special relationship between a band, its rapidly expanding fan base that came to include most Canadians in the summer of 2016, and the country in which they all cohabit. Just as importantly, however, it was also an acknowledgement that Canada was in good shape and could, at long last, take comfort in its own cultural and artistic productions.

SUGGESTIONS FOR FURTHER READING

Michael Barclay. *The Never-Ending Present: The Story of Gord Downie and The Tragically Hip*. Toronto: ECW Press, 2018.

Corey Ross Cole. *Hard Canadian: A Completist's Guide to Gord Downie and The Tragically Hip*. CreateSpace Independent Publishing Platform, 2018.

Gordon Downie. *Coke Machine Glow*. Toronto: Vintage Canada, 2001.

Ryan Edwardson. *Canuck Rock: A History of Canadian Popular Music*. Toronto: University of Toronto Press, 2009.

Bob Mersereau. *The History of Canadian Rock 'n' Roll*. Lanham, MD: Backbeat Books, 2015.

Marc Shapiro. *What is Hip? The Life and Times of The Tragically Hip*. Riverdale, NY: Riverdale Avenue Books, 2017.

SUGGESTIONS FOR FURTHER VIEWING

Jennifer Baichwal and Nicholas de Pencier. *Long Time Running*. Elevation Pictures & Bell Media, 2017.

Andy Keen. *The Tragically Hip in Bobcaygeon*. Universal Music Canada & Regular Horse Productions, 2013.

Pierre and François Lamoureux. *That Night in Toronto*. Universal Music Canada, 2005.

David Russell. *The Tragically Hip: A National Celebration* (DVD of their final concert). CBC & Insight Production Company, 2016.

10

MARCH 8 2018

A New Ten-Dollar Bill

IN KEEPING WITH THE TENOR OF THE LAST CHAPTER, and echoing one of its major themes, we would do well to remember that sharing a border with the United States creates a number of issues. We see this most clearly when it comes to the topic of race. Because of the latter country's history of slavery, its increasing return to overt forms of racism, and wanton police violence against African Americans, there is a tendency for Canadians to pat themselves on the back while boldly proclaiming that when it comes to racism, we have it all figured out. Canada, we are told, is a tolerant country based on the virtues of multiculturalism. A quick look at white Canada's treatment of Indigenous populations, as seen in chapter 8, should quickly put such a congratulatory attitude to rest. Residential schools, political disenfranchisement, abysmal conditions on reserves, and excessive rates of incarceration for Indigenous populations tell a much different—indeed, a much more uncomfortable—story than many want to hear.

To this, it is also necessary to add the story of Black Canadians.[1] We could point, as many inevitably do, to the fact that the British government promised freedom to Black Loyalists during the American War of Independence, or that Nova Scotia was home in the late eighteenth century to the largest free Black community in British North America, or that many slaves in the United States escaped to freedom in Canada through the Underground Railroad. While all this is certainly true, it unfortunately overlooks many of the real problems—social, structural, institutional, political—that Black Canadians have faced over the decades, and that they continue to face.

Coinciding with this overly rosy narrative there exists a much different one. While Black Loyalists were welcome in Nova Scotia, they encountered unfair and unequal treatment compared to white Loyalists. They were, for example, given much smaller plots of land and fewer provisions than their white counterparts—if they received land and provisions at all. Black labourers were paid lower wages than white labourers. Local towns often passed discriminatory bylaws that penalized Black people for "offences" such as dancing or loitering. And then there is the case of Halifax's Africville, where Black Haligonians lived in cramped conditions with none of the services afforded to their white counterparts.

The date that this chapter celebrates is a little more amorphous than those in previous chapters. While it might have been useful to use a date when, say, "Jim Crow" laws were repealed in Canada, we never really had such laws. Likewise, it would be convenient to use a date when systemic racism in Canada was clear to all, such as happened in the United Kingdom with the murder of Stephen Lawrence and the subsequent inquiry into his death, but again, there is no such date. While racism in Canada is everywhere, connecting it to a specific date is difficult. Indeed, that would seem to be the whole point with structural and institutional racism. I have chosen March 8, 2018, because it commemorates injustice and, just as importantly, hopefully illuminates the path to a more just future.

When federal finance minister Bill Morneau and Bank of Canada governor Stephen Poloz unveiled the new ten-dollar bill in a historic ceremony in Halifax on March 8, 2018—International Women's Day—Viola Desmond (1914–1965) became both the first woman (other than the Queen) and the first Black Canadian to appear on regular Canadian currency.[2] The purple polymer bill—the first vertically oriented banknote issued in Canada—also included an old map of Halifax's north end, the city's historic Black neighbourhood, in the background behind Desmond. On the reverse side was a picture of the Canadian Museum for Human Rights in Winnipeg, an eagle feather, and a quotation from section 15 of the Charter of Rights and Freedoms: "Every individual is equal before and under the law and has the right to the equal protection and equal benefit of the law without discrimination."

The new ten-dollar bill was meant to showcase the important but often overlooked role of women in Canada's past, while simultaneously acknowledging the wrongs committed against visible minorities. The new bill, in other words, draws our attention, even if symbolically, to the problems inherent in Canadian society, including the various institutions that perpetuate such wrongs. March 8, 2018, then, is another one of those days that represents the culmination of injustice and the desire to move forward. As with the release of the Executive Summary of the Truth and Reconciliation Committee, however, it remains to be seen what kind of forward movement there will be. It could be symbolic and reduced to a colourful banknote, or it could be structural and create positive change in Canadian society.

I

Black communities have existed in Canada since before Confederation. The earliest were established by those individuals who arrived in New France in the seventeenth century, either as free persons serving in the French navy or as indentured servants of various colonial administrators. When New France was ceded to England, French colonists were allowed to retain their slaves, despite the fact that slaves could no longer be bought or sold.

The American War of Independence (1775–1783) saw the arrival of both Black slaves who came with white Loyalists—namely, those American colonists who had stayed loyal to the British Crown—and Black Loyalists, who had escaped slavery and joined other Loyalists because of the British promise of freedom. Many of the latter arrived in Nova Scotia, where they were promised land grants and supplies to help them resettle. Between April and November 1783 roughly three thousand Black Loyalists made their way to Nova Scotia, which at the time also included modern-day

New Brunswick.[3] These Black Loyalists founded settlements throughout the region, the largest being at Birchtown, near Shelburne in the southwest part of Nova Scotia. With an initial population of about 1,500, Birchtown would come to be the largest free Black community in British North America. Another community, Preston, in the greater Halifax area, is today the place with the highest per capita number of Black residents in Canada, with 69.4 per cent of the population identifying as Black.

Upon their arrival in Nova Scotia, Black Loyalist settlers faced many difficulties because of discrimination. They received less land (if they received any at all), were provided with fewer provisions, and were paid lower wages than white Loyalists. Since many had come from the much warmer climates of colonies such as Virginia and South Carolina, they found the cold climate to be particularly challenging. After a few years, roughly 1,200 decided to leave Canada and set sail for Africa. There, on March 11, 1792, they formed the core of a group of former slaves that founded Freetown in the new British colony of Sierra Leone.[4]

The War of 1812, fought between the United States and Britain, witnessed a second wave of Black migration to what would become Canada. This wave included a large number of former slaves entering the country. These individuals, often referred to as Black refugees, numbered as many as thirty thousand, with most arriving alone or in small groups. Though many formed communities in Upper Canada, which would later become Ontario, the majority of these Black refugees settled in the rural areas around Halifax, with the largest communities established at Preston, Hammonds Plains, and Beechville. Though pleased to have escaped servitude and to be establishing communities of their own, they too faced social and governmental prejudice. The local government, for example, did not give the Black refugees outright grants to the land they inhabited, but instead offered them tickets of location or licences of occupation. This denied the Black refugees the opportunity to own the land on which they lived or to sell it for a profit. The lots provided by the government were limited to ten acres and tended to be located on rocky, infertile soil, which made farming difficult. In such conditions, the crops planted by Black refugees repeatedly failed.

To make matters worse, the white population of Nova Scotia resented the Black refugees' dependence on the government and, just as significantly, refused to accept them as equal members of society.

Provincial authorities protested that the refugees were "unfitted by nature to this climate, or to an association with the rest of His Majesty's Colonists."[5] In 1821, colonial authorities attempted to remove the Black refugees from Nova Scotia by pressuring them to resettle in Trinidad, but the majority refused to relocate to any place where slavery was still legal. White society seems to have had difficulty accepting the new immigrants as free settlers because, in their minds, the colour of their skin was associated with slavery. As a result, the Black refugees were largely excluded from Nova Scotian society. When compared to life in the United States at the time, things may well have been theoretically better for Black immigrants, but practically, social, political, and legal discrimination made their lives difficult.

In 1829, the American government requested the extradition of a person who had helped a slave escape to the colony. In response to the request, the executive council of Lower Canada replied, "The state of slavery is not recognized by the Law of Canada...Every Slave therefore who comes into the Province is immediately free whether he has been brought in by violence or has entered it of his own accord."[6] Four years later, in 1833, the British government formally outlawed slavery throughout its Empire.

Unlike in the southern United States, there were no "Jim Crow" laws—that is, laws designed to maintain racial segregation—in Canada at the federal level of government, and, outside of education, none at the provincial level of government.[7] Instead, segregation tended to be dependent on the prejudices of local school board trustees, businessmen, union leaders, and landlords. In those circles, there was plenty of prejudice to go around. The Common School Act of 1850, for example, imposed segregation in Canada West (later Ontario), and the Education Act of 1865 did the same thing in Nova Scotia. In 1911, the federal government went so far as to pass Order-in-Council 1911-1324, which was intended to stop the entry of Black immigrants to Canada:

> His excellency in Council, in virtue of the provisions of Sub-section (c) of Section 38 of the Immigration Act, is pleased to Order and it is hereby Ordered as follows: For a period of one year from and after the date hereof the landing in Canada shall be and the same is prohibited

> of any immigrants belonging to the Negro race, which race is deemed unsuitable to the climate and requirements of Canada.[8]

Though this regulation was not written into the Immigration Act, it nevertheless attests to the government's desire to prevent Black settlement

in Canada. In addition, Canadian authorities paid for agents to give presentations in the United States to warn African Americans that Canada would be an unsuitable destination.[9]

Canada's first female magistrate and suffragist Emily Murphy (1868–1933)—also known by her pen name "Janey Canuck"—was highly critical of non-white immigrants. She accused "the Negro," for example, of both drug use and drug dealing, and described Chinese Canadians as opium peddlers "of fishy blood." Both of these groups, she argued, were out to undermine the white race.[10] "Negros," according to Murphy, were "obstinately wicked persons, earning their livelihood as free-ranging peddlers of poisonous drugs. Even when deported, they make their way back to Canada carrying on their operations in a different part of the country."[11] It was prejudices such as Murphy's that established a connection between Black Canadians, drug use, and crime in the minds of many white Canadians—a connection that persists to the present. It is also because of such disturbing comments that when the shortlist of women being considered to appear on the new ten-dollar bill was announced, her name was nowhere to be found.

During the global economic hardships of the 1930s and 1940s, many Black Canadian villages and hamlets in both Ontario and Nova Scotia, which had been founded in the previous century as Loyalist settlements, were abandoned as their inhabitants moved to cities in search of work. This led to an increase in anti-Black racism as Black Canadians encountered informal "Jim Crow" restrictions in many restaurants, bars, hotels, and theatres, with many landlords refusing to rent to Black tenants.

Today the overwhelming majority of Black Canadians live in cities, with many Black immigrants settling in provinces where the language of their country of origin is spoken. For example, 90 per cent of Canadians of Haitian origin live in Quebec,[12] and some 85 per cent of Canadians of Jamaican origin live in Ontario.[13] According to the 2016 census, Black

Canadians form the third-largest visible minority group in Canada, after South Asian and Chinese Canadians, with close to 1.2 million Black Canadian individuals.[14]

II

Despite the lengthy history of Black settlement in Canada, there have been—and this is clear even from the quick historical survey above—numerous systemic problems inherent in mainstream (read: white) Canadian society that have put Black Canadians at a disadvantage. Nowhere is this on clearer display than in the unfortunate situation that unfolded in Africville.

In 1848, William Brown Sr. and William Arnold, two Black refugees, were the first to purchase land on the southern shore of the Bedford Basin in Halifax.[15] People from the Black refugee communities at Hammonds Plains and Preston began settling there, and the area gradually became known as Africville. In spite of Black residents' determination, the City of Halifax neglected the community at every turn, failing to provide the same infrastructure and services given to other Haligonians. Residents of Africville, for example, were denied access to clean water, sanitation, paved roads, street lights, and garbage removal. The city also began to use the area as an industrial site, introducing a waste-treatment facility, an infectious disease hospital, a prison, and a dump nearby. Due to poverty, exacerbated by the poor infrastructure and the nearby waste-treatment facility, many of the residents of Africville struggled with poor health and lack of access to proper medical facilities.

In January 1964, without any consultation with residents, the City of Halifax announced it would relocate Africville's inhabitants to newer and better housing. "In this country, when you own a piece of land," said resident Joe Skinner at the time of the eviction, "you are not a second-class citizen."[16] Those who could not supply deeds to their properties, and many could not, were offered $500 cash, with the last house destroyed in January 1970. Though many of the homes in the community had reached a state of disrepair, the destruction of Africville also happened to coincide with an expansion of the Port of Halifax and development of the nearby A. Murray MacKay Bridge, which links the Halifax Peninsula with neighbouring Dartmouth.

It was an unfortunate period in Canadian history that saw a marginalized community with little to no infrastructure displaced to make way for construction that would privilege a white majority. The destruction uprooted an historic community and undermined the social bonds that it had created. Many of Africville's former inhabitants faced racism from white neighbours in their new homes, including local petitions that wanted to keep communities all white. In the 1980s, the Africville Genealogy Society was established and sought compensation for former residents because of the suffering they had endured from the destruction of their community.

Soon after this, former residents and activists began a long protest on the site against their treatment. On July 5, 2002, federal heritage minister Sheila Copps declared the former neighbourhood a national historic site.[17] And finally, on February 24, 2010, some thirty years after the community's destruction, Halifax mayor Peter Kelly offered a public apology to former residents and their descendants. "We realize words cannot undo what has been done," he said, "but we are profoundly sorry and apologize to each and every one of you. The repercussions of what happened to Africville linger to this day. They haunt us in the form of lost opportunities for the young people who never were nurtured in the rich traditions, culture and heritage of Africville."[18] The apology also came with a pledge of $5 million. In 2017, the Seaview Baptist church, which had functioned as the heart of the community, was rebuilt. It now houses the Africville Museum.[19]

When award-winning playwright George Elliott Clarke was interviewed in Halifax on the opening of his play *Settling Africville*, he told the interviewer that, though the community ultimately ended tragically, it was nevertheless important to be aware of some of the positive developments in that place. Africville, like other Black communities in Nova Scotia, he noted, "was less about awful land grants than it was about ex-African Americans determining to build free lives—together—even if on poor land."[20] This perseverance, including the creation of strong and vibrant communities, unfortunately took place on the margins of Canadian society because of that society's institutional racism.

III

Eighteen years before the razing of Africville, and nine years before Rosa Parks famously refused to give up her seat on a bus in Montgomery, Alabama, one of Canada's most notorious and publicized incidents of racial discrimination unfolded in a New Glasgow movie theatre. Viola Desmond, a resident of Halifax, was an unlikely candidate to be the catalyst for jump-starting the modern civil rights movement in Canada. The daughter of a Black mother and a white father, she grew up aware of the absence of hair and skin-care products for Black women. In order to rectify the situation, she sought, at a young age, to become a beautician. Since she was not allowed to train in Halifax because of the colour of her skin, she went to study in Montreal, Atlantic City, and New York to receive the proper training. Upon completion of her training, she returned to Halifax to start her own hair salon.[21]

Desmond was an astute business woman. She opened the Desmond School of Beauty Culture so that Black women would not have to travel as far as she had to receive proper instruction. Her goal was to train other women who had been denied admission to white beauty schools. She then encouraged her former pupils to open their own businesses, which would, in turn, provide jobs for other Black women within their communities. In addition to all this, Desmond also started her own line of hair and skin-care products, called Vi's Beauty Products, which she marketed and sold herself.

On November 8, 1946, Viola Desmond set out from Halifax by car to travel to Sydney in Cape Breton to sell her beauty products. Her car broke down in New Glasgow, and when she was told that she would have to wait a day before the parts to fix it became available, she decided to pass the time by going to see a movie at a local cinema. Though there were no formal laws enforcing segregation in movie theatres in New Glasgow, it was unofficial policy that main floor seats were reserved solely for the use of white patrons, so Desmond was sold a ticket in the balcony. Since there was no sign informing patrons of the "rule," Desmond, unaware of the theatre's policy, decided to find a seat on the main floor so she could be closer to the screen because of her nearsightedness. When she was asked to move, she refused owing to the better view the floor seat afforded her. She was then forcibly removed from the theatre and arrested. She spent the night in jail, was not informed of her right to legal advice, a lawyer, or legal counsel, and the next day was convicted of tax evasion. The tax on the balcony ticket was two cents, whereas the tax on the floor ticket was three cents, so she was convicted of having deprived the Government of Nova Scotia one cent in tax. Desmond was fined twenty dollars.

With the help of her church and the Nova Scotia Association for the Advancement of Coloured People, Desmond hired a lawyer to represent her in an appeal of the decision, but they did so on the grounds that Desmond had been wrongfully accused of tax evasion rather than arguing that racial discrimination had taken place.[22] In dismissing the appeal, Justice William Lorimer Hall wrote:

> Had the matter reached the court by some other method than *certiorari* [judicial review of the reasons for the original conviction] there might have been an opportunity to right the wrong done this unfortunate woman. One wonders if the manager of the theatre who laid the complaint was so zealous because of a bona fide belief that there had been an attempt to defraud the province of Nova Scotia of the sum of one cent, or was it a surreptitious endeavour to enforce a Jim Crow rule by misuse of a public statute.[23]

Hall seems to intimate here that had Desmond's lawyer appealed on the basis of racial discrimination, the outcome of the appeal might well have been different.

Desmond and her lawyer also tried, unsuccessfully, to file a lawsuit against the Roseland Theatre in New Glasgow. After the trial and appeal, Desmond left Halifax for Montreal and eventually died in New York City at the age of fifty in 1965.

Reflecting on the case fifteen years later, William Pearly Oliver, Desmond's minster at the Cornwallis Street Baptist Church in Halifax, remarked:

> This meant something to our people. Neither before or since has there been such an aggressive effort to obtain rights. The people arose as one and with one voice. This positive stand enhanced the prestige of the Negro community throughout

the Province. It is my conviction that much of the positive action that has since taken place stemmed from this.[24]

It was only on April 14, 2010—sixty-four years after her conviction and fifty-five years after her death—that Desmond was granted a posthumous pardon, the first ever to be granted in Canada.[25] The Government of Nova Scotia also apologized the following day for prosecuting her for tax evasion and acknowledged she was rightfully resisting racial discrimination when the arrest had occurred.[26]

Viola Desmond thus came to play a crucial role in the modern civil rights movement in Canada. She is sometimes referred to as "Canada's Rosa Parks." This is unfortunate as it overlooks her own unique story and erases what she accomplished here, transforming her into a footnote to the American civil rights movement. If anything—given the fact that Viola Desmond's arrest and trial occurred several years before that of Parks—Parks is, in many ways, "America's Viola Desmond."

The fact that Canadians are more likely to have heard of Rosa Parks, to return us to one of the themes of the previous chapter, reveals yet again the hold that American popular culture has on Canada. It also reflects, and this is even more important, a Canadian unwillingness to admit that this country has its own race problem. "Every year I ask my graduate students, 'Who has heard of Viola Desmond?' And only a sprinkling of hands go up," says Constance Backhouse, a law professor at the University of Ottawa and author of *Colour-Coded: A Legal History of Racism in Canada*, 1900–1950. "Everybody knows about Rosa Parks and the history of racism in the United States, but it seems that nobody wants to own up to the racist history here in Canada."[27] As Viola Desmond shows, the struggle for civil rights is by no means exclusive to the United States. It is also a very Canadian struggle. And it is important that we not forget that.

IV

That denial of racism in Canada and the refusal to admit those racist aspects of our history come with a cost. While the majority of Canadians might be willing to acknowledge the poor treatment of Indigenous peoples—on full display in the horrors of the residential school system—many are less forthcoming when it comes to other communities, especially that of Black Canadians. We assume that Canada is a multicultural oasis with no race problem. The denial of racism, however, means that we do not address it. And if left unaddressed, it risks festering. This has been on clear display in Canadian society in the years *since* Desmond's image adorned the ten-dollar bill.

On May 25, 2020, police in Minneapolis killed George Floyd, a Black man, during an arrest for allegedly using a counterfeit bill.[28] The image of the white police officer kneeling on Floyd's neck for several minutes spurred massive protests across the world, including in Canada. Though Floyd's murder was but the latest installment of white police murdering young Black men, the protests were, in many ways, unprecedented. Even in the midst of the COVID-19 pandemic, protesters took to the streets with the aim of drawing attention to systemic racism in the United States and beyond, but also calling for the defunding of police departments and instead using the money to fund grassroots community networks.

In the immediate aftermath of the George Floyd murder, Marie-Claude Landry, the chief commissioner of the Canadian Human Rights Commission, issued a statement on anti-Black racism here. "It is time for all Canadians to acknowledge that anti-Black racism is pervasive in Canada," she said. "In fact, the belief that there is little to no racism in Canada is in itself a barrier to addressing it."[29] Her statement continued:

> Now is the time for all Canadians, but especially non-racialized Canadians, to listen, learn and reflect on how white privilege and systemic racism contribute to injustice and inequality in this country. We need to look inwards and challenge our biases, fears, assumptions and privilege. We need to have difficult and uncomfortable conversations. We must recognize and respect the leadership of voices from the Black community, and learn from lived experiences of anti-Black racism.

Indeed, the statistics appear to confirm Landry's assessment. Indigenous and Black Canadians, for example, are more likely to be victims of crime than white or non-racialized Canadians. The murder rate among Indigenous people is seven to eight times higher than the overall rate, despite the fact that they make up roughly 4 per cent of the population.

A similar statistic emerges from Toronto, the city with the largest community of Black Canadians, where Black people, who make up 4 per cent of the population, account for as much as 40 per cent of murder victims.

The John Howard Society, which is committed to the reform of the criminal justice system, notes that Black youth, especially males, report being stopped regularly or searched by police at roughly double the rate for white youth. Based on an analysis of ten thousand arrests in Toronto, the society also showed that Blacks were 50 per cent more likely to be taken to a police station for processing after arrest, and 100 per cent more likely to be held overnight than were whites, regardless of criminal history and age. When given bail, Black Canadians had more conditions imposed.[30] It is for these reasons that the protests surrounding justice and equality for African Americans in the United States have caught on in Canada. Just as organizations like Black Lives Matter have tried to expose the structural and systemic problems inherent in the American criminal justice system, and work for positive change, similar organizations have arisen in Canada. One crucial difference between the movements in these two countries, however, is that in Canada the movement for anti-Black racism is intimately connected to the rights of Indigenous Canadians, with an acknowledgement that Indigenous land claims need to be addressed. This has led to a common cause and understanding that Black and Indigenous individuals and communities have both suffered from systemic racism and its effects. According to the Canadian chapter of Black Lives Matter (BLM), for example,

> In our movement for Black liberation, we join calls to decolonize Turtle Island and Nunavut Nunangat. Our struggles are tied up with the struggles of the Indigenous people of the land on which many of our ancestors were brought and forced into brutalization—a living apocalypse. There is no Black Liberation without Indigenous Liberation on Turtle Island.[31]

Significantly, BLM Canada here uses "Turtle Island," an Indigenous name for North America, and Nunangat, a term used to denote the traditional home of the Inuit in northern Canada. The common cause, as this quotation nicely makes clear, is that while the Indigenous populations of

Canada had their land taken from them against their will, the ancestors of Black Canadians were forced to the New World against their will.

If much of the early struggle for Black civil rights in Canada occurred in the context of Nova Scotia and its historical Black community, the epicentre of the movement today—now organized under the rubric of BLM—is focused in larger urban centres, such as Toronto and Montreal.

V

As it did with everything else, the COVID-19 pandemic further exposed these structural problems in Canadian society. As was seen in other multi-racial and multicultural countries, people from Black and other ethnic communities tended to be harder hit by the virus than whites. In Toronto, for example, Black people and other people of colour made up 83 per cent of reported COVID-19 cases, despite the fact that these communities account for only half of Toronto's population.[32] This has less to do with race than it has to do with the impediments Black Canadians and other people of colour face on a daily basis that make them more susceptible to the disease. For example, they live in poorer neighbourhoods, work lower-level jobs, have to take public transportation, and have worse access to the healthcare system than do non-racialized communities.[33]

A study by the Edmonton-based African Canadian Civic Engagement Council and Innovative Research Group that looked at the health and economic impacts of COVID-19 from the perspective of Black Canadians bears this out. The study found that Black Canadians are more likely than other Canadians to be infected or hospitalized by the virus, and nearly three times more likely to know someone who has died after contracting COVID-19. Black Canadians reported at higher rates that their jobs require them to work face-to-face with people, and that no matter how well they protect themselves, they feel their daily routine puts them at high risk of infection. Those who worked in front-line jobs, such as cashiers, personal support workers, nurses, and drivers, and those who relied on public transit to get to work, reported they felt most at risk.[34]

COVID-19, in other words, has amplified the disparities in Canadian life. Unlike the United States, however, Canada's medical system does not collect data based on race.[35] Despite the fact that there have been many studies that show correlations between race and income on one hand and access to healthcare on the other, Canadian hospitals tend not to track this. The result is that we do not see the adverse effects that the Canadian system has on its most vulnerable citizens.

VI

Viola Desmond is on the ten-dollar bill because the Canadian government was determined to have a woman on it. The other four shortlisted contenders were the poet and writer E. Pauline Johnson (1861–1913); Elizabeth (Elsie) MacGill (1905–1980), the world's first female aircraft designer; gold-medal-winning Olympic athlete Fanny (Bobbie) Rosenfeld (1905–1969); and Idola Saint-Jean (1880–1945), Quebec journalist, educator, and feminist who fought for the women's vote in Quebec. However, Desmond is also on the bill because she was Black. Her unfair treatment by the law was the result of the colour of her skin, and her subsequent fight for civil rights was a landmark event in Canadian history.

The roots of anti-Black racism and systemic discrimination in Canada run deep. They are, as Desmond's life reveals, historically embedded in Canadian society, culture, laws, and—perhaps most dangerously—in our attitudes. They are built into our institutions and perpetuate the social and economic disparities that exist in everything from education and healthcare to housing and employment. All of these can change only with a change in attitude and acknowledgement of historical wrongs. This is what the appearance of Viola Desmond on the ten-dollar bill signifies.

In an anti-racism and defund-the-police demonstration at Place du Canada in Montreal on August 29, 2020, protesters toppled a statue of John A. Macdonald, Canada's first prime minister. They did so as a denunciation of his racism toward Indigenous populations, with demonstrators blaming him for, among other things, the establishment of the residential school system.

Quebec premier François Legault wrote on Twitter that "whatever one might think of John A. Macdonald, destroying a monument in this way is unacceptable. We must fight racism, but destroying parts of our history is not the solution. Vandalism has no place in our democracy and the statue must be restored."[36] Justin Trudeau also went on record as saying that he was "deeply disappointed" with the toppling of the statue. "We are a country of laws, and we are a country that needs to respect those laws even as we seek to improve and change them," he said two days after the event.[37] While organizers of the demonstration were on record as saying, "These racist monuments don't deserve space," Trudeau struck a more conciliatory tone. "We have an awful lot to do as a country," he said, "and part of it needs to have a clearer eye towards the past and mistakes made by previous generations of people who built this country."[38]

Echoing the first date featured in this book, October 13, 1970, and the demands by members of the FLQ, the organizers of the demonstration at Place du Canada—the Coalition for BIPOC (Black, Indigenous, [and] People of Colour) Liberation—listed their own set of demands: the removal of all statues, plaques, and emblems that commemorate "perpetrators of racism and slavery"; a 50 per cent reduction in police budgets, which could then be invested in grassroots organizations dealing with Black and Indigenous communities; and the demilitarization of the police.[39]

In the immediate aftermath of the event, the city of Montreal was uncertain about the fate of the statue—not sure if it would be restored to the same spot in Place du Canada, if a contextual plaque would be added to begin a conversation about Canada's racist past, or if the statue would be moved to a museum. Regardless, when Viola Desmond's portrait replaced that of John A. Macdonald's on Canada's ten-dollar bill on March 8, 2018, a significant recognition took place. As was the case with the Executive Summary of the Truth and Reconciliation Commission (chapter 8), it remains to be seen if this change will be merely symbolic or much more tangible and structural.

SUGGESTIONS FOR FURTHER READING

Constance Backhouse. *Colour-Coded: A Legal History of Racism in Canada, 1900–1950*. Toronto: University of Toronto Press, 1999.

Desmond Cole. *The Skin We're In: A Year of Black Resistance and Power*. Toronto: Doubleday Canada, 2020.

Cecil Foster. *They Call Me George: The Untold Story of Black Train Porters and the Birth of Modern Canada*. Windsor, ON: Biblioasis, 2019.

Lawrence Hill. *The Book of Negroes*. Toronto: HarperCollins, 2007. (Also made into a miniseries with the same name.)

Glenn Reynolds. *Viola Desmond's Canada: A History of Blacks and Segregation in the Promised Land*. Halifax: Fernwood Publishing, 2016.

Barrington Walker. *The African Canadian Legal Odyssey: Historical Essays*. Toronto: University of Toronto Press, 2012.

Robin Winks. *The Blacks in Canada: A History*. 2nd Edition. Montreal and Kingston: McGill-Queen's University Press, 1997.

SUGGESTIONS FOR FURTHER VIEWING

Sylvia Hamilton. *Speak It! From the Heart of Black Nova Scotia*. National Film Board of Canada, 1992.

Shelagh Mackenzie. *Remember Africville*. National Film Board of Canada, 1991.

Roger McTair. *Journey to Justice*. National Film Board of Canada, 2000.

Brian Murray. *Long Road to Justice: The Viola Desmond Story*. Communications Nova Scotia, 2011.

Sandamini Rankaduwa. *Ice Breakers*. National Film Board of Canada, 2019. (A documentary about a Black hockey league in Atlantic Canada).

Acknowledgements

AS A CANADIAN ACADEMIC who has spent the last decade in the United States, I have thought a lot about Canada, what it means to be a Canadian, and how all too often—at conferences, at dinner parties, at swimming lessons with children—I have had to listen to Americans talk about themselves. In all of these conversations, I frequently find my eyes glazing over while asking myself questions like: What does it mean to be a Canadian? What dates and events have shaped us as a nation? As luck would have it, my wife is Italian and now resides in the US. Like many Europeans, she thought of "North America" as some generic unit where we all share the same culture, history, and problems. She literally had no window onto what I like to call "the genius of Canada." This book is, among other things, something I wanted to write for her, to introduce her to a country I am proud to call my own. A country that has shaped me, and made me into the person I am. Thankfully, she liked it. And when I lost faith in it, she encouraged me to keep writing. She would read every chapter as I finished and wait for the next one to appear. I dedicate this book to her.

I would also like to thank the National Endowment for the Humanities, which funded a year of research at the University of Oxford. While they thought they were funding a project on the history of medieval Islam, the world, alas, had other ideas. When COVID-19 brought so much of what we thought was normalcy to a halt, and the libraries closed in Oxford as they did pretty much everywhere, I finally found the time to write this book, which I had wanted to do for a number of years. *10 Days That Shaped Modern Canada* not only helped me get through those very difficult times, but it also rekindled my love for Canadian history.

My ideal reader for this book is not fellow academics, but everyone with an interest—passing or passionate—in things Canadian. My 84-year-old mum in Edmonton and my 16-year-old daughter in Calgary became my test audience. They read chapters and, usually of little interest to an academic more focused on technical prose and jargon, they liked what they read! Their comments were supplemented by those of two very generous and anonymous readers for the press. The grace with which they read the manuscript—and the many, many helpful suggestions they made—have truly improved this book. I thank them all very much.

In addition to these individuals, of course, I would like to acknowledge a number of colleagues with whom I talked about this, many of whom wondered why I would want to write such a book in the first place. Some got it. Some did not. They will know where they fit. Regardless, I thank them all: Leonardo Ambasciano, Dustin Atlas, Ken Ehrenberg, Alex Henley, Daniel Herskovitz, Timothy Langille, Michael Levine, Russell McCutcheon, Lauren Morrey, and Elliot Wolfson. In addition, several pleasant conversations with Jake Gold, The Tragically Hip's Manager, proved helpful in sorting through the band's history.

I would be remiss if I did not acknowledge and thank Audrey McClellan, who expertly copyedited the entire manuscript. Finally, I am grateful for the care and attention that my editor at the press, Michelle Lobkowicz, gave to this manuscript. I have worked with a number of editors over the years and can honestly say that her expertise and professionalism are among the best I have encountered.

Notes

1 | OCTOBER 13, 1970

1. See the survey of this position in Ian McKay, "The Liberal Order Framework: A Prospectus for a Reconnaissance of Canadian History," *The Canadian Historical Review* 81.4 (2000): 616–45.
2. On the fifty-year anniversary of the phrase, including a short video clip of the speech in question, see Andrea Bellemare, "Charles de Gaulle's Infamous 'Vive le Québec libre speech' Feted, 50 Years On," CBC News, July 24, 2017, www.cbc.ca/news/canada/montreal/charles-de-gaulle-speech-50th-annivesary-1.4218130.
3. The term "two solitudes," popularized by MacLennan's novel *Two Solitudes* (Toronto: Macmillan, 1945), refers to a perceived lack of communication (or a lack of will to communicate) between anglophones and francophones in Canada.
4. For requisite background, see Gustave Lanctot, *A History of Canada*, vol. 3: *From the Treaty of Utrecht to the Treaty of Paris, 1713–1763*, trans. Margaret M. Cameron (Cambridge, MA: Harvard University Press, 1965).
5. Robert Bothwell, *The Penguin History of Canada* (Toronto: Penguin, 2006), 149–99. More specifically in terms of Lower Canada and Upper Canada, see 165–68.
6. Lord Durham, *Report on the Affairs of British North America* (Ottawa, 1839), 12. The full report may be found online at www.canadiana.ca/view/oocihm.32374/1?r=0&s=1.

7. Durham, *Report on the Affairs of British North America*, 12–13.
8. Durham, *Report on the Affairs of British North America*, 12.
9. The full Act of Union may be consulted at www.solon.org/Constitutions/Canada/English/PreConfederation/ua_1840.html.
10. Bothwell, *Penguin History of Canada*, 183–86.
11. Indeed, in an attempt to ameliorate these tensions, it was arranged for leadership of the new province to be shared by an anglophone from Canada West and a francophone from Canada East.
12. Government of Canada, "Appendix 1: The Terms of Reference," in *Report of the Royal Commission on Bilingualism and Biculturalism: Book 3* (Ottawa: Queen's Printer, 1969), 571, https://publications.gc.ca/site/eng/9.699864/publication.html.
13. Government of Canada, "Appendix 1: The Terms of Reference," 572.
14. Even years later, the tensions remain. See William Johnson, "English-Speaking Quebecers Must Wake Up and Defend Their Rights," *Montreal Gazette*, August 31, 2007.
15. Judy M. Torrance, *Public Violence in Canada, 1867–1982* (Kingston and Montreal: McGill-Queen's University Press, 1986), 35.
16. The book offers an interesting first-hand account of a particular perspective at a particular time, but, as can be gleaned from the title alone, the author's goal is not to provide an objective historical account of the situation.
17. Tom Diaz and Barbara Newman, *Lightning Out of Lebanon: Hezbollah Terrorists on American Soil* (New York: Random House, 2006), e-book (no page number).
18. An English translation of the FLQ Manifesto, reviewed and edited by Damien-Claude Bélanger, may be found at http://faculty.marianopolis.edu/c.belanger/quebechistory/docs/october/documents/FLQManifesto.pdf.
19. Bélanger, FLQ Manifesto.
20. Tim Ralfe, "Interview with Pierre Elliott Trudeau," CBC Television News, October, 13, 1970. A clip of the interview can be found on the CBC digital archives at www.cbc.ca/player/play/1241195075951.
21. Marc Montgomery, "History: Oct. 13, 1970—How Far Would You Go? Just Watch Me," Radio-Canada International, October 13, 2015, www.rcinet.ca/en/2015/10/13/history-oct-13-1970-how-far-would-you-go-just-watch-me/.
22. Pierre Elliott Trudeau, "Notes for a National Broadcast, October 16, 1970." The text may be found at greatcanadianspeeches.ca/2020/10/09/pierre-trudeau-october-crisis-1970/.
23. "Gallup Poll of Canada: 87% Approve the Invoking of the War Measures Act," *Toronto Star*, December 12, 1970; Blair Kirby, "Extend the War Measures Act Bill, Public Tells TV Pollsters," *Globe and Mail*, November 16, 1970. A convenient survey of Canadian newspaper responses appeared for American readers in "Editorial Comment from Canadian Newspapers on the War Measures Act," *New York Times*, October 18, 1970.
24. As quoted, for example, in Rod Bantjes, *Social Movements in a Global Context: Canadian Perspectives* (Toronto: Canadian Scholars' Press, 2007), 201.

25. René Lévesque, "Statement on the War Measures Act," October 17, 1970. The text may be found at http://faculty.marianopolis.edu/c.belanger/quebechistory/docs/october/levesque.htm.
26. For Cross's account of the ordeal, see David North, "James Cross Remembers," *Maclean's*, October 21, 1985.
27. Jay Walz, "Cross Free as Kidnappers Fly to Cuba," *New York Times*, December 4, 1970.
28. Michael T. Kaufman, "Quebec Rebuffed on Power of Veto," *New York Times*, December 7, 1982.
29. Leyland Cecco, "October Crisis: 50 Years After Bloody Spasm That Nearly Tore Canada Apart," *The Guardian*, October 16, 2020.
30. Michael D. Behiels and Matthew Hayday, eds., *Contemporary Quebec: Selected Readings and Commentaries* (Montreal and Kingston: McGill-Queen's University Press, 2011), 210.
31. Dominique Clément, *Canada's Rights Revolution: Social Movements and Social Change, 1937–82* (Vancouver: UBC Press, 2008), 109.
32. Province of British Columbia, Order-in-Council, October 22, 1970. The document may be found at www.bclaws.gov.bc.ca/civix/document/id/oic/arc_oic/3560_1970/search/CIVIX_DOCUMENT_ROOT_STEM:(%22no%20person%20teaching%20or%20instructing%20our%20youth%22)?1#hit1.
33. Tom Hawthorn, "Former Editor Recalls Frightening Fight for Liberty," *Globe and Mail*, October 7, 2005.
34. Hawthorn, "Former Editor Recalls Frightening Fight for Liberty."
35. Arthur Blakely, "Question of ID Cards Stalls on Trial Run in Commons," *Montreal Gazette*, October 15, 1971.
36. Behiels and Hayday, eds., *Contemporary Quebec*, 212.
37. For example, Vincent Gogolek, "War Measures Act Less Onerous than Bill C-51," *Victoria Times Colonist*, March 8, 2015.
38. Lorne Nystrom, "The End of Innocence: Canadians Reflect on the Crisis," *Maclean's*, October 15, 1990.

2 | SEPTEMBER 28, 1972

1. Quoted in Gerald Eskenazi, "Once They Stopped Laughing, Things Got Serious Fast," *New York Times*, September 1, 2012.
2. These numbers derive from the very useful QuantHockey website, www.quanthockey.com/nhl/nationality/canadian-nhl-players-1972-73-stats.html.
3. The interview may be found in the documentary *Cold War on Ice: Summit Series '72*, directed by George Roy (NBC Sports Network, 2012), www.youtube.com/watch?v=WPzaVDilFEI.
4. See J.L. Granatstein and David Stafford, *Spy Wars: Espionage and Canada from Gouzenko to Glasnost* (Toronto: Key Porter, 1990).
5. Rose's biography may be found in David Levy, *Stalin's Man in Canada: Fred Rose and Soviet Espionage* (New York: Enigma Books, 2011).
6. John English, *Citizen of the World: The Life of Pierre Elliott Trudeau*, vol. 1: 1919–1968 (Toronto: Knopf Canada), 166.

7. Robert Bothwell and J.L. Granatstein, *Trudeau's World: Insiders Reflect on Foreign Policy, Trade, and Defence, 1968–84* (Vancouver: UBC Press), 263.
8. Arthur Blakely, "PM Hopeful Hull Will Play," *Montreal Gazette*, July 14, 1972.
9. Father David Bauer, "Reasons to Expect TOTAL Victory," *Toronto Sun*, September 2, 1972.
10. Roy MacSkimming, *Cold War: The Amazing Canada-Soviet Hockey Series of 1972* (Vancouver: Greystone Books, 1996), 27.

11. Quoted in MacSkimming, *Cold War*, 58.
12. Harry Sinden, *Hockey Showdown: The Canada-Russia Hockey Series* (Toronto: Doubleday Canada, 1972), 13.
13. Tim Burke, "They Beat Us Almost Everywhere—Sinden," *Montreal Gazette*, September 4, 1972.
14. Eskenazi, "Once They Stopped Laughing."
15. Burke, "They Beat Us Almost Everywhere."
16. Burke, "They Beat Us Almost Everywhere."
17. Burke, "They Beat Us Almost Everywhere."
18. "Game-End Incident 'Mistake,'" *Montreal Gazette*, September 4, 1972.
19. MacSkimming, *Cold War*, 77.
20. From the documentary *Cold War on Ice: Summit Series '72*.
21. From *Cold War on Ice*.
22. Both quotations come from Ted Blackman, "Canada Edges Russians, Refs: Never Gonna Beat Us Again," *Montreal Gazette*, September 25, 1972.
23. "Paul Henderson Sorry for Criticizing Clarke," CBC Sports, October 7, 2002, www.cbc.ca/sports/hockey/paul-henderson-sorry-for-criticizing-clarke-slash-1.320565.
24. Both quotations come from Jeff Z. Klein, "In 1972, Hockey's Cold War Boiled Over," *New York Times*, September 1, 2012.
25. Klein, "In 1972, Hockey's Cold War Boiled Over."
26. Klein, "In 1972, Hockey's Cold War Boiled Over."
27. From the documentary *Cold War on Ice: Summit Series '72*.
28. Brian McFarlane, *Team Canada 1972: Where Are They Now?* (Toronto: Winding Stair Press, 2001), 10.
29. Government of Canada, Order-In-Council, PC 1967-1616 (1967). The document may be found at https://pier21.ca/research/immigration-history/immigration-regulations-order-in-council-pc-1967-1616-1967.
30. Reg Whitaker, "Canadian Immigration Policy Since Confederation" (Ottawa: Canadian Historical Association, 1991), 19.
31. The text of the Immigration Act (1967) may be found at https://pier21.ca/research/immigration-history/immigration-act-1976.
32. Wes Judd, "Why the Ice Is White," *Pacific Standard*, June 19, 2015 (updates June 14, 2017), https://psmag.com/social-justice/why-is-hockey-so-white.
33. "Year in the Sports Media Report: 2013" (Nielsen, 2014), www.nielsen.com/us/en/insights/report/2014/year-in-the-sports-media-report-2013/#.

34. "Hockey Pundit Don Cherry Fired by Sportsnet over Xenophobic Rant," *The Guardian*, November 11, 2019.
35. Roughly six months after Cherry's outburst, K'Andre Miller, an African American draft choice for the New York Rangers, was subject to hostile racist abuse in an online videoconference set up by the Rangers. See Erica L. Ayala, "A Black Hockey Player Faced Racial Taunts. Some Fans Aren't Surprised," *New York Times*, April 17, 2020.
36. "Hockey Night in Canada's Punjabi Broadcast Seeks to Reunite Fans After Don Cherry's Firing," CBC Radio, November 15, 2019.
37. Duncan Mackay, "Lewis: 'Who cares I failed drug test?'" *The Guardian*, April 23, 2003.
38. "Ben Johnson: A Hero Disgraced," CBC Radio, September 19, 2013, www.cbc.ca/radio/rewind/ben-johnson-a-hero-disgraced-1.2801243.
39. The Dominion Institute is now Historica Canada, www.historicacanada.ca/.
40. Anne McIlroy, "Confederation Wins the Vote for the Greatest Event in Our History," *Globe and Mail*, September 18, 2000.

3 | APRIL 17, 1982

1. Martina Bet, "Royal Scandal: How Canadian Leader Made Queen Laugh with X-Rated Language," *Daily Express*, May 1, 2020.
2. The entire British North America Act, 1867, may be found online at www.legislation.gov.uk/ukpga/Vict/30-31/3/contents.
3. Quoted in "The Night of Long Knives," CBC History, www.cbc.ca/history/EPISCONTENTSE1EP17CH1PA3LE.html. For Lévesque's assessment of the situation, see René Lévesque, *Memoirs*, trans. Philip Stratford (Toronto: McClelland and Stewart, 1986).
4. Ron Graham, "The Myth of the Long Knives," *Globe and Mail*, November 4, 2011.
5. For example, see William Johnson, "Charest's a Federalist?" *Globe and Mail*, July 11, 2006.
6. Graham, "The Myth of the Long Knives."
7. As an example, in 2000, Alberta tried, unsuccessfully, to invoke the clause to limit its Marriage Act to opposite-sex partnerships. The Supreme Court of Canada ruled that the definition of marriage was federally mandated and not at the discretion of provincial legislatures.
8. Pierre Elliott Trudeau, *Memoirs* (Toronto: McClelland and Stewart, 1993), 322.
9. Joseph F. Fletcher and Paul Howe, "Public Opinion and Canada's Courts," in *Judicial Power and Canadian Democracy*, eds. Paul Howe and Peter H. Russell (Montreal and Kingston: McGill-Queen's University Press, 2001), 255–96.
10. The text of the Charter of Rights and Freedoms can be found online at https://laws-lois.justice.gc.ca/eng/Const/page-12.html#h-40.
11. *R. v. Oakes* 1986, 1 SCR 103, para. 61.
12. Steve Paikin, "Interview with Jean Chrétien, Roy Romanow, and Roy McMurtry," on *The Agenda with Steve Paikin*, TVO, April 18, 2012. Online at www.youtube.com/watch?v=-15a773nqnQ.

13. Paikin, "Interview with Chrétien, Romanow, and McMurtry."
14. The English-language text of the Quebec Charter of Rights and Freedoms may be found online at www.legisquebec.gouv.qc.ca/en/document/cs/c-12.
15. The Constitution Act, 1982, section 35. It may be found online at https://laws-lois.justice.gc.ca/eng/Const/page-13.html#h-53.
16. Though there is one section of the Charter of Rights and Freedoms that deals explicitly with Aboriginal rights. Section 25 reads as follows:

> 25. The guarantee in this Charter of certain rights and freedoms shall not be construed so as to abrogate or derogate from any aboriginal treaty or other rights or freedoms that pertain to the aboriginal peoples of Canada including
> (a) any rights or freedoms that have been recognized by the Royal Proclamation of October 7, 1763; and
> (b) any rights or freedoms that now exist by way of land claims agreements or may be so acquired.

Despite this, section 35 is usually seen as providing the most important constitutional protection.
17. Government of Canada, "The Government of Canada's Approach to Implementation of the Inherent Right and the Negotiation of Aboriginal Self-Government," www.rcaanc-cirnac.gc.ca/eng/1100100031843/1539869205136#wccf.
18. John Borrows, "Measuring a Work in Progress: Canada, Constitutionalism, Citizenship and Aboriginal Peoples," in *Box of Treasures or Empty Box? Twenty Years of Section 35*, eds. Ardith Walkem and Halie Bruce (Penticton, BC: Theytus, 2003), 225.
19. Janyce McGregor, "'We Are Not Opening the Constitution': Trudeau Pans Quebec's Plans," CBC News, June 1, 2017.
20. "Canada Must Alter Constitution for Indigenous Leaders to Play Real Role in First Ministers Conference: AFN," *National Post*, December 9, 2016.
21. "Prime Minister to Host First Ministers' Meeting and Meeting with National Indigenous Leaders," press release from the Prime Minister's Office, https://pm.gc.ca/en/news/news-releases/2020/02/27/prime-minister-host-first-ministers-meeting-and-meeting-national.
22. Pierre Elliott Trudeau, "Say Goodbye to the Dream of One Canada," *Toronto Star*, May 27, 1987.
23. Trudeau, "Say Goodbye to the Dream of One Canada." For a much more negative portrayal of Trudeau's motives, see Guy Laforest, *Trudeau and the End of a Canadian Dream*, trans. Paul Leduc Browne and Michelle Weinroth (Montreal and Kingston: McGill-Queen's University Press, 1995), 115–18.
24. Bruce Wallace and Ross Laver, "War Over Words: Quebec's Move to Restrict the Use of English Signs Provoked a Crisis Across Country," *Maclean's*, January 2, 1989.

25. "Will It Be Yes or No to the Charlottetown Accord?" CBC News, October 1992, www.cbc.ca/player/play/2295082883. For a set of academic responses, see Kenneth McRoberts and Patrick Monahan, eds., *The Charlottetown Accord, the Referendum, and the Future of Canada* (Toronto: University of Toronto Press, 1993).
26. Susan Delacourt, "Charlottetown Accord's Demise Marked End of Canadians' Faith in Each Other," *Toronto Star*, October 26, 2012.
27. It should be noted in the present context that, although the accord failed, several of its central concepts—perhaps most notably defining Quebec as a "distinct society"—were subsequently adopted by Parliament, though outside the context of the Constitution. See chapter 7.
28. Richard Albert, "A Constitution for Canada and One for Quebec," *Ottawa Citizen*, March 14, 2016.
29. Pierre Elliott Trudeau in the documentary *Fundamental Freedoms: History of the Canadian Charter of Rights and Freedoms*, directed by Ian Thompson, Sailor Jones Media, 2006. Online at www.youtube.com/watch?v=LArINRMNptM.
30. For an example, see Grant Huscroft, "Yes. The Charter of Rights Has Given Judges Too Much Power," *Globe and Mail*, April 19, 2012.
31. Louise Arbour, "How the Charter Helped Define Canada," *Globe and Mail*, April 16, 1982.
32. F.L. Morton and Rainer Knopff, *The Charter Revolution and the Court Party* (Toronto: Broadview Press, 2000).
33. "The Turban That Rocked the RCMP: How Baltej Singh Dhillon Challenged the RCMP—and Won," CBC Archives, May 11, 2017, www.cbc.ca/2017/canadathestoryofus/the-turban-that-rocked-the-rcmp-how-baltej-singh-dhillon-challenged-the-rcmp-and-won-1.4110271.
34. Lauren Collins, "Surrey's Baltej Dhillon, First Mountie to Wear a Turban, Speaks About Acceptance," *Surrey Now-Leader*, September 28, 2019.
35. Douglas Quan, "Mounties Update Uniform to Allow Navy Blue Hijabs in Bid to Attract Muslim Women to the Force," *National Post*, August 24, 2016.
36. "Royal Canadian Mounted Police Allows Muslim Officers to Wear Hijab," *The Guardian*, August 24, 2016.
37. Philip Saunders, "The Charter at 20," CBC News, April 2002, https://web.archive.org/web/20060307194214/http:/www.cbc.ca/news/features/constitution/.
38. Pierre Elliott Trudeau, "Speech to the Nation at the Signing Ceremony," CBC Television news special, April 17, 1982. The speech may be found online at www.cbc.ca/archives/entry/proclamation-of-canadas-constitution.
39. Adam Liptak, "'We the People' Loses Appeal with People Around the World," *New York Times*, February 6, 2012.
40. David S. Law and Mila Versteeg, "The Declining Influence of the United States Constitution," *New York University Law Review* 87.3 (2012): 762–858.
41. Law and Versteeg, "Declining Influence of the United States Constitution," 811.
42. Law and Versteeg, "Declining Influence of the United States Constitution," 820–21.

43. For technical legal studies that reveal this influence, see Sujit Choudhry, "Globalization in Search of Justification: Toward a Theory of Comparative Constitutional Interpretation," *Indiana Law Journal* 74.3 (1999): 819–92; Lorraine Weinrib, "The Canadian Charter as a Model for Israel's Basic Laws," *Constitutional Forum* 4.85 (1993): 85–87; Paul Rishworth, "The Inevitability of Judicial Review under 'Interpretive' Bills of Rights: Canada's Legacy to New Zealand and Commonwealth Constitutionalism," *Supreme Court Law* Review 135 (2004).

44. Pierre Elliott Trudeau, "There's No Place for the State in the Bedrooms of the Nation," archived at CBC, www.cbc.ca/player/play/1811727781.

4 | JULY 21, 1988

1. While legislation would eventually define three founding cultures—French, English, *and* Indigenous—the latter has been largely ignored, especially in the nineteenth century. See chapter 8.
2. See John Ralston Saul, *Louis-Hippolyte Lafontaine and Robert Baldwin* (Toronto: Penguin Canada, 2010), 152–60.
3. For a general survey, see Freda Hawkins, *Canada and Immigration: Public Policy and Public Concerns*, 2nd ed. (Montreal and Kingston: McGill-Queen's University Press, 1988), 89–118.
4. Ninette Kelley and Michael Trebilcock, *The Making of the Mosaic: History of Canadian Immigration Policy*, 2nd ed. (Toronto: University of Toronto Press, 2010), 316–351. On more specific populations, see Helen Ralston, "Canadian Immigration Policy in the Twentieth Century: Its Impact on South Asian Women," *Canadian Woman Studies* 19.3 (1999): 33–37; and Ali Kazimi, *Undesirables: White Canada and the Komagata Maru — An Illustrated History* (Vancouver: Douglas and McIntyre, 2011). For a documentary, see *Continuous Journey*, directed by Ali Kazimi, TVOntario, 2004.
5. Stephanie Bangarth, "'We Are Not Asking You to Open Wide the Gates for Chinese Immigration': The Committee for the Repeal of the Chinese Immigration Act and Early Human Rights Activism in Canada," *Canadian Historical Review* 84.3 (2003): 395–422. See also K.W. Taylor, "Racism in Canadian Immigration Policy," *Canadian Ethnic Studies* 23.1 (1991): 1–20.
6. Kate A. Foster, *Our Canadian Mosaic* (Toronto: Dominion Council of the YWCA, 1926).
7. John Murray Gibbon, *Canadian Mosaic: The Making of a Northern Nation* (Toronto: McClelland and Stewart, 1938), viii.
8. Government of Canada, *Report of the Royal Commission on Bilingualism and Biculturalism*, Appendix 1: *The Terms of Reference* (Ottawa: The Queen's Printer, 1963), 173, https://primarydocuments.ca/report-of-the-royal-commission-on-bilingualism-and-biculturalism-book-1-the-official-languages-2/.
9. Hugh Donald Forbes, "Canada: From Bilingualism to Multiculturalism," *Journal of Democracy* 4.4 (1993): 69–84.
10. The comments were made by Yuzyk at the preliminary and public hearing stages of the Royal Commission on Bilingualism and Biculturalism in a set of remarks

titled "The Emerging New Force in the Emerging New Canada," which was delivered at the Thinkers' Conference on Cultural Rights, December 13–15, 1968. The transcript may be found at R5366-2-4-E, Box 9, Folder 12(1), Library and Archives Canada, Ottawa, ON.

11. Government of Canada, *Report of the Royal Commission on Bilingualism and Biculturalism*, Appendix 1, 174.
12. Sarah V. Wayland, "Immigration, Multiculturalism and National Identity in Canada," *International Journal of Group Rights* 5.1 (1997): 33–58; Freda Hawkins, *Critical Years in Immigration: Canada and Australia Compared*, 2nd ed. (Montreal and Kingston: McGill-Queen's University Press, 1991), 218; Michael Temelini, "Multicultural Rights, Multicultural Virtues: A History of Multiculturalism in Canada," in *Multiculturalism and the Canadian Constitution*, ed. M. Temelini (Vancouver: UBC Press, 2007), 43–60.
13. Hugh Donald Forbes, "Trudeau as the First Theorist of Canadian Multiculturalism," in Temelini, *Multiculturalism and the Canadian Constitution*, 27–42.
14. Rt. Hon. P.E. Trudeau (Prime Minister), "Announcement of Implementation of Policy of Multiculturalism within Bilingual Framework," in House of Commons, *Debates*, 28th Parliament, 3rd Session, vol. 8 (October 8, 1971), 8545–48. The policy document is appended on pages 8580–85. Online at www.pier21.ca/research/immigration-history/canadian-multiculturalism-policy-1971.
15. Trudeau, "Announcement of Implementation of Policy of Multiculturalism within Bilingual Framework."
16. Trudeau, "Announcement of Implementation of Policy of Multiculturalism within Bilingual Framework."
17. It is often read in conjunction with section 15 of the Charter, which says:

    15. (1) Every individual is equal before and under the law and has the right to the equal protection and equal benefit of the law without discrimination and, in particular, without discrimination based on race, national or ethnic origin, colour, religion, sex, age or mental or physical disability.
    (2) Subsection (1) does not preclude any law, program or activity that has as its object the amelioration of conditions of disadvantaged individuals or groups including those that are disadvantaged because of race, national or ethnic origin, colour, religion, sex, age or mental or physical disability.

18. *Canadian Multiculturalism Act* (R.S.C., 1885, c. 24 [4th Supp.]). The text of the act may be found online at https://laws.justice.gc.ca/eng/acts/C-18.7/page-1.html.
19. Jeffrey Simpson, "Balking at Multiculturalism," *Globe and Mail*, September 29, 1989.
20. Rich Morin, "The Most (and Least) Culturally Diverse Countries in the World," Pew Research Center, July 18, 2013. African countries (such as Chad) are often at the very top of the list of culturally diverse nations because of the various cultural groups that are found within.
21. One study is Forbes, *Global Diversity Rankings by Country, Sector and Occupation* (2012); another is Oxford Economics, *The Global Diversity Report* (2011).

22. These numbers may be found on the Immigration, Refugees and Citizenship website at www.canada.ca/en/immigration-refugees-citizenship/corporate/reports-statistics/statistics-open-data.html.
23. Kathleen Harris, Chris Hall, Peter Zimonjic, "Canada to Admit Nearly 1 Million Immigrants over Next 3 Years," CBC News, November 1, 2017.
24. Ministry of Immigration, Refugees and Citizenship, *2019 Annual Report to Parliament on Immigration* (Ottawa: The Ministry, 2020). Online at www.canada.ca/en/immigration-refugees-citizenship/corporate/publications-manuals/annual-report-parliament-immigration-2019.html#s3.
25. Jonathan Tepperman, "Canada's Ruthlessly Smart Immigration Policy," *New York Times*, June 28, 2017.
26. Andrew Griffith, *Multiculturalism in Canada: Evidence and Anecdote* (Toronto: Anar Press, 2015), 50.
27. Environics Institute, *Focus Canada* 2012, 18. Online at www.environicsinstitute.org/projects/project-details/focus-canada-2012.
28. Environics Institute, *Focus Canada* 2012, 20.
29. "Canadian Attitudes Towards Immigration Hardening, Poll Suggests," *Toronto Star*, November 7, 2017.
30. Mitch Potter, "Maxime Bernier Vows to Slash Immigration and Impose a Values Test on Newcomers," *Toronto Star*, July 24, 2019.
31. Lina Dib, "Bernier Promises to Build Border Fences if Elected PM," CTV News, July 24, 2019.
32. Lise Ravary, "Multiculturalism, Interculturalism and Quebec," *Montreal Gazette*, August 12, 2019.
33. It came as a surprise to many that, in admitting defeat on the eve of losing the 1995 Quebec referendum, Parti Québécois leader Jacques Parizeau blamed the loss to "l'argent et des votes ethniques" ("money and ethnic votes"). Many took this as code for blaming "Jews" (Montreal has one of Canada's largest populations of Jewish people) and immigrants. He resigned the following day. This is discussed in more depth in chapter 7.
34. Gérard Bouchard, "What Is Interculturalism?" *McGill Law Journal/Revue de droit de McGill* 56.2 (2011): 441.
35. Bouchard, "What Is Interculturalism?" 467.
36. Ann Carroll, "Let the Debate Begin," *Montreal Gazette*, August 15, 2007.
37. "Let's Move On, Says Quebec Accommodation Commission," CBC News, May 23, 2008, www.cbc.ca/news/canada/montreal/let-s-move-on-says-quebec-accommodation-commission-1.709976.
38. "Un logo tout bleu pour le virage nationaliste de la CAQ," Radio-Canada, May 11, 2015, https://ici.radio-canada.ca/nouvelle/748259/caq-logo-multicolore-remplace-bleu-virage-nationaliste.
39. "La CAQ veut évaluer les immigrants au bout de trois ans," Radio-Canada, March 16, 2015.
40. Cecilia Keating, "What Just Happened in Quebec? Seven Things You Need to Know about François Legault's Historic Victory," *National Observer*, October 2, 2018,

www.nationalobserver.com/2018/10/02/analysis/what-just-happened-quebec-seven-things-you-need-know-about-francois-legaults.

41. Keith Archer and Faron Ellis, "Opinion Structure of Party Activists: The Reform Party of Canada," *Political Science/Revue Canadienne de science politique* 27.2 (1994): 277–308, at 292.
42. Archer and Ellis, "Opinion Structure of Party Activists," 296. Interestingly, though, when asked the question "When Canada admits immigrants, it should take them from all ethnic and racial groups," 68.9 per cent agreed (with 22.5 per cent disagreeing and 8.6 per cent undecided).
43. Roger Hewitt, *White Backlash and the Politics of Multiculturalism* (Cambridge: Cambridge University Press, 2005), 137.
44. Something that is, of course, paradoxical, since the Official Languages Act was instituted to break the stranglehold of anglophone elitism in Ottawa.
45. S. Patten, "Citizenship, the New Right and Social Justice: Examining the Reform Party's Discourse on Citizenship," *Socialist Studies Bulletin* 57–58 (1999): 25–51.
46. Maura Forrest, "Thirty Years After the Birth of the Reform Party, Its Legacy Lives in Conservative Leadership Results," *National Post*, May 31, 2017.
47. Rod Mickleburgh, "Harper Defends Canadian Diversity," *Globe and Mail*, June 20, 2006.
48. This move was later reversed by the Liberal government of Justin Trudeau, who returned the Ministry of Multiculturalism to Canadian Heritage.
49. This coincided with an often unequivocal endorsement of the right-wing prime minister of Israel, Benjamin Netanyahu, and his government's poor treatment of Arab minorities and Palestinians in that country.
50. "Niqab Ban for Public Servants Would Be Considered: Stephen Harper," CBC News, October 6, 2015, www.cbc.ca/news/politics/stephen-harper-niqab-ban-public-servants-1.3258943. On the use of the phrase "old stock Canadians," see Tristen Hopper, "Taking Stock of 'Old Stock Canadians': Stephen Harper Called a 'Racist' After Remark During Debate," *National Post*, September 19, 2015.
51. "Refugee Crisis, Drowned Syrian Boy Shift Focus of Election Campaign," CBC News, September 3, 2015. See also the damning indictment in Martin Lukacs, "Harper's Canada Has More Than One Refugee Death on Its Hands," *The Guardian*, September 4, 2015.
52. "Canadian Election Results 2015: A Riding-by-Riding Breakdown of the Vote," *National Post*, October 19, 2015.
53. Douglas Todd, "Growing Ethnic Enclaves Hurt Sense of Canadian 'Belonging,'" *Vancouver Sun*, September 11, 2010. This piece was republished on the website of Immigration Watch Canada, a right-wing group that states, "[Immigration] should never be a social engineering experiment that is conducted on Canada's mainstream population in order to make it a minority." Online at http://immigrationwatchcanada.org.
54. For example, Daniel Stoffman, *Who Gets In? What's Wrong with Canada's Immigration Program, and How to Fix It* (Toronto: Macfarlane Walter & Ross, 2002).

For a more academic critique of multiculturalism, see Phil Ryan, *Multicultiphobia* (Toronto: University of Toronto Press, 2020).

55. Robert Fulford, "How We Became a Land of Ghettos," *National Post*, June 12, 2006.
56. Neil Bissoondath, *Selling Illusions: The Cult of Multiculturalism in Canada* (Toronto: Penguin Books, 1994).
57. Pierre Elliott Trudeau, *The Essential Trudeau*, ed. Ron Graham (Toronto: McClelland and Stewart, 1998), 16–20.

5 | DECEMBER 6, 1989

1. Details in this section come from the *Report of the Coroner's Investigation*, which provides English translations of the dialogue between the killer and his victims. It may be accessed online at https://web.archive.org/web/20160303180531/http:/www.diarmani.com/Montreal_Coroners_Report.pdf.
2. Four years earlier, in Lennoxville, Quebec, five members of a motorcycle gang had been murdered. While tragic, it was nothing like the scale of the massacre at École Polytechnique.
3. For a treatment that supplies brief and touching biographies of the victims, see Anne Thériault, "Remember the Women of the Montreal Massacre by More Than Just Their Names," *Flare*, December 6, 2017.
4. Kate Fillion, "*Maclean's* Interview: Monique Lépine," *Maclean's*, October 24, 2008.
5. Monique Lépine and Harold Gagné, *Aftermath*, trans. Diana Halfpenny (Toronto: Viking Canada, 2008), 150–55.
6. *Report of the Coroner's Investigation*, 11.
7. *Report of the Coroner's Investigation*, 14.
8. The English translation of the letter may be found at https://en.wikipedia.org/wiki/Marc_Lépine#Suicide_statement. For the French original, see www.philo5.com/Feminisme-Masculisme/890612%20Lettre%20de%20Marc%20Lepine.htm.
9. "Woman Shot in Montreal Massacre Watches Classmates' Funeral," interview with Michael Enright, *As It Happens*, CBC Radio, December 11, 1989, www.cbc.ca/archives/entry/woman-shot-in-montreal-massacre-watches-classmates-funeral.
10. "Witness History: The Montreal Massacre," BBC Sounds, December 6, 2012, www.bbc.co.uk/sounds/play/p0116v7f.
11. Marian Scott, "Polytechnique Massacre: Lives Forever Changed," *Montreal Gazette*, December 6, 2014.
12. Katherine Wall, "Persistence and Representation of Women in STEM," Statistics Canada, May 2, 2019. The report may be accessed online at www150.statcan.gc.ca/n1/pub/75-006-x/2019001/article/00006-eng.htm.
13. "Montreal Massacre Survivor Welcomes New Recognition It Was an 'Anti-Feminist Attack,'" *The Current*, CBC Radio, December 6, 2019, www.cbc.ca/radio/thecurrent/the-current-for-dec-6-2019-1.5385684/montreal-massacre-survivor-welcomes-new-recognition-it-was-an-anti-feminist-attack-1.5385686.
14. "30 Years After Polytechnique Massacre, New Memorial Park Sign to Recognize Killings as 'Antifeminist,'" CBC Montreal, November 4, 2019.
15. Scott, "Polytechnique Massacre: Lives Forever Changed."

16. Scott, "Polytechnique Massacre: Lives Forever Changed."
17. Denis Villeneuve's award-winning feature film *Polytechnique* (Remstar Media Partners, 2009), a fictional and thoughtful portrayal of the events, lists the names of the victims at the end of the film and appends to them the name of Blais.
18. "Survivors Recall École Polytechnique Shooting," *Maclean's*, December 4, 2009.
19. "Survivors Recall École Polytechnique Shooting."
20. "Woman Shot in Montreal Massacre Watches Classmates' Funeral."
21. Adina Bresge, "Nova Scotia Mass Murder 'Catalyst' Highlights an 'Eerily Familiar Threat of Domestic Violence,' Experts Say," *National Post*, April 26, 2020.
22. "New Gun Law in Wake of Montreal Massacre," *Canada at Five*, CBC Radio, July 27, 1992.
23. The Coalition for Gun Control website may be found at http://guncontrol.ca. Rathjen has written about her struggle, with co-author Charles Montpetite, in *December 6: From the Montreal Massacre to Gun Control* (Toronto: McClelland and Stewart, 1999).
24. René Bruemmer, "Polytechnique Shootings 30 Years On: Rearming After Gun-Control Wins and Losses," *Montreal Gazette*, December 7, 2019.
25. Jeff Davis, "Conservatives and Enthusiasts Cheer the End of the Long-Gun Registry," *National Post*, February 15, 2012.
26. Tonda MacCharles, "Montreal Massacre Survivor Slams Plan to Scrap Long-Gun Registry," *Toronto Star*, November 24, 2011.
27. Julia Page, "Survivors of Quebec Mass Shootings Plead for Ban on Assault Weapons," CBC News, May 22, 2018.
28. Bruemmer, "Polytechnique Shootings 30 Years On."
29. "Four-in-Five Canadians Support Complete Ban on Civilian Possession of Assault Style Weapons," Angus Reid Institute, May 1, 2020. The poll may be found online at http://angusreid.org/assault-weapons ban/?fbclid=IwAR3fX2wFKH7OUDgbVGaOSnU2XI9JsMJ__-h2PhrsQZMAnon_sjncnJHCyMU.
30. Barbara Kay, "Lone Gunman: The École Polytechnique Massacre Was a Freak Tragedy. So Why Is Every Man Made to Feel Guilty for It?" *National Post*, December 6, 2006.
31. Louise Desmarais and Marie Mathieu, "Chantale Daigle, la victoire d'une femme pour toutes les femmes," *Le Devoir*, August 8, 2019.
32. Julie Bindel, "The Montreal Massacre: Canada's Feminists Remember," *The Guardian*, December 3, 2012.
33. Status of Women Subcommittee of the Standing Committee on Health, Welfare, Social Affairs, Seniors and the Status of Women, *The War Against Women* (Ottawa: Minister of Supply and Services, 1991), 1.
34. Lise Gotell, "A Critical Look at State Discourse on 'Violence against Women': Some Implications for Feminist Politics and Women's Citizenship," in *Women and Political Representation in Canada*, eds. Caroline Andrew and Manon Tremblay (Ottawa: University of Ottawa Press, 1998), 39–84, at 55.

35. Health and Welfare Canada, "New Family Violence Initiative Underway / La nouvelle initiative contre la violence familiale bat son plein," *Canadian Woman Studies* 12.1 (1991): 111.
36. Statistics Canada, *National Survey on Violence Against Women: Survey Highlights* (Ottawa: Statistics Canada, 1993).
37. "National Day of Remembrance and Action on Violence Against Women," on the archived Status of Women Canada website, https://web.archive.org/web/20130812210657/http://www.swc-cfc.gc.ca/dates/vaw-vff/index-eng.html.
38. *Stolen Sisters: A Human Rights Response to Discrimination and Violence Against Indigenous Women in Canada* may be found online at www.amnesty.ca/sites/default/files/Stolen%20Sisters%202004%20Summary%20Report_0.pdf. A second report by Amnesty International, five years later, further documented the crimes and the inaction. *No More Stolen Sisters: The Need for a Comprehensive Response to Discrimination and Violence Against Indigenous Women in Canada* may also be found online at www.amnesty.ca/sites/default/files/amr200122009en.pdf.
39. Tina Hotton Mahony, Joanna Jacob, and Heather Hobson, "Women and the Criminal Justice System" (Ottawa: Statistics Canada, 2017). The report may be found online at www150.statcan.gc.ca/n1/pub/89-503-x/2015001/article/14785-eng.pdf.
40. Royal Canadian Mounted Police, "Missing and Murdered Aboriginal Women: 2015 Update to the National Operational Overview." The report may be found online at www.rcmp-grc.gc.ca/en/missing-and-murdered-aboriginal-women-2015-update-national-operational-overview.
41. For example, Ian Austen and Dan Bilefsky, "Canadian Inquiry Calls Killings of Indigenous Women Genocide," *New York Times*, June 3, 2019; Drew Brown, "Canada Complicit in Genocide: MMIWG Report," *The Independent*, June 4, 2019.
42. 2SLGBTQQIA is an acronym for "Two-Spirit, lesbian, gay, bisexual, transgender, queer, questioning, intersex, and asexual."
43. National Inquiry into Missing and Murdered Indigenous Women and Girls, *Executive Summary of the Final Report*, 3. The report may be found online at www.mmiwg-ffada.ca/wp-content/uploads/2019/06/Executive_Summary.pdf.
44. Evan Dyer, "MMIWG Final Report Quietly Altered After CBC Inquired About Errors," CBC News, September 3, 2019, www.cbc.ca/news/politics/missing-murdered-indigenous-women-inquiry-statistics-1.5176756.
45. National Inquiry into Missing and Murdered Indigenous Women and Girls, *Executive Summary of the Final Report*, 2.
46. For example, Arthur White-Crummey, "MMIWG Finding of 'Race-Based Genocide' Gets Differing Reception in Sask.," *Regina Leader-Post*, June 4, 2019; Rob Breakenridge, "Use of the Word 'Genocide' Undermines MMIWG Report," Global News, June 8, 2019, https://globalnews.ca/news/5366507/mmiwg-genocide-debate/.
47. Both remarks may be found in Adina Bresge, "Explained: Why the MMIWG Commission Invoked 'Canadian Genocide,'" *National Post*, June 3, 2019.

48. Douglas Quan and Steve McKinley, "The Nova Scotia Shootings Began with an Act of Domestic Abuse—and There Were Red Flags That Came Before," *Toronto Star*, April 23, 2020.
49. "Neighbour Who Warned RCMP About N.S. Shooter's Domestic Violence Says She Was 'Scared to Death' of Him," *As It Happens*, CBC Radio, May 13, 2020.
50. Maire Sinha, "Section 3: Intimate Partner Violence," in *Family Violence in Canada: A Statistical Profile, 2011* (Statistics Canada, 2013), 38–59. The report may be accessed online at www150.statcan.gc.ca/n1/pub/85-002-x/2013001/article/11805-eng.htm.
51. Zoran Miladinovic and Leah Mulligan, "Homicide in Canada, 2014" (Statistics Canada, 2015). The report may be found online at www150.statcan.gc.ca/n1/pub/85-002-x/2015001/article/14244-eng.htm#a9.
52. Jane Gerster, "Did We Miss the Nova Scotia Shooting Warning Signs—or Dismiss Them," Global News, March 23, 2020.
53. Michael Tutton, "How N.S. Mass Shooting Could Bring Law That Makes Abusers' Tactics a Crime," CTV News, May 24, 2020.
54. Quan and McKinley, "The Nova Scotia Shootings Began with an Act of Domestic Abuse."
55. Even the most notorious case of wrongful conviction in Canada involves violence against women. David Milgaard was released from prison after twenty-three years. He was wrongly convicted for the rape and murder of Gail Miller, a young nursing student in Saskatoon. The real killer was Larry Fisher, a serial rapist with an extreme hatred for women.
56. Stacy May Fowles, "When Paul Bernardo Stalked My Neighbourhood," *The Walrus*, November 11, 2013.
57. Nicole Brockbank, "Alex Minassian Reveals Details of Toronto Van Attack in Video of Police Interview," CBC News, September 27, 2019.
58. Leyland Cecco, "Toronto Van Attack Suspect Says He Was 'Radicalized' Online by 'Incels,'" *The Guardian*, September 27, 2019.
59. Caroline Van Vlaardingen, "Polytechnique: Male Survivor Talks About Guilt and Lessons He'll Pass On," CTV News Montreal, December 3, 2019.
60. Statistics Canada, "Women in Corporate Canada: Who's at the Top?" May 7, 2019, www150.statcan.gc.ca/n1/pub/11-627-m/11-627-m2019028-eng.htm.
61. Rachelle Pelletier, Martha Patterson, and Melissa Moyser, "The Gender Wage Gap in Canada: 1998 to 2018" (Statistics Canada, 2019). The report may be found online at www150.statcan.gc.ca/n1/pub/75-004-m/75-004-m2019004-eng.htm.
62. Mélissa Blais, "Les parallères entre la tuerie de Polytechnique et le massacre de la mosquée de Québec," *Le Devoir*, January 20, 2018.
63. Les Perreaux and Eric Andrew-Gee, "Quebec City Mosque Attack Suspect Known as Online Troll Inspired by French Far-Right," *Globe and Mail*, January 30, 2017.
64. Guillaume Piedboeuf, "Bissonnette s'était replié sur lui-même," *Le Soleil*, January 30, 2017.

6 | MAY 25, 1995

1. John Ibbitson, "Everett Klippert's Story: The Long, Late Redemption of a Man Punished for Being Gay in the 1960s," *Globe and Mail*, February 27, 2016; Nikki Wiart, "Everett Klippert: An Unlikely Pioneer of Gay Rights in Canada," *Maclean's*, June 10, 2016.
2. *Klippert v. The Queen*. The judgment may be found online at https://scc-csc.lexum.com/scc-csc/scc-csc/en/item/4738/index.do?r=AAAAAQAFeW91dGgAAAAAAAAB.
3. House of Commons, *Debates*, 27th Parliament, 2nd Session, vol. 4 (November 8, 1967), 4036–37. Online at http://parl.canadiana.ca/view/oop.debates_HOC2702_04/538?r=0&s=1. The report of the Wolfenden Commission recommended, among other things, that "homosexual behaviour between consenting adults in private should no longer be a criminal offence."
4. He subsequently avoided publicity and even married his friend Dorothy Hagstrom. In 2016, the government of Justin Trudeau indicated that it planned to recommend a posthumous pardon of Klippert's conviction. See https://calgarygayhistory.ca/2021/03/11/everett-klippert-coda/.
5. *Canada v. Mossop*. The ruling may be found online at https://scc-csc.lexum.com/scc-csc/scc-csc/en/item/969/index.do.
6. Miriam Smith, *Lesbian and Gay Rights in Canada: Social Movements and Equality-Seeking, 1971–1995* (Toronto: University of Toronto Press, 1999), 90.
7. He was also the subject of Heritage Canada's first LGBTQ2S Heritage Minute. It may be found online at www.youtube.com/watch?v=a3e5jC7yZeo.
8. James Egan, *Challenging the Conspiracy of Silence: My Life as a Canadian Gay Activist*, ed. Donald W. McLeod (Toronto: The ArQuives / Homewood Books, 1998), 45. On Egan's place in LGBTQ2S activism more generally, see Tom Warner, *Never Going Back: A History of Queer Activism in Canada* (Toronto: University of Toronto Press, 2002).
9. "Elderly B.C. Couple Say They Are Ideal Test Case on Spousal Rights," *Montreal Gazette*, December 29, 1994.
10. *Egan v. Canada*, 515. The ruling may be found online at https://scc-csc.lexum.com/scc-csc/scc-csc/en/item/1265/index.do.
11. *Egan v. Canada*, 567. Italics in original.
12. *Egan v. Canada*, 567.
13. *Egan v. Canada*, 528.
14. In 2016, the Province of Ontario ruled that same-sex parents in Ontario who use assisted reproduction to conceive would no longer have to formally adopt their own children born using this process. Prior to this, same-sex couples had to do this, while heterosexual couples who conceived using reproductive technologies did not. See Rob Ferguson, "Ontario Same-Sex Couple No Longer Have to Adopt Their Own Children," *Toronto Star*, September 29, 2016.
15. *M v. H*. The ruling may be found online at www.canlii.org/en/ca/scc/doc/1999/1999canlii686/1999canlii686.html.
16. Martha McCarthy, "How a Canadian Case Pushed Along 20 Years of Progress in Same-Sex Equality," *Globe and Mail*, January 3, 2020.

17. "Ottawa Nixes Same-Sex Marriage," CBC News, June 9, 1999.
18. Andy Clark, "Toronto Pastor Who Officiated Canada's First Legal Same-Sex Marriage Retires," *Globe and Mail*, December 24, 2017. See also "Brent Hawkes, Pastor Who Officiated Canada's First Legal Gay Marriages, Delivers Final Christmas Eve Sermon," CBC News, December 25, 2017.
19. Sylvain Larocque, *Gay Marriage: The Story of a Canadian Social Revolution*, trans. Robert Chodos, Louisa Blair, and Benjamin Waterhouse (Toronto: Lorimer, 2006), 51.
20. Larocque, *Gay Marriage*, 50–52.
21. Anne McIlroy, "Canadian Government to Defy Church on Gay Marriage," *The Guardian*, August 11, 2003.
22. Christopher Mason, "Gay Marriage Galvanizes Canada's Right," *New York Times*, November 19, 2006.
23. Mason, "Gay Marriage Galvanizes Canada's Right."
24. Quoted in Katherine Harding, "Alberta Plans to Fight Gay Marriage," *Globe and Mail*, December 10, 2004.
25. The issue has also caused deep division in the Anglican Church of Canada. After passing a motion to accept same-sex marriage at its general assembly in 2016, the church failed to pass a second vote at the next assembly three years later, as required by the church's rules, so same-sex marriages were not affirmed. See Maryse Zeidler, "Anglican Church Rejects Same-Sex Marriage Approvals in Vote," CBC News, July 13, 2019.
26. Claude J. Summers, "United Church of Canada," GLBTQ Archives, www.glbtqarchive.com/ssh/united_church_canada_S.pdf.
27. McIlroy, "Canadian Government to Defy Church on Gay Marriage."
28. Andrew Parkin, "A Country Evenly Divided on Gay Marriage," *Policy Options* (October 1, 2003), https://policyoptions.irpp.org/magazines/who-decides-the-courts-or-parliament/a-country-evenly-divided-on-gay-marriage/.
29. Frank Bruni, "On Same-Sex Marriage, Catholics Are Leading the Way," *New York Times*, May 27, 2015.
30. Parkin, "A Country Evenly Divided on Gay Marriage."
31. Parkin, "A Country Evenly Divided on Gay Marriage."
32. Katherine Harding, "Gay-Rights Activists Bide Time in Alberta," *Globe and Mail*, November 10, 2004.
33. Harding, "Alberta Plans to Fight Gay Marriage."
34. Harding, "Alberta Plans to Fight Gay Marriage."
35. "Alberta To Recognize Validity of Same-Sex Marriages," CBC News, April 17, 2014.
36. "Regina MP Canned over Comments on Gays," CBC News, November 27, 2003.
37. "Canada's Political Right Unites," BBC News, December 7, 2003.
38. "Comuzzi Quits Cabinet over Same-Sex Bill," CBC News, June 28, 2005.
39. Mason, "Gay Marriage Galvanizes Canada's Right."
40. "Comuzzi Quits Cabinet over Same-Sex Bill."
41. "Comuzzi Quits Cabinet over Same-Sex Bill."
42. "Harper Reopens Same-Sex Marriage Debate," CBC News, 29th November, 2005.
43. "MPs Defeat Bid to Reopen Same-Sex Marriage Debate," CBC News, December 7, 2006.

44. "MPs Defeat Bid to Reopen Same-Sex Marriage Debate."
45. Aaron Wherry, "Why the Liberals Turned Scheer's Same-Sex Marriage Speech into a Political Weapon," CBC News, August 23, 2019.
46. Alex Boutilier, "Andrew Scheer Urged to End 'Boycott' of Gay Pride Events After 2005 Speech on Same-Sex Marriage Comes to Light," *Toronto Star*, August 22, 2019.
47. Subcommittee on Equality Rights, *Equality for All: Report of the Parliamentary Committee on Equality Rights* (Ottawa: Queen's Printer, 1985).
48. Quoted in Gary Kinsman and Patrizia Gentile, *The Canadian War on Queers: National Security as Sexual Regulation* (Vancouver: UBC Press, 2010), 400.
49. Kinsman and Gentile, *The Canadian War on Queers*, 400.
50. "Appeal Dismissed in Challenge to Alberta Gay-Straight Alliance Law," Global News, April 29, 2019; Amanda Coletta, "Alberta's New Conservative Government Revisits Gay-Straight Student Alliance," *Washington Post*, July 6, 2019.
51. CBC/Ekos Poll for the CBC Sunday News, "Public Attitudes Toward Same-Sex Marriage," www.ekospolitics.com/articles/CBCSundayNews6.pdf.
52. The poll may be found online at Mario Canseco, "Almost Two-Thirds of Canadians OK with Same-Sex Marriage," ResearchCo., August 1, 2019, https://researchco.ca/2019/08/01/i-want-the-world-to-know-got-to-let-it-show/. See also Simon Little, "1 in 4 Canadians Still Oppose Full Same-Sex Marriage Rights: Poll," Global News, August 1, 2019.

7 | OCTOBER 30, 1995

1. Clyde H. Farnsworth, "Quebec Separatists Win Provincial Election, Ending the Liberal Party's 9-Year Reign," *New York Times*, September 13, 1994.
2. "Lucien Bouchard Says There's No Way to Repair Friendship with Brian Mulroney," *National Post*, October 21, 2014.
3. In an opinion piece in the referendum's aftermath, former prime minister Trudeau wrote that "the so-called '[night of the] long knives,' [is] a label shamelessly borrowed from Nazi history by separatists suffering from acute paranoia." Pierre Elliott Trudeau, "Trudeau Accuses Bouchard of Betraying Quebecers," *Montreal Gazette*, February 3, 1996.
4. Anne F. Bayefsky, *Self-Determination in International Law: Quebec and Lessons Learned* (The Hague: Kluwer Law International), 10.
5. Chantal Hébert with Jean Lapierre, *The Morning After: The 1995 Referendum and the Day That Almost Was* (Toronto: Knopf Canada, 2014).
6. Andrew Phillips, "The Choice in Quebec," *Maclean's*, October 30, 1995.
7. J. Patrick Boyer, *Forcing Choice: The Risky Rewards of Referendums* (Toronto: Dundurn, 2017), 241.
8. "A Message from the Prime Minister," appended to "Draft Bill Respecting the Future of Quebec" (the version mailed to every household). It may be found online at www.solon.org/misc/referendum-bill.html.
9. "Draft Bill Respecting the Future of Quebec."
10. Quotations from "High Stakes in the 1995 Quebec Referendum," CBC Archives, October 1, 2018.

11. Boyer, *Forcing Choice*, 241.
12. Barry Came, "'We the People': Jacques Parizeau Unveils Quebec's Referendum Question," *Maclean's*, September 18, 1995.
13. Parizeau would later express regret that the agreement had to be cited in the question, but noted that the June 12, 1995, agreement had been sent to every registered voter in the province.
14. Came, "'We the People': Jacques Parizeau Unveils Quebec's Referendum Question."
15. André Picard, "Parizeau Promises to 'Exact Revenge' for Sovereigntist Loss," *Globe and Mail*, October 31, 1995.
16. Both quotations come from André Picard, "From the Archives: Parizeau Promises to 'Exact Revenge' for Sovereigntist Loss," *Globe and Mail*, October 30, 2015.
17. Clyde H. Farnsworth, "Quebec's Premier Quits After Loss on Independence," *New York Times*, November 1, 1995. See further Charles Trueheart, "Polarized Quebec Votes No on Separation," *Washington Post*, October 31, 1995.
18. In 2006, the House of Commons voted in support of a motion—"That this House recognize that the Quebecois form a nation within a united Canada"—introduced by Conservative prime minister Stephen Harper, thereby replacing the idea of Québec as a "distinct society." See, for example, Gloria Galloway and Brian Laghi, "A Nation Within Canada," *Globe and Mail*, November 23, 2006; "House Passes Motion Recognizing Quebecois as Nation," CBC News, November 27, 2006.
19. Clyde H. Farnsworth, "Ottawa Unity Plan Draws Fire from Both Quebec and West," *New York Times*, December 1, 1995.
20. David Bercuson and Barry Cooper, *Deconfederation: Canada Without Quebec* (Toronto: Key Porter Books, 1991).
21. Nearly 2 per cent of the votes cast during the 1995 referendum were rejected. Ridings such as Chomedey in Laval, a predominantly federalist riding, had more than one in ten ballots not counted. "Spoiled Referendum Ballots on Display in Quebec," CBC News, August 2, 2000.
22. "Citizenship Blitz in Quebec," *Montreal Gazette*, August 31, 1995; Pierre O'Neill, "Le Camp du NON a-t-il vole le referendum de 1995," *Le Devoir*, August 11, 1999.
23. Claire Durand and André Blais, "Why Did the Polls Go Wrong in the 1988 Quebec Election? The Answer from Post Election Polls," *Bulletin of Sociological Methodology/Bulletin de Méthodolgie Sociologique* 62.2 (1999): 43–47.
24. The CAQ government of François Legault, elected in 2018, has signalled its intention to hold a referendum, but on electoral reform and *not* on separation. See Benjamin Shingler, "CAQ Government Wants to Hold a Referendum over Electoral Reform Plan," CBC News, September 25, 2019.
25. Dan Bilefsky, "The Reawakening of Quebec's Nationalism," *New York Times*, November 1, 2019.
26. "Francois Legault Says CAQ Would 'Never' Hold a Referendum," CTV News, April 10, 2014.
27. Ingrid Peritz, "After 50 Years, Parti Québécois Pushed to Political Margins as Lisée Loses Montreal Seat and Resigns," *Globe and Mail*, October 1, 2018.
28. Chris Hall, "New Leader Blanchet Steering Bloc Back to Relevance in Quebec," CBC News, October 12, 2019.

29. Bilefsky, "The Reawakening of Quebec's Nationalism."
30. "Le Bloc Québécois veut taxer les géants du web," *La Presse*, September 14, 2019.
31. Bilefsky, "The Reawakening of Quebec's Nationalism."
32. Bilefsky, "The Reawakening of Quebec's Nationalism."
33. Anthony Depalma, "Canadian Court Rules Quebec Cannot Secede on Its Own," *New York Times*, August 21, 1998.
34. Depalma, "Canadian Court Rules Quebec Cannot Secede on Its Own."

35. "Canadians' Reaction to the Quebec Referendum," Ipsos news release about Angus Reid/Southam News poll, November 4, 1995. Online at www.ipsos.com/en-ca/news-polls/canadians-reaction-quebec-referendum.
36. See, for example, Clyde H. Farnsworth, "Quebec Vote Bares Latent Ethnic Anger," *New York Times*, November 5, 1995.
37. "History Through Our Eyes: Oct. 30, 1995, Money and Ethnic Votes," *Montreal Gazette*, October 30, 2019.
38. Andrew Stark, "Adieu, Liberal Nationalism," *New York Times*, November 2, 1995.
39. Charles Truehart, "Quebecer Damages Separatist Cause with Remark on Low Province Birthrate," *Washington Post*, October 18, 1995. After the referendum, former prime minister Pierre Elliott Trudeau wrote a scathing review: "Trudeau Accuses Bouchard of Betraying Quebecers," *Montreal Gazette*, February 3, 1996.
40. Stark, "Adieu, Liberal Nationalism."
41. "Mr. Bouchard's Ethnic Nationalism," *Globe and Mail*, October 17, 1995.
42. Jill Wherrett, *Aboriginal Peoples and the 1995 Québec Referendum: A Survey of the Issues* (Ottawa: Parliament of Canada, 1996).
43. The James Bay and Northern Quebec Agreement (JBNQA) was signed on November 11, 1975, by the Government of Quebec, the Government of Canada, Hydro-Québec, the Grand Council of the Crees of Quebec, and the Northern Quebec Inuit Association.
44. Matthew Coon Come, *Sovereign Injustice: Forcible Inclusion of the James Bay Crees and Cree Territory into a Sovereign Quebec* (Nemaska: Grand Council of the Crees, 1995), 62.
45. "The Cree of Quebec Hold Their Own Referendum," *The National*, CBC TV, October 24, 1995.
46. Charles Trueheart, "Quebec's Natives Almost Unanimous in Opposition to Secession from Canada," *Washington Post*, October 26, 1995.
47. "First Nations Weigh in on Quebec Sovereignty Debate," CBC News, March 18, 2014.
48. "Territorial Integrity Quebec: You Are Forgetting the Right of First Nations to Self-Determination," *Cision*, April 10, 2019, www.newswire.ca/news-releases/territorial-integrity-quebec-you-are-forgetting-the-right-of-first-nations-to-self-determination-832112449.html.
49. The Declaration on the Rights of Indigenous Peoples may be found online at www.un.org/esa/socdev/unpfii/documents/DRIPS_en.pdf.
50. On talk of Alberta secession after the 2019 federal election—nicknamed "Wexit" in reference to Brexit, the British "exit" from the European Union—see Lisa Johnson,

"Wexiters Rally at Alberta Legislature to Push for Secession," *Edmonton Journal*, January 12, 2020; Leyland Cecco and David Agren, "Wexit: Alberta's Frustration Fuels Push for Independence from Canada," *The Guardian*, November 25, 2019.
51. Rheal Seguin, "Bouchard Reviles Unity Proposal: Plan Would Abolish Quebec Reality," *Globe and Mail*, September 17, 1997.
52. The Calgary Declaration may be found online at www.exec.gov.nl.ca/currentevents/unity/unityr1.htm.
53. Stéphane Dion, "What, Exactly, Do We Mean by 'Nation'?" *National Post*, October 26, 2006.
54. Giuseppe Valiante, "Quebec's 1995 Referendum Far from Last Gasp for Sovereignty Hopes," CBC News, October 28, 2015; Giuseppe Valiante and Pierre St-Arnaud, "1995 Quebec Referendum: 20 Years Later, Canada Still Standing, But So Is Sovereignty," *Huffington Post Canada*, October 28, 2015.
55. "PQ Defends Against Attacks from Lucien Bouchard," CTV News Montreal, February 17, 2010.
56. Dan Bilefsky, "A Quebec Ban on Religious Symbols Upends Lives and Careers," *New York Times*, March 7, 2020.

8 | JUNE 2, 2015

1. Department of the Interior, *Annual Report for the Year Ended 30th June, 1876* (Parliament, Sessional Papers, No. 11, 1877), xiv.
2. The criteria for a successful and unsuccessful application for status may be found on the Indigenous Services Canada website at www.sac-isc.gc.ca/eng/1100100032463/1572459644986.
3. Here it is worth mentioning that initially the Indian Act was little interested in either Métis or Inuit peoples. Both groups, along with First Nations, were recognized officially in the Constitution Act of 1982. However, this recognition did not mean that the Métis or the Inuit were granted the rights conferred by status.
4. Statistics Canada, "Aboriginal Peoples in Canada: First Nations People, Métis and Inuit," from the National Household Survey, 2011, 10–12. The report may be found online at www12.statcan.gc.ca/nhs-enm/2011/as-sa/99-011-x/99-011-x2011001-eng.pdf.
5. Métis, Inuit, and non-status Indians have never been granted the same recognition and rights provided to those status Indians living on reserves, including access to healthcare and educational programs, and the ability to hunt/trap/fish on public lands. In 2013 the Federal Court ruled that these individuals could be recognized as "Indians" according to the Constitution. The federal government appealed, but the appeal was turned down in the Federal Court of Appeals the following year. The Federal Court ruling has not yet translated into actual benefits for these individuals. See, for example, "Court of Appeal Upholds Landmark Ruling on Rights of Métis," CBC News, April 17, 2014.
6. The complexities around issues of "status" have been nicely portrayed by Howard Adler's short film *Status* (2014) for the CBC.

7. Especially sec. 15 of the Charter, which states that that "every individual is equal before and under the law and has the right to the equal protection and equal benefit of the law without discrimination...based on race, national or ethnic origin, colour, religion, sex, age, or mental or physical disability."
8. Tim Fontaine, "Indian Act Turns 140, But Few Celebrating," CBC News, April 12, 2016.
9. Fontaine, "Indian Act Turns 140, But Few Celebrating."

10. According to Statistics Canada, 24.3 out of every 100,000 Indigenous individuals commit suicide compared to eight out 100,000 for non-Indigenous people. Eric Stober, "First Nations Suicide Rate 4 Times Higher Than for Non-Indigenous People: StatsCan," Global News, June 30, 2019.

    On rates of substance abuse, see the study by the World Health Organization titled "Indigenous Peoples and Substance Abuse." It may be found online at www.who.int/substance_abuse/activities/indigenous/en/.
11. Quoted in Truth and Reconciliation Commission of Canada, *Honouring the Truth, Reconciling for the Future: Summary of the Final Report of the Truth and Reconciliation Commission of Canada*, 2. The document may be found online at https://nctr.ca/records/reports/#trc-reports.
12. A convenient map that locates these schools may be found at the University of Manitoba's National Centre for Truth and Reconciliation. The map may be found online at https://nctr.ca/map.php.
13. The numbers were calculated and released in TRC, *Honouring the Truth, Reconciling for the Future*, 3–4.
14. "Crimes Against Children at Residential School: The Truth About St. Anne's," *The Fifth Estate*, CBC TV, March 3, 2019, www.youtube.com/watch?v=ep7AW2K4Xww. See also "Recounting the Horrors of St. Anne's Residential School," CBC News. The clip may be found at www.youtube.com/watch?v=QJ9qhYATUmo.
15. TRC, *Honouring the Truth, Reconciling for the Future*, 4–5.
16. Amanda Coletta, "Thousands of Canada's Indigenous Children Died in Church-Run Boarding Schools. Where Are They Buried?" *Washington Post*, October 21, 2018.
17. Gord Downie and Jeff Lemire (illustrator), *Secret Path* (Toronto: Simon and Schuster, 2016).
18. Ian Adams, "The Lonely Death of Charlie Wenjack," *Maclean's*, February 1, 1967.
19. The full United Church apology may be found at https://united-church.ca/sites/default/files/apologies-response-crest.pdf.
20. The full Presbyterian apology may be found at https://presbyterian.ca/healing/.
21. The full Anglican apology may be found at www.anglican.ca/tr/apology/. The later apology may be found at www.anglican.ca/news/an-apology-for-spiritual-harm/30024511/.
22. TRC, *Honouring the Truth, Reconciling for the Future*, 330.
23. Tanya Talaga, "The Catholic Church Needs To Do More Than Apologize over Residential Schools," *Toronto Star*, January 17, 2019.

24. A transcription of the full papal apology may be found in the CBC archives at https://www.cbc.ca/news/world/francis-apology-full-text-1.6404953. For an Indigenous breakdown of the apology, see Melissa Ridgen, "Accept or Decline? Breaking Down the Pope's Apology," *InFocus*, APTN News, April 6, 2022, https://www.aptnnews.ca/infocus/accept-or-decline-breaking-down-the-popes-apology/. While this apology marks a historically important shift in the Catholic Church's position on residential schools, it does not fulfill the TRC's call 58, which calls for the apology to be "delivered by the Pope in Canada." The pope is expected to visit Canada in July 2022.

25. "Statement of Apology to Former Students of Indian Residential Schools," June 11, 2008, available on the Government of Canada website, www.rcaanc-cirnac.gc.ca/eng/1100100015644/1571589171655. The apology in the House may be watched on YouTube at www.youtube.com/watch?v=xCpn1erz1y8.
26. "Government Apologizes for Residential Schools in 2008," CBC Archives, June 25, 2018.
27. "Recounting the Horrors of St. Anne's Residential School," CBC News, April 3, 2018, www.youtube.com/watch?v=QJ9qhYATUm0.
28. Heather Scoffield, "Four Years Later, Harper's Apology for Residential Schools Rings Hollow for Many," *Toronto Star*, June 11, 2012.
29. "Shawn Atleo Resigns as AFN National Chief," CBC News, May 2, 2014.
30. Standing Committee on Aboriginal Affairs and Northern Development, "Evidence," March 7, 2013. The transcript of Valcourt's remarks is available online at www.ourcommons.ca/DocumentViewer/en/41-1/aano/meeting-63/evidence.
31. See, for example, Jorge Barrera, "Woman Denied Settlement for Sexual Assault on Way to Residential School Because She Wasn't Yet a Student," CBC News, January 20, 2020; Jorge Barrera, "Man's Residential School Claim Rejected, Then Identified for Compensation, Then Rejected Again," CBC News, February 3, 2020.
32. "GG Relaunches Truth and Reconciliation Commission," CBC News, October 15, 2009.
33. The webpage of the National Centre for Truth and Reconciliation may be found at https://nctr.ca/map.php.
34. The Calls to Action may be found online at https://ehprnh2mwo3.exactdn.com/wp-content/uploads/2021/01/Calls_to_Action_English2.pdf.
35. "Truth and Reconciliation: Looking Back on a Landmark Week for Canada," CBC News, June 6, 2015.
36. "PM Harper Won't Implement TRC Recommendation on UN Declaration on Indigenous Peoples," APTN News, June 2, 2015; Bill Curry, "Government Remains Silent on Truth and Reconciliation Recommendations," *Globe and Mail*, June 3, 2015.
37. Susana Mas, "Trudeau Lays Out Plan for New Relationship with Indigenous People," CBC News, December 8, 2015. Though it is worth noting that the police response to the National Inquiry into Missing and Murdered Indigenous Women

and Girls has been uneven at best. See Olivia Stefanovich, "Police Co-Ordination Still Lacking a Year After Inquiry Report on Missing and Murdered Indigenous Women," CBC News, June 3, 2020.

38. Joanna Smith, "Trudeau Defends Record on Indigenous Issues, as Stump Speech Mentions Are Brief," CBC News, October 20, 2019.

39. Susan Delacourt, "Indigenous Protests Put Justin Trudeau's Good Intentions on a Collision Course with Reality," *Toronto Star*, February 12, 2020.

40. Of course, not everyone in the Wet'suwet'en First Nation was opposed to the $6.6-billion-dollar pipeline. See Rafferty Baker, "A Who's Who of the Wet'suwet'en Pipeline Conflict," CBC News, February 26, 2020.

41. Recent cases as of July 2020 include the police killings of Chantal Moore and Rodney Levi in New Brunswick, eight days apart. See Shane Magee, "Investigation of Shooting Death of Chantel Moore Could Take Months," CBC News, June 5, 2020; Logan Perley and Hadeel Ibrahim, "Mi'kmaq Community Holds Healing Walk in Memory of Rodney Levi," CBC News, June 19, 2020.

42. The NHS was a voluntary survey mailed to approximately 4.5 million homes, seeking information on immigration, citizenship, place of birth, religion, education, housing costs, income, and Indigenous peoples, among other things. The results of the survey may be found online at www12.statcan.gc.ca/nhs-enm/2011/dp-pd/prof/help-aide/aboutdata-aproposdonnees.cfm?Lang=E.

43. These statistics are from Statistics Canada, "Aboriginal Peoples in Canada," from the National Household Survey. The report may be found online at www12.statcan.gc.ca/nhs-enm/2011/as-sa/99-011-x/99-011-x2011001-eng.cfm.

44. TRC, *Honouring the Truth, Reconciling for the Future*, 151.

45. The Declaration on the Rights of Indigenous Peoples may be found online at www.un.org/esa/socdev/unpfii/documents/DRIPS_en.pdf.

46. *Honouring the Truth, Reconciling for the Future*, 154.

47. Ian Austin, "Vast Indigenous Land Claims in Canada Encompass Parliament Hill," *New York Times*, November 12, 2017.

48. Courtney Dickson, "Nisga'a Treaty Trailblazers Reflect on Agreement 20 Years After It Went into Effect," CBC News, May 11, 2020.

49. Dickson, "Nisga'a Treaty Trailblazers Reflect on Agreement 20 Years After It Went into Effect."

50. Amber Hildebrandt, "Supreme Court's Tsilhqot'in First Nation Ruling a Game-Changer for All," CBC News, June 27, 2014.

51. Hildebrandt, "Supreme Court's Tsilhqot'in First Nation Ruling a Game-Changer for All."

52. David P. Ball Raven's Eye, "Tla'amin Sign $30M Self-GovernmentTreaty, But Tensions Remain," *Aboriginal Multi-Media Society*, 32.1 (2014). Online at www.ammsa.com/publications/ravens-eye/tla'amin-sign-30m-self-government-treaty-tensions-remain.

53. Raven's Eye, "Tla'amin Sign $30M Self-Government Treaty, But Tensions Remain."

54. Brendan Kergin, "TteS Comments on Arrests," Castanet, October 18, 2020, www.castanet.net/news/Kamloops/313730/Tk-emlups-te-Secwepemc-leadership-releases-statement-on-TMX-arrests.

55. Justin Brake, "Tiny House Warriors Establish New Village to Resist Pipeline, Assert Secwepemc Sovereignty," APTN News, July 19, 2018, www.aptnnews.ca/national-news/tiny-house-warriors-establish-new-village-to-resist-pipeline-assert-secwepemc-sovereignty/.
56. "Supreme Court Dismisses First Nations' Challenge Against TransMountain Pipeline," CBC News, July 2, 2020.
57. Office of the Correctional Investigator, "Indigenous People in Federal Custody Surpasses 30%," news release, January 21, 2020. The release may be found online at www.oci-bec.gc.ca/cnt/comm/press/press20200121-eng.aspx.
58. A 2019 study also found that 22 per cent of all murders in Canada in 2018 were committed against Indigenous individuals. See Kat Eschner, "Indigenous People Much More Likely To Be Murdered Than Other Canadians," *The Guardian*, July 23, 2019.
59. Office of the Correctional Investigator, "Indigenous People in Federal Custody Surpasses 30%."
60. Leyland Cecco, "'National Travesty': Report Shows One Third of Canada's Prisoners are Indigenous," *The Guardian*, January 22, 2020.
61. Lynn A. Stewart, Geoff Wilton, Sebastian Baglole, and Ryan Miller, "A Comprehensive Study of Recidivism Rates Among Canadian Federal Offenders," Correctional Services Canada. The report may be found online at www.csc-scc.gc.ca/research/005008-r426-en.shtml#2.
62. National Inquiry into Missing and Murdered Indigenous Women and Girls, *Executive Summary of the Final Report*, 2. The report may be found online at www.mmiwg-ffada.ca/wp-content/uploads/2019/06/Executive_Summary.pdf.
63. Jorge Barrera, "Indigenous Child Welfare Rates Creating a 'Humanitarian Crisis' in Canada, Says Federal Minister," CBC News, November 2, 2017. The interview may be found online at www.cbc.ca/player/play/1088963651546.
64. The federal NDP made this a priority in their 2019 election campaign. See, for example, "Jagmeet Singh Commits to Funding Clean Drinking Water in Indigenous Communities," *Globe and Mail*, October 5, 2019.
65. "Aboriginal Homelessness an 'Epidemic,' York Researcher Says," CBC News, March 28, 2014. See also "Homelessness, One Lasting Impact of Indian Residential Schools," CBC News, March 27, 2014.
66. Jorge Barrera, "Chantel Moore's Home First Nation Says Edmunston Police Officer Should Be Charged with Murder," CBC News, June 24, 2020.
67. Judith Kekinusuqs Sayers, Ardith Walpetko We'dalx Walkem, and Doug White III Kwulasultan, "Indigenous People Have a Plan for Achieving True Justice. When Will Canada Act?" *Globe and Mail*, July 7, 2020.
68. Sayers, Walkem, and Kwulasultan, "Indigenous People Have a Plan for Achieving True Justice."
69. Robert Fife, "Brian Mulroney Calls for Bold Social Changes to Prepare Canada for a World After COVID-19," *Globe and Mail*, June 29, 2020.

9 | AUGUST 20, 2016

1. Natasha Rudnick, "The Tragically Hip: 10 Essential Songs," *Rolling Stone*, August 19, 2016, www.rollingstone.com/music/music-lists/the-tragically-hip-10-essential-songs-97420/
2. In addition to one live album, one compilation album, two video albums, and a boxed set.
3. From the band's website, which has been archived at https://web.archive.org/web/20111111095932/http://www.thehip.com/HipArchive/hypercd/tth-early.htm.
4. "Tragically Hip: The Most Canadian Band in the World," *BBC Magazine*, October 18, 2017, www.bbc.com/news/magazine-36399891.
5. "Gord Downie Appointed to Order of Canada," CBC News, June 19, 2017.
6. "Gord Downie Appointed to Order of Canada"; "Gord Downie Appointed to Order of Canada for Work on Indigenous Issues," *Toronto Star*, June 19, 2017.
7. Rachel West, "The Tragically Hip Talk Life After Gord Downie: 'We're All Still Adjusting,'" Global News, July 6, 2018.
8. "Dan Aykroyd on the Tragically Hip, the Blues, Ghosts and the Caesar," CBC Radio, May 16, 2019.
9. Personal Correspondence with Jake Gold, The Tragically Hip's manager, August, 30, 2021.
10. Quoted in Marc Shapiro, *What is Hip? The Life and Times of The Tragically Hip* (Riverdale, NY: Riverdale Avenue Books, 2017), e-book.
11. Chris Jancelewicz, "Justin Trudeau Delivers Emotional, Tearful Tribute to Gord Downie," Global News, October 18, 2017.
12. "Tragically Hip Wins Fans By 'Doing Its Thing,'" *Edmonton Journal*, November 27, 1992.
13. Lance Hornby, "The Late Gord Downie Helped Us Remember Bill Barilko," *Toronto Sun*, October 18, 2017.
14. Amara McLaughlin, "Maple Leafs Honour Gord Downie Before Game at ACC," CBC News, October 18, 2017. More generally, see "Hockey World Mourns Gord Downie's Death," ESPN.com, October 18, 2017.
15. Adrian Lee, "Searching for The Tragically Hip's Mythical Bobcaygeon," *Maclean's*, July 15, 2016.
16. "Courage References," archived at www.hipmuseum.com/hugh.html.
17. Andrea Warner, "Why One Fan Says The Tragically Hip Is a Feminist Band and Not Just for 'Bros,'" CBC Radio, August 19, 2016.
18. I owe this point to my son, Gabriel Hall-Hughes.
19. Dave Kaufman, "How Gord Downie and The Tragically Hip Became a Part of Our Landscape, and Experience in What It Means To Be Canadian," *National Post*, July 21, 2016.
20. Simon Vozick-Levinson "Gord Downie, a Canadian Rock Legend, Sings Goodbye," *The New York Times* October 18, 2017.
21. Gordon Downie, *Coke Machine Glow* (Toronto: Vintage Canada, 2001).
22. "Toboggan Hill" from *Coke Machine Glow* by Gordon Downie, copyright © 2001 Wiener Art Inc. Reprinted by permission of Vintage Canada, a division of Penguin Random House Canada Limited. All rights reserved. Any third party use of this

material, outside of this publication, is prohibited. Interested parties must apply directly to Penguin Random House Canada Limited for permission.

23. The animated film of *The Secret Path* and a panel discussion that followed its original airing may be found on YouTube at www.youtube.com/watch?v=yGd764YU9yc.
24. "Tragically Hip Rocks Fort Albany School Gym," CBC News, February 17, 2012, www.cbc.ca/news/canada/sudbury/tragically-hip-rocks-fort-albany-school-gym-1.1192855.
25. The Gord Downie and Chanie Wenjack Foundation's website is www.downiewenjack.ca.
26. A video of the ceremony is available at John Paul Tasker, "'Man Who Walks Among the Stars': AFN Honours Tearful Gord Downie," CBC News, December 6, 2016, www.cbc.ca/news/politics/gord-downie-tragically-hip-afn-honoured-1.3883618.
27. David Friend, "Gord Downie Chosen as Top Canadian Press Newsmaker for Second Consecutive Year," *Globe and Mail*, December 19, 2017.
28. Jancelewicz, "Justin Trudeau Delivers Emotional, Tearful Tribute to Gord Downie."
29. Canadian Press, "Tragically Hip Tour Raises More Than $1M for Canadian Brain Cancer Research," *Toronto Star*, September 19, 2016.
30. James R. Perry "Behind the Scenes with Gord Downie's Doctor on The Tragically Hip's Last Tour," *Globe and Mail*, October 16, 2018.
31. The tour was profiled in the 2017 documentary film *Long Time Running* by Jennifer Baichwal and Nicholas de Pencier. The final concert was also released on DVD under the title *A National Celebration* on December 24, 2017.
32. Bruce Arthur, "Love-in for The Hip at Rio's Canada House," *Toronto Star*, August 20, 2016.
33. Tania Kohut, "The Tragically Hip Invited Justin Trudeau to Kingston Concert: PMO," Global News, August 23, 2016.
34. Steven Marche, "Watching Canada's Biggest Rock Band Say a Dramatic Goodbye," *The New Yorker*, August 20, 2016.
35. "Tragically Hip: The Most Canadian Band in the World."
36. Brian C. Thompson, *Anthems and Minstrel Shows: The Life and Times of Calixa Lavallée* (Montreal and Kingston: McGill-Queen's University Press 2015), 228.
37. Quoted in Michelle Dean and Nicole Cliffe, "Explaining the Importance of The Tragically Hip's Final Show," *The Guardian*, August 23, 2016.
38. Caroline Catherman and Christina Zdanowicz, "Neil Young Is Finally a US Citizen After He Says His Love of Weed Delayed Application," CNN, January 24, 2020; Angie Martoccio, "54 Tears After Moving to America, Neil Young Is Now a U.S. Citizen," *Rolling Stone*, January 23, 2020.
39. Andy Greene, "Neil Young Pens Open Letter to Donald Trump: 'You Are a Disgrace to My Country,'" *Rolling Stone*, February 19, 2020. My italics.
40. This is not to say there are no other bands that sing about Canadian issues. In addition to Stompin' Tom mentioned above there are also bands like the Rheostatics or Spirit of the West. While popular, they never had the same kind of mainstream success as The Tragically Hip.

41. Michael Barclay, *The Never-Ending Present: The Story of Gord Downie and the Tragically Hip* (Toronto: ECW Press, 2019).
42. Jacob Poushter, "Canadians Satisfied with U.S. Relationship," Pew Research Center, October 6, 2015.
43. Frank Newport and Julie Ray, "G6 Plus One Mindset Existed Before Summit," Gallup, June 12, 2018, https://news.gallup.com/opinion/polling-matters/235541/plus-one-mindset-existed-summit.aspx.

44. Aaron Hutchins, "While Trump Eyes Tariffs, Americans Really Want More Canada," *Maclean's*, June 23, 2020.
45. Hutchins, "While Trump Eyes Tariffs, Americans Really Want More Canada."
46. Spencer Gallichan-Lowe, "Strong Majority of Canadians View Trump as Racist: Poll," *CityNews*, June 16, 2020. Percentages add up to more than 100 per cent due to rounding.
47. Laura Dawson, "Notes from a Disillusioned Canadian: Our Friendship with the U.S. May Never Be the Same," *Globe and Mail*, September 7, 2018.
48. Catherine Porter, "Prime Minister Justin Trudeau Won't Cross the Border for Washington Summit," *New York Times*, July 6, 2020. On the "sniffles" remark, see Domenico Montanaro, "Some People 'Have the Sniffles': Trump Downplays the Coronavirus's Severity," National Public Radio News, July 19, 2020.
49. The letter from Congress may be found at https://higgins.house.gov/sites/higgins.house.gov/files/6-3-20%20NORTHERN%20BORDER%20LETTER.pdf.
50. Rachel Gilmore, "Canadians Push Back as U.S. Congress Pressures Canada to Reopen Shared Border," CTV News, July 10, 2020.

10 | MARCH 8, 2018

1. I have opted to use the term "Black Canadian" as opposed to African Canadian, which mimics African American, because many Canadians of Afro-Caribbean origin maintain that "African Canadian" obscures their own unique history and culture. "Black Canadian" thus functions as an umbrella term under which various other national terms—such as Jamaican Canadian or Ghanaian Canada—sit.
2. Technically, Viola Desmond was not the first non-monarchical female on Canadian currency. In 2017, to mark the 150th anniversary of Confederation, Agnes MacPhail (1890–1954), Canada's first female MP, appeared along with three men on a commemorative note with a small print run. But Viola Desmond is the first woman to appear alone and the first to appear on a regular banknote.
3. John N. Grant, "Black Immigrants into Nova Scotia, 1776–1815," *The Journal of Negro History* 58.3 (1973): 253–70.
4. See James W. St. G. Walker, *The Black Loyalists: The Search for a Promised Land in Nova Scotia and Sierra Leone 1783–1870* (New York: Africana Publishing Co., 1976).
5. "Address of the House of Assembly to Lieutenant Governor Sherbrooke Opposing Black Refugee Immigration," April 1, 1815, Nova Scotia Archives. Online at https://novascotia.ca/archives/Africanns/archives.asp?ID=76.
6. This quotation comes from "Notes on Slavery in Canada," *The Journal of Negro History* 4.4 (1919): 396–411, at 399. This article collects numerous documents from

the Department of Archives in Ottawa that bear on the question of slavery in Upper Canada.

7. Graham Reynolds, *Viola Desmond's Canada: A History of Blacks and Racial Segregation in the Promised Land* (Black Point, NS: Fernwood Publishing, 2016), 50.
8. The Order-in-Council is available online at https://pier21.ca/research/immigration-history/order-in-council-pc-1911-1324.
9. R. Bruce Shepard, "Diplomatic Racism: Canadian Government and Black Migration from Oklahoma, 1905–1912," *Great Plains Quarterly* 3:1 (1983): 5–16, at 5–6.
10. Emily F. Murphy, *The Black Candle* (Toronto: Thomas Allen, 1922), 175.
11. Murphy, *The Black Candle*, 189.
12. "The Haitian Community in Canada," Statistics Canada, www150.statcan.gc.ca/n1/pub/89-621-x/89-621-x2007011-eng.htm.
13. "The Jamaican Community in Canada," Statistics Canada, www150.statcan.gc.ca/n1/pub/89-621-x/89-621-x2007012-eng.htm.
14. Information generated from "Census Profile, 2016 Census" on the Statistics Canada website. Online at www12.statcan.gc.ca/census-recensement/2016/dp-pd/prof/etailscfm?Lang=E&Geo1=PR&Code1=01&Geo2=PR&Code2=01&SearchText=Canada&SearchType=Begins&SearchPR=01&B1=Visible%20minority&TABID=1&type=0.
15. Elissa Barnard, "Africville from the Beginning," *Halifax Chronicle Herald*, September 18, 2014.
16. "Africville Is an Eyesore," *Close-Up*, CBC TV, June 24, 1962, www.cbc.ca/archives/entry/africville-is-an-eyesore.
17. "Africville Declared a National Historic Site," *The World at Six*, CBC Radio, July 5, 2002, www.cbc.ca/archives/entry/africville-declared-a-national-historic-site.
18. "Halifax Apologizes for Razing Africville," CBC News, February 24, 2010.
19. Anjuli Patil, "Africville Church Commemorated, 50 Years after Demolition," CBC News, May 31, 2017.
20. Quoted in Barnard, "Africville from the Beginning."
21. A convenient biography of Desmond may be found at the Nova Scotia Museum website, https://ojs.library.dal.ca/NSM/article/view/5762/5140.
22. Constance Backhouse, *Colour-Coded: A Legal History of Racism in Canada, 1900–1950* (Toronto: *University of Toronto Press*, 1999), 266.
23. For the archive of the trial, see https://novascotia.ca/archives/Desmond/archives.asp?ID=5&Page=201501014&Language=.
24. Colin A. Thomson, *Born With a Call: A Biography of Dr. William Pearly Oliver, C.M.* (Halifax: Black Cultural Centre for Nova Scotia, 1986), 84.
25. Paul Darrow, "In Rare Posthumous Pardon, Nova Scotia Apologizes for Black Woman's 1946 Arrest," *Globe and Mail*, April 15, 2010.
26. "Apology a Dream for Sister of 'Canada's Rosa Parks,'" CTV News, April 16, 2010.
27. Kathryn Blaze Carlson, "'Canada's Rosa Parks,' Viola Desmond, Posthumously Pardoned," *National Post*, April 14, 2010.
28. Evan Hill, Ainara Tiefenthäler, Christiaan Triebert, Drew Jordan, Haley Wallis, and Robin Stein, "How George Floyd Was Killed in Police Custody," *New York*

Times, May 31, 2020. For a Canadian take on the story, see Carolyn Dunn, "Anger, Grief and Exhaustion: A City Is Left Raw after George Floyd's Death," CBC News, June 4, 2020.

29. Marie-Claude Landry, "Statement—Anti-Black Racism in Canada: Time to Face the Truth," Canada Human Rights Commission. The statement may be found online at www.chrc-ccdp.gc.ca/en/resources/anti-black-racism-canada-time-face-the-truth.
30. John Howard Society, "Race, Crime and Justice in Canada," October 19, 2017. Online at https://johnhoward.ca/blog/race-crime-justice-canada/.
31. From the BLM website at https://blacklivesmatter.ca.
32. Jessica Cheung, "Black People and Other People of Colour Make Up 83% of Reported COVID-19 Cases in Toronto," CBC News, July 30, 2020.
33. Andrea Huncar, "Black Canadians Hit Hard by COVID-19, New National Study Shows," CBC News, September 2, 2020.
34. Huncar, "Black Canadians Hit Hard by COVID-19, New National Study Shows."
35. Shree Paradkar, "Unlike Canadians, Americans At Least Know How Black People Are Faring with COVID-19 (Very Badly)," *Toronto Star*, April 8, 2020.
36. "Canada Statue of John A. Macdonald Toppled by Activists in Montreal," BBC News, August 30, 2020.
37. Rachel Gilmore, "Trudeau 'Deeply Disappointed' After Demonstrators Topple John A. Macdonald Statue," CTV News, August 31, 2020.
38. Emerald Bensadoun, "Trudeau 'Disappointed' by Toppling of John A. Macdonald Statue during Weekend Rallies," Global News, August 31, 2020.
39. Gilmore, "Trudeau 'Deeply Disappointed' After Demonstrators Topple John A. Macdonald Statue."

Index

OTHER TITLES FROM UNIVERSITY OF ALBERTA PRESS

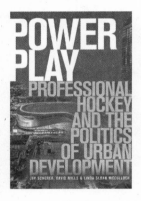

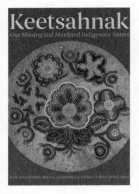

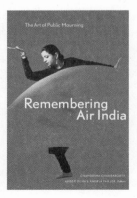